THE GREAT BOOK OF
BOMBERS

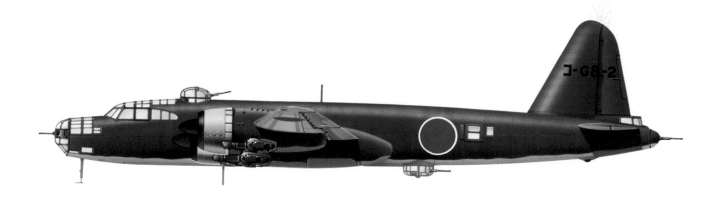

THE GREAT BOOK OF
BOMBERS

The world's most important bombers from
World War I to the present day

JON LAKE

SALAMANDER

A Salamander Book

8 Blenheim Court
Brewery Road
London N7 9NY
England

A member of Chrysalis Books plc

9 8 7 6 5 4 3 2 1

ISBN 1 84065 353 1

CREDITS
Cover Design by John Heritage
Interior Design by Heather Moore, John Heritage, Cara Hamilton
Index Compiled by Chris Bernstein
Production: Susannah Straughan
Editorial Director: Charlotte Davies
Editor: Antony Shaw
Colour Reproduction: Anorax Imaging Ltd
Printed in Taiwan

PRELIM CAPTIONS
page 1: A Nakajima G8N 3rd PROT.

page 2 and 3: Boeing B-17 Flying Fortresses of the US Army 8th Air Force leave their marks in the sub-stratosphere. The curved trails, leading upward, were made by the fighters accompanying the B-17s on the raid.

page 4: A Convair B-36 of the 7th B.G.(H)

CONTENTS

INTRODUCTION

THIS BOOK DESCRIBES history's most important, influential and interesting bomber aircraft. Some are legendary, having achieved great success and distinction in war, but others were fascinating failures, and a handful are 'might have beens'—great aircraft which promised to revolutionize aerial warfare, but which ultimately failed to enter operational service. Our definition of a bomber is deliberately quite loose—encompassing some aircraft designed to do nothing but drop bombs on the enemy, and others which may have been designed with other roles in mind, but which may have also been used in the bomber role. Some are even what we might think of as fighters—though we have tended to include only those fighters which can also carry the ultimate weapon—an atomic bomb.

But before examining these individual bomber aircraft, it is perhaps appropriate to quickly recount the history of the bomber, and to illustrate how and when it has changed the world in which we live.

The most far-sighted military thinkers had foreseen the use of 'flying machines' to drop bombs even before the Wright Brothers made their historic first powered flight at Kitty Hawk in 1903. Perhaps surprisingly, there is no documented instance of armies dropping offensive weapons from the balloons which they used for observation and artillery spotting

during the 19th Century, although there is no doubt that military thinkers did consider how the balloon might be turned into a more offensive weapon.

Legend has it that Napoleon Bonaparte favored the idea of using balloons to drop bombs during his war against Britain (1793–1815). He envisaged they would fly effortlessly across the narrow stretch of water which divided France and Britain. Napoleon's enthusiasm waned rapidly, when it was pointed out that prevailing winds would actually make it much easier for the British to use balloons against France.

The military in most countries were remarkably slow in exploiting the offensive potential of the aeroplane, using it first as an observation and reconnaissance platform, and then as a means of attacking enemy aircraft. Things moved more quickly in Italy where an expeditionary Air Flotilla of nine aircraft was dispatched as part of a force sent to eject Ottoman Turk forces from the Libyan capital of Tripoli (1911–12). The Italians quickly developed artillery spotting tactics

Inset, top: *The first bombs were dropped out the cockpit of the aeroplane. Bombing was initally a sporadic affair.*
Right: *World War II saw rapid development of the bomber. The superb Consolidated B-24 Liberator was built in large numbers but has been overshadowed by the largely inferior Boeing B-17.*

(dropping messages to the gunners in tins!) and, on November 1, 1911, began dropping small bombs from aircraft. Lieutenant Giulio Gavotti became the world's first bomber pilot, lobbing three 4.4-lb (2-kg) grenades from his Etrich Taube monoplane at Taguira Oasis. By the end of the campaign, Italian airmen were even dropping specially constructed aerial bombs by night.

Bombing was initially a sporadic affair during World War I (1914–18), and largely a matter of individual initiative. Lt Franz von Hiddeson, a German pilot, dropped two light bombs from his Taube over Paris on August 13, 1914. Another German dropped the first bomb on British soil (in a garden in Dover, southeast England) on Christmas Eve, 1914. On October 8, 1914, two British pilots, flying Sopwith Tabloids, attacked the railroad station in Köln, western Germany, and nearly destroyed a enemy Zeppelin during a raid on the west central city of Düsseldorf.

On the Western Front, the battle line running from Belgium to the Swiss border, bombing operations were largely limited to tactical targets for most of World War I. Lightweight bombs were dropped on enemy forces in the field and immediately behind the front. This was 'tactical bombing' whereby aircraft attack the manifestations of enemy armed strength in the immediate vicinity of the actual fighting—and also strike at the sources of that fighting.

German Zeppelin airships made the first 'strategic' bombing attacks. They began with a raid on Antwerp, the leading port of Belgium, on the night of September 2/3, 1914 during which LZ17 (operating from Köln) dropped three 200-lb (90.7-kg) bombs on the city. Another Zeppelin dropped the first bombs on London on May 31, 1915, and the campaign soon intensified, with the lumbering airships carrying bombs of up to 600-lb (272-kg) —far larger than could be carried by contemporary bomber aeroplanes.

The first use of heavier than air strategic bombers was made by Russia during their campaign against the Germans in eastern Europe. Russia introduced the four-engined Sikorsky bombers on February 15, 1915. In Italy, the Corpo Aeronautica Militaire launched its strategic bomber offensive against Austro-Hungarian targets on August 20, 1915. The Germans were not far behind, and established frontline heavy bomber wings in early 1916, for attacks behind French and Russian lines. True strategic operations began on May 25, 1917, with the first raid, by 23 Gotha G IVs, on Britain. Gothas and Zeppelin Staaken R-planes quickly took over the bombing campaign against Britain from the Zeppelins, and although the damage they caused was fairly minor, it caused a public outcry, and fighter squadrons had to be rushed home from the Western Front to provide air defense for the capital. This forced a switch to night-bombing operations, which proved harder to intercept, though the accuracy of the German bombing also

Below, top: *Two Royal Flying Corps 'erks' fuse a bomb before flight. Most World War I bombs were small and lacked lethality.*

Below: *The Handley Page V/1500 was just too late to play a part in World World I. It did, however, take part in colonial policing operations during the interwar period.*

fell dramatically. The larger German bombers could at last carry weapons of a meaningful size, and a Staaken R VI dropped a 2,204-lb (1000-kg) bomb on the Royal Hospital, London, on February 16/17, 1918. It was the largest bomb to fall on Britain.

Strategic bombing operations by Britain only really began after the establishment of the Independent Force, initially as No.41 Wing, Royal Flying Corps (RFC), in October 1917. The force operated a range of aircraft

types, from FE.2bs and DH.4s to the larger Handley Page O/100s, and attacked a number of targets far in the German rear, and in Germany itself. The size and weight of bombs carried increased with the introduction of the O/400 and V/1500, and as the war ended, three of the massive V/1500s were 'bombed up' and waiting to take off for the first Royal Air Force (RAF) attack on Berlin.

There was a broad acceptance that strategic bombing had failed to meet

Right: *Lord Trenchard was the 'father of the Royal Air Force'. He was the first champion of the strategic bomber, and of bombing for psychological effect.*
Below: *General Billy Mitchell ended up being court-martialled for his efforts to promote the bomber, and to outline the poor state of the US Army's infant Air Corps.*
Opposite page, top: *General Giulio Douhet's 1921 book,* The Command of the Air *foresaw air power being used as the dominant force in destroying an enemy's ability and will to fight.*
Opposite page, bottom: *Buildings damaged by air attacks during the Spanish Civil War. The effect of the bombing was shocking at the time although its use was limited.*

its full potential in World War I, because navigation, bomb-aiming, and target marking techniques and equipment were immature and inadequate, while bombloads were too small to have much effect. Even the bombers' most dedicated adherents in Britain claimed that their effect on Germany had been more psychological (sapping the will of German civilians) than material, although they did claim that this 'moral effect' had been significant and worthwhile. These supporters, however, overlooked the obvious failure of German bombing to undermine British morale. Despite the shortcomings of the bomber offensives during World War I, Hugh Trenchard, first Chief of the Air Staff, remained a firm supporter of strategic bombing.

Between the World Wars, the RAF

proved its value time and again in the Colonial Policing role, using light bombers in the 'Air Control' role, mounting punitive raids and shows of force far more cheaply than conventional forces on the ground could have done. But while these light, tactical bombers flew the missions which gave the interwar RAF its *raison d'etre*, the Air Marshals concentrated their attentions on heavy strategic bombing, endlessly refining the Trenchard doctrine, which rapidly assumed the status of holy writ.

Under this doctrine, it was affirmed that the army's purpose was to 'defeat the enemy army' while that of the air force was to 'defeat the enemy nation'. It was an article of faith that the 'Bomber would always get through', beating off any attacks by fighters without undue difficulty and it was widely believed that once it reached its target it would be devastatingly effective. Peacetime exercises tended to support such conclusions. Fighter pilots' claims were dismissed as being 'over-enthusiastic'. Assurances by bomber crews that they would have got through unscathed, and that 'yes, they would have hit the target' were accepted almost without question.

Even the more pessimistic observers believed that all that a bomber would need to do to guarantee 'getting through' would be to attack by night,

though the day bombing of centres of population, 'for moral effect', remained the official doctrine.

The RAF's theories and doctrine were echoed elsewhere. In Italy (which had virtually invented the bomber) General Giulio Douhet published the influential *The Command of the Air* in 1921. This work set out his vision of aerial warfare, in which air power would defeat the enemy air force and then smash its industrial capacity, directing air attacks primarily at population centres and the national infrastructure. The destruction of 'governing bodies, banks and other public services in a single day' he believed, would plunge the enemy into 'terror and confusion'.

Remarkably, perhaps, the strategic theories of Douhet had little effect on Italian bomber development. Italy's World War I Caproni bombers had led the world, but in the interwar period, Italian industry produced a range of tactical bombers notable mainly for their mediocrity.

The United States had entered World War I belatedly, and its bomber force had played little part in the conflict. Postwar isolationism forced the United States Army Air Corps (USAAC) to concentrate on home defence (and the reinforcement of overseas territories such as Hawaii and the Philippines). The bomber's role focused on attacking enemy warships as part of maritime defense. This drove forward a concentration on precision bombing (a moving ship on the moving sea is nothing if not a pinpoint target!). William 'Billy' Mitchell, the leading army pilot and aviation pioneer, demonstrated the bombers' potential as a ship-killer by sinking a number of captured German ships, before being court martialled for raising accusations that the air arm was being 'neglected'. The early emphasis on precision bombing, however, survived, and was carried over even when the USAAC adopted a strategic bombing role.

Actual combat operations seemed to reinforce the complacent confidence of the peacetime 'Bomber Barons', even though the interwar conflicts they studied were hardly representative of the conditions that would be faced by long-range strategic bombers in a European war. In the Spanish Civil War (1936–39), in Italian operations in Abyssinia (1935–41) and during the Sino-Japanese War (1937–45) bombers mainly operated in the tactical role. When the bombers were not, they tended to be operating against virtually undefended targets, over very short ranges, in conditions of air superiority or air supremacy.

The perceived effectiveness of bombing was also distorted because it was such a new and shocking form of warfare, and by the phenomenon of Guernica. The destruction of this Republican northern Spanish city during the country's civil war was profiled by artists, poets and internationally condemned. The devastation attributed to Nazi bombers that were pro-Nationalist, however, may have actually been partly largely due to well-placed explosives on the ground!

In fact, many now view the Spanish Civil War as being the precursor of the modern, post Cold War air campaign, since the outside powers involved fought it in a very limited manner, with self imposed restrictions on the nature and extent of forces committed, and on targeting, in an effort to restrict the extent of the conflict.

Left: *German bombers like the Junkers Ju 88 and Dornier Do 17 had compact cockpits in which the whole crew were grouped together.*
Below: *The Dornier Do 19 was built to meet a German requirement for a long range heavy bomber. The aircraft, however, was abandoned in favour of lighter, shorter ranged tactical bombers.*
Opposite page: *The Junkers Ju 87 proved effective only where the Luftwaffe enjoyed complete air superiority.*

Despite its extensive experience of strategic bombing operations during World War I, Germany concentrated on tactical air power during the 1930s and 1940s. Overall German military doctrine during the period placed great emphasis on the need for momentum, which was now seen as the only way by which the stagnation

of the Western Front could have been broken. From this was developed the theory of the Blitzkrieg (literally 'Lightning War'), in which highly mobile and powerful forces, supported by mobile firepower and air power would 'breakthrough' before any defending forces could react. Led and shaped by a celebrated World War I fighter pilot (Hermann Goering) and with a number of other fighter pilots and even infantry soldiers in its high ranks (Erhard Milch, Ernst Udet and Albert Kesselring, for example), the Luftwaffe's outlook was perhaps inevitably narrowly focused around the use of air power to directly support the army.

Nazi Germany did begin a strategic bomber program, based around aircraft such as the Dornier Do 19 and Junkers Ju 89, but this was abandoned after the death of its chief adherent, General Walther Wever, in an air crash in 1936.

Various interwar campaigns may have alerted the air forces of Germany,

Italy and Japan to the relative value and practicality of tactical and strategic bombing. When World War II broke out in September 1939, however, the Royal Air Force's Bomber Command, optimized for strategic bombing operations, received a rude awakening. Its bombers were cut to pieces by flak and fighters by day, and proved unable to reliably hit (or sometimes even find) their targets with any degree of accuracy by night. Mechanical reliability was poor, and the aircrew were inadequately trained, and poorly protected from the cold. Many aircraft failed to return even without any action on the part of the

enemy. Nor were contemporary RAF bombs powerful enough to do much damage even when they did find their targets.

The initial reaction was to limit Bomber Command to leaflet-dropping, and to peripheral operations against shipping and port facilities, where the risk of collateral damage to civilians could be minimized. But it was soon argued that civilian morale was a legitimate target, and that the enemy workers who manufactured weapons were as valid a target as the soldiers who carried them. The old Trenchardian doctrine of bombing cities for what he referred to as 'moral

effect' was soon back in the ascendant, embraced with enthusiasm by senior Air Staff officers including Charles Portal and Arthur 'Bomber' Harris.

The spectacular success of the Allied heavy bombers in the closing stages of the war provided ample 'evidence' to be used by the bomber adherents. The destruction of cities like Dresden in southeast Germany and the attendant loss of life, seemed to confirm the efficacy of the strategic bomber, and this impression was only reinforced by the horrific destruction of the Japanese cities of Hiroshima and Nagasaki by the new atomic bomb.

But in fact, for much of the war, the

heavy bomber had been an extremely inefficient means of carrying the war to the enemy, causing modest levels of destruction at a barely sustainable cost in men and machines, and generally with insufficient accuracy to be of no use except as a terror weapon. Throughout 1942 and 1943, night after night, RAF 'heavies' would set out against a German city suffering heavier casualties than they caused, and losing tens of aircraft for the damage (and sometimes, when they were lucky, the destruction) of a handful of houses. Meanwhile, bombers of the USAAF were scarcely any more effective (and no more accurate) when operating by day. The USAAF did maintain the fiction that it was conducting precision attacks against pinpoint industrial targets until the end of the war, even when weather conditions forced it to bomb on radar from above cloud, and when the aim point

Opposite page: The crew of an RAF Vickers Wellington prepare for a sortie, donning their cumbersome flying kit.
Left: Bombsights on US aircraft allowed extraordinary precision in clear weather. In combat, however, USAAC bombing accuracy was lamentable.
Below: The Vickers Wellington was arguably the most effective of the Royal Air Force bombers during the first years of World War II. It earned an enviable reputation for rugged dependability.

of a marshalling yard (say) was a convenient cover for what was in all but name an area attack against a city's industrial heart, or when navigational accuracy was barely adequate to find the target city, let alone the desired target. That such poor navigation was rife within the US Eighth Air Force was dramatically demonstrated in March 1945, when 15 bombers of USAAF accidentally attacked Basle

and Zurich in neutral Switzerland. Postwar research even suggests that the RAF tended to concentrate more of its bombs around its aiming points (inevitably military or industrial targets) than did the USAAF, even though it accepted that it was actually going to destroy whole areas of a city around that aim point. But until the end Dwight D. Eisenhower, supreme commander of the Allies in Europe, and Carl Spaatz, commander of the US Strategic Air Forces in Europe, categorically denied that the USAAF conducted area bombing missions.

If the bomber offensive achieved anything before 1943, it was in diverting German resources from the frontline to the defence of the homeland, and in providing a highly visible (if largely tokenistic) retaliation for German attacks. The effect on German industrial output was rela-

tively unimportant throughout the war, and the RAF and USAAF were never able to destroy the morale of the German civilian population.

Had resources been diverted from the heavy bomber campaign to a more effective prosecution of the war against the U-Boat, and to attacking German targets using smaller, faster, more survivable light bombers (such as the Mosquito) and even fighter bombers (such as the Westland Whirlwind) it is likely that Germany's war effort would have suffered more severe damage, that Allied losses of men and matériel would have been reduced and that the war might have been shortened. In every theatre, tactical bombing (on both sides) proved to be a battle-winning weapon, whether by destroying enemy capital ships in harbour or at sea, or by bottling up and destroying enemy armour, railway

Above: *Avro Lancasters take shape on the assembly line. With heavy attrition on the frontline, just keeping pace with losses was by no means easy, yet Avro managed to produce sufficient aircraft for a massive expansion of Bomber Command.*

Opposite page, top: *Several Boeing B-17s survive in airworthy condition to this day, and the type has become emblematic of the USAAF's bomber war. The aircraft formed the backbone of the US Eighth Air Force operating from British bases during World War II.*

Opposite page, bottom: *A B-17 of the 390th Bomb Group ('Wittan's Wallopers') sits waiting its bombload at a US airbase in England. The B-17E was the variant used to launch the Eighth Air Force's 'precision daylight bombing' campaign against the Third Reich in August 1942. In fact, in most weather conditions, the accuracy of the B-17s was no better than that achieved by the RAF's Bomber Command at night.*

locomotives, or aerodromes.

Allied strategic bombing accuracy improved exponentially during the final year of the war, and losses plummeted as the Luftwaffe lost command of the skies over the Fatherland. The RAF and USAAF at last began inflicting levels of damage and destruction that far exceeded their own losses. But despite this, German industry kept producing, and the German population's morale did not collapse.

Ironically, in view of the bomber commanders' widespread hostility to 'diversions' from their single-minded campaign against enemy cities and industrial centers, the finest moment of the wartime heavy bombers came during the invasion period, when they provided accurate and often extremely timely support to Allied troops, often bombing enemy positions within a few hundred yards of the Allied front lines. The main thrust of the Allied heavy bomber campaign in Europe, by contrast, achieved little, beyond winning its participants a reputation for enormously courageous self-sacrifice and

its commanders a less well deserved reputation for single-minded ruthless brutality. Some postwar observers have even sought to portray some bombing raids (like the infamous fire-raids on Hamburg and Dresden in Germany) as being war crimes, as Wing Commander John Tipton, a former RAF Bomber Command navigator, explained. "Postwar generations have the conviction that the bomber campaign was unnecessary, wasteful and evil...Harris and, by association, his crews have been branded as war criminals. I'm sure that we would all have preferred to fly Spitfires in defence of the White Cliffs of Dover to universal approval, but, though the fighter pilots of 1940 saved us from defeat it was the endurance of the bomber crews that ensured our victory." In truth, while the bomber aircrew and their commanders were not war criminals, nor did they win the war in Europe for the Allies, and their sacrifice may have been disproportionate to their achievements.

The bomber war in the Pacific was

quite different, in that the dispersal and small scale of Japanese industry (and poor target intelligence) forced the USAAF to embrace an area bombing policy from the start, quite deliberately targeting industry, its workers and their housing with indiscriminate fire-raids against Japan's wooden houses. Though less well known, these proved even more costly (in terms of human life on the ground) than the RAF's attacks on Dresden. Between the end of 1944, when Japan's cities finally came within the USAAF's range, and the beginning of August 1945, between 300,000 and 600,000 Japanese civilians were killed and a quarter of the urban population (8 million people) lost their homes.

Against this background, the atomic bomb was a logical progression, and on August 6, 1945 the B-29 'Enola Gay' opened the atomic age. Horrified by the destruction in Hiroshima, Spaatz (newly arrived as commander of US Strategic Air Forces in the Pacific) pressed for the second bomb to be dropped outside a city, to reduce

Opposite page: *A stick of bombs tumble from a B-17 over Dresden on Valentine's Day 1945. Large parts of the city were still ablaze after the RAF's raid the night before.*
Right: *B-17Gs of the 384th Bomb Group at Grafton Underwood, central England, release their bombs on railway centers in Dresden on April 17, 1945.*
Below *Colonel Paul Tibbets and some of the air and groundcrew of the B-29 'Enola Gay'. The nuclear bomb they dropped on Japan in 1945 opened the atomic age.*

the devastation. He was overruled and three days after the first strike, Nagasaki followed the same way. This ended the war, and Japan surrendered, thereby saving the millions who would have perished on both sides had the Allies been forced to invade and conquer Japan conventionally.

The atomic bomb opened a new era, in which a single large bomber could finally inflict untold damage on a target. This saw the beginning of the end of the era of massed formations of

Opposite page, top: *The 9,000-lb (4,082-kg) 'Little Boy' dropped on the Japanese city of Hiroshima in 1945 was estimated to be as effective as 20,000 tons of high explosive.*

Opposite page, bottom: *One of a series of atmospheric nuclear weapons tests carried out during the early years of the Cold War. The threat of mutual nuclear destruction maintained an uneasy peace throughout the period.*

Below: *Oil storage tanks explode during an attack by US Navy A-4 Skyhawks during the Vietnam War.*

bomber aircraft being sent out against a single target. This enormously destructive power was increased exponentially with the introduction of the hydrogen bomb.

While the pace of the Cold War was governed by the developments in atomic warfare, a number of conflicts outside Europe (some of them connected with the European withdrawal from Empire, and some of them Cold War proxy conflicts) also provided some food for thought for bomber

strategists, although the lessons provided by these minor wars were not always more widely applicable.

Even in Vietnam (1965–73), where the surface-to-air-missile (SAM) and anti-aircraft artillery (AAA) threat eventually became intensive, the bombers were able to operate under conditions of local air superiority, without a significant fighter threat, and against enemy forces that could not respond in kind. Most of the bombing in Vietnam was tactical, with

the US political leadership exercising tight control over targeting during Operation Rolling Thunder, which lasted from 1965 to 1968, before imposing a 'Bombing Halt' which ended in 1972. A massive bombing campaign, spearheaded by B-52s, was launched in April 1972, in response to a full scale offensive by North Vietnam. Operation Linebacker ended on October 24 when the Vietnamese called for negotiations, but resumed (as Linebacker II) between December 18–29, 1972 when the B-52 force engaged in a brief but devastating orgy of destruction against targets in and around Hanoi and Haiphong. The campaign forced the Vietnamese back to the negotiating table, and with the release of its PoWs, America was able to disengage from the conflict.

With the development of a Soviet inter-continental nuclear strike capability, the Cold War's opposing sides were capable of 'Mutually Assured Destruction' and reached a terrifying but ultimately stable balance of terror. But while the spectre of nuclear Armageddon was sufficient to maintain an uneasy peace for a while, nuclear strategies and doctrines changed, and bomber development continued apace. An all-out nuclear response to a limited attack became less and less credible, while the availability of larger numbers of smaller tactical nuclear weapons led to the adoption of a strategy of flexible response, in which retaliation short of all-out war was possible, and in which

Above, top: *The Tupolev Tu-16 'Badger' was the Soviet Union's equivalent to the Boeing B-47 Stratojet. The aircraft entered service in late 1953 and was an important part of the Soviet Cold War armory.*
Above: *Weapons such as the SAM-2 missile removed the protection once afforded by high altitude flight.*

it even became possible to envisage fighting a limited nuclear war.

The first nuclear weapons had been bulky and heavy, and strategic targeting had dictated that they should be carried by long range aircraft. The new tactical weapons were much smaller, and might be aimed against targets just behind enemy lines, and so they could be carried by smaller light and medium bombers, and even by

modified fighter bombers.

Heavy defensive armament had already been proven to be of limited utility during World War II, and bomber designers sought to provide protection by endowing their aircraft with superior performance, and especially by flying very high—above the reach of enemy ground defenses. The development of high altitude Surface-to-Air Missiles (SAMs) removed the sanctuary of high altitude. Bombers were now forced to fly at very low altitude, penetrating enemy air defenses by flying 'under-the-radar'. These low-level tactics were quickly adopted by all offensive aircraft, from large strategic bombers to small fighter-bombers and strike/attack aircraft.

Today's fighters can often carry heavier bombloads than most World War II bombers, and can deliver their weapons with pinpoint accuracy, in all weathers. Some fighter-sized aircraft are built to fulfill what our fathers and grandfathers would recognize as a 'pure bomber' role, and have little or no air-to-air capability. Some, like the F-111 and F-117, even have fighter designations. When the SEPECAT Jaguar entered RAF service in the mid-1970s, commentators were astonished that an 'aircraft with the wingspan of a Spitfire could take off from East Anglia and clobber a pinpoint target in Germany with a Lancaster-sized

payload, and all in eight eighths clag!' The fact that the same Jaguar could have flown an even longer mission carrying a single atomic bomb, with more destructive power than an entire 1,000 Bomber Raid, was left unsaid.

Such aircraft formed the backbone of the opposing North Atlantic Treaty Organization (NATO) and Warsaw Pact airforces throughout the Cold War, while the importance of long range strategic bombers declined with the introduction of submarine-launched ballistic missiles and land-based Intercontinental Ballistic Missiles (ICBMs). But bombers retained a vital role, because they kept a 'man in the loop'. As such, manned bombers could be more flexible than missiles, searching for and evaluating targets before they were attacked. Manned bombers could switch to attacking a secondary target, and could even be recalled after launch.

The increasing sophistication of air defence radars and SAMs, the introduction of Airborne Early Warning aircraft, and fighters with look-down radar, made low altitude penetration increasingly fraught with danger and difficulty. One solution was the development of dedicated radar and SAM suppression aircraft, optimized to attack and disable enemy air defenses in order to open up 'sanitized' corridors through enemy air space.

Above: *The Jaguar is typical of today's ground attack aircraft, combining high speed at very low level with sophisticated avionics and a knockout punch.*

Another solution, pursued throughout the 1970s by the United States, was to design specialized bombers with very low radar cross sections, which would be effectively invisible to enemy radar, at least until they were too close to their targets to be detected and engaged. These 'Stealthy' aircraft were not invisible to radar, but their very low radar signatures meant that the range of enemy radar was dramatically reduced. The first operational Stealth warplane, the F-117A, was designed as a 'Silver Bullet' able to attack targets undetected, and perhaps even to be used 'deniably', or to spearhead attacks against an enemy's air defenses, or even to attack high value, heavily defended targets on the 'first night' of any war. To maintain its potential 'deniability' the F-117A's very existence was a closely guarded secret until some years after it had entered service. The later B-2 bomber was much larger, with inter-continental range, but its existence was always admitted and acknowledged. At one time, it seemed likely that the B-2 would be procured in large numbers, and would become the spearhead of the USAF's manned bomber force,

Opposite page, top: The Northrop B-2 is the world's most sophisticated bomber, combining stealth technology with sophisticated target-finding systems.

Opposite page, middle: The ageing B-52 (seen here dropping bombs over Vietnam) remains in service today. The aircraft is a popular and useful work-horse.

Opposite page, bottom: The F-117 Nighthawk, although it has an F- for fighter designation, is a dedicated stealth bomber. The type became operational in 1983.

able to attack the most difficult and heavily defended targets. The end of the Cold War saw procurement scaled back dramatically, leaving the type equipping only a single specialized Bomb Wing.

In the post Cold War world, the bomber role has changed again. The Superpowers (and a handful of other nations) retain nuclear weapons, but have put them beyond immediate use, and huge fleets of nuclear strike aircraft are no longer held 'cocked' on alert, ready to launch and unleash Armageddon at a moments notice.

Massive fleets of strategic bombers have been retired and carefully dismantled under the terms of a succession of international treaties and agreements. In the baking heat of the Arizona desert, countless B-52s have been cut into sections using giant guillotines, then left in pieces for prowling Russian satellites to photograph, before finally being processed into aluminium ingots. Behind the former Iron Curtain, Russian heavy bombers have met the same fate.

Surviving strategic bombers have embraced new roles, gaining new conventional attack capabilities using a wide range of non-nuclear weapons, from simple 'dumb' iron bombs to laser-guided and Global Positioning System-guided (GPS) bombs or even sophisticated cruise missiles.

Post Cold War conflicts have been marked by a great concentration on accuracy, and by a desire to avoid what is euphemistically referred to as 'collateral damage' (the death of enemy civilians). This has been accompanied by an unwillingness to accept aircrew losses. These two factors have driven a move towards campaigns in which (usually old-fashioned and rather primitive) enemy air defenses are carefully sanitized (usually by Cruise Missiles, specialized defense suppression aircraft and standoff weapons) before a second phase in which 'main force bombers' deliver Precision Guided Munitions (PGMs) from medium level.

The increasing squeamishness of political leaders has led to a distaste for excessive casualties even among enemy frontline troops (perhaps especially where they can be seen as being relatively innocent pawns of a dictator or a despotic regime). This has led to a concentration on attacking the enemy's military infrastructure, and command and communication facilities, rather than troops in the field, hitting strategic targets rather than tactical. Any tactical air campaign would also tend to require greater use of low level tactics, and might be expected to generate heavier casualties, which are no longer tolerable.

During the Gulf War of 1991, there were relatively few constraints on Allied bombers and fighter-bombers, and as a result, the air campaign was extremely effective. Some dispute whether air power alone could have forced Iraq's dictator, Saddam Hussein, to disengage his forces from positions which threatened Kuwait had the bombing campaign gone on longer. This can be acknowledged, however, as a distinct possibility, and there is no doubt that bombing played a decisive part in the Allied victory.

Similarly, Operation Deliberate Force in Bosnia in 1995 saw air power achieve a coercive victory against the Bosnian Serb leadership, who were forced to accede to NATO demands after a brief but intensive air campaign which was aimed against both strategic and tactical targets.

In Kosovo in 1999, NATO bombers were primarily targeted against strategic objectives. The Yugoslav army in the field in Kosovo was relatively untouched, and 85% of it returned to Serbia unscathed at the end of the war, having lost 13 tanks or less. Moreover, an air campaign planned to last for about a week, and involving 300 aircraft, dragged on for 78 days, 'sucking in' some 900 aircraft. Meanwhile, as the campaign dragged on, the Serbs were free to continue their murderous campaign of ethnic cleansing.

Even though every attempt was made by NATO to avoid collateral damage, Serbia suffered civilian casualties of between 500 and 1,200 out of a total population of 22 million. On a daily basis, compared to British civilian casualties during World War II, and measured as a percentage of total population, the Serbian casualty rate was extremely similar. There were also a number of high profile incidents in which civilian casualties seemed to be the result of reckless targeting, during attacks on bridges far from the war zone, and during the attack on the Serbian state TV station. If the Gulf War marked the high-point of air power and bombing, then Kosovo marked its most recent low-point.

As these words were written, US bombing missions were underway against the Taliban regime in Afghanistan, as part of the retaliation for the terrorist attacks on the World Trade Center and Pentagon building in the United States on 11 September 2001. USAF long-range strategic bombers, including the Northrop B-2, Boeing B-52H and Rockwell B-1B were augmented by carrierborne F/A-18 and F-14 aircraft, and seemed to be targeted primarily against very small and limited semi-strategic targets. It will be interesting to analyze the results of the air campaign mounted by the United States against the Taliban forces from October 2001, to assess whether the lessons of Kosovo have been learned.

EARLY RFC AND RNAS BOMBERS

THE BRITISH WERE by no means the first to use aircraft to drop bombs 'in anger', but do have some grounds for claiming to be the first to make effective use of aerial bombs. Italian bombing in Libya in 1911 was of little more than nuisance value, while German bombs dropped during the first few months of the World War I were generally of little significance, making little impact except on Allied newspaper editors.

But on October 8, 1914, Britain's RNAS launched a historic raid against strategic German targets. Taking off from Antwerp, northern Belgium, two RNAS pilots, flying Sopwith Tabloids, attacked Köln and Düsseldorf. At Köln, Squadron Commander Grey attacked the railroad station, while Flt Lt Marix attacked the Zeppelin sheds at Düsseldorf, destroying a newly completed airship. Some six weeks later, the RNAS sent three Avro 504s to bomb the Zeppelin factory in the southwestern city of Friedrichshafen, causing significant damage and destroying the hydrogen gas plant. In floatplane form, the Tabloid had won the Schneider Trophy in April 1914, but the type's service life was short, and it soon gave way to more powerful two-seaters.

One such was the Short 184, derived from a prewar floatplane designed for a 'Circuit of Britain' race. The aircraft featured folding wings (for shipboard use) and were optimized to carry torpedoes. Later the 184's wings were fitted with bomb racks and they were used in the bomber role on a number of occasions.

More importantly, perhaps, the Short 184 formed the basis of a land-plane bomber (known simply as the Short Bomber) with a new wing and a lengthened fuselage. These aircraft re-equipped No.7 Wing, RNAS, at Coudekerque, northern France, and went into action in November 1916, when four aircraft, each carrying eight 65-lb (29.4-kg) bombs, attacked U-boat pens at the Belgian port of Zeebrugge. The type subsequently equipped the RNAS No.3 Wing at Luxeuil (attacking targets in the Saar industrial region on the Franco-German border) and 14 were transferred to the RFC.

Early bombers were not purpose-built, but tended to be hasty in-the-field modifications of general purpose (eg reconnaissance) aircraft. In the early months of World War I, units had a mix of types. The RNAS Squadron based in Belgium used BEs, Bleriots, a Bristol TB.8 and a mix of Shorts and Sopwiths.

The most successful of Britain's early bombers began life as a Scout, or fighter, arguably the best of the RFC's early fighters, and the most effective counter to the Fokker scourge. This was the Royal Aircraft Factory FE.2b, which was adapted to the bomber role from mid-1916. With its generous, high lift wing and long range, the FE.2b was pressed into service as a bomber, finding particular

Right: *The Sopwith Tabloid had been a successful pre-war racing seaplane, but was successfully adapted as a land-based bomber. More powerful two-seaters soon replaced it.*

success with No.100 Squadron at night. Some of these aircraft were armed with a quick-firing Vickers One-pounder gun, and these were sent out against enemy road and rail transport. Others carried heavy bombs, of up to 230lb (104kg) in weight.

Left: *No.100 Squadron's FE.2bs were used with signal success in the night intruder role.*
Below: *The Short bomber was based on the Short 184 seaplane. The aircraft formed the backbone of the RFC's early bomber force during World War I.*

RUSSIA'S EARLY HEAVY BOMBERS

TODAY, THE NAME of Igor Sikorsky is associated with the development of the helicopter in the United States. But the young Sikorsky began his career in Russia, designing aircraft for the Tsar, becoming the aeroplane designer with the Russo-Baltic Wagon Factory (RBVZ) at St Petersburg, the capital, during the Spring of 1912.

At Sikorsky's urging, the factory built an enormous aircraft, the Bolshoi Baltiskii or Grand, flying this on March 15, 1913 (March 2 according to the old Julian Calendar then still in use in Imperial Russia). Initially flown as a twin-engined aircraft, the type subsequently gained two more engines (at first mounted as pushers, behind the original engines, then further out along the wing, as tractors).

This aircraft formed the basis of a production aeroplane, named Il'ya Muromets (a legendary Ukrainian

Left: *The Ilya Muromets served with distinction in the bomber role. Only two of these Russian aircraft were lost in action—one after downing three attackers!*
Below: *A Ilya Muromets bomber with the red, white and blue tricolour of the Imperial Russian Air Service.*

hero) and some 80 were eventually delivered. Many were used as passenger carriers, but some formed the world's first dedicated strategic bomber unit, the EVK (Squadron of Flying Ships) formed under the command of MV Shidlovsky, chairman of the RBVZ.

The aircraft tended to operate with a crew of five or six, and carried up to six defensive machine guns of various types, with one aircraft even carrying a 37-mm Hotchkiss cannon. The Il'ya Muromets could carry a bomb load of up to 2,205lb (1,000kg). This consisted of bombs of up to 500lb (226.8kg) in weight.

The unit fought long and hard, operating from the Russian cities of Lida, Gatchina, Pskov and finally Vinnitsa. They flew extraordinary long-range bombing missions with only two losses to enemy action. One of these force-landed successfully and the other first shot down three German fighters. Following Russia's 1917 Revolution, surviving bombers were taken over by the Bolsheviks. These aircraft remained in service into the 1920s, as transports, airliners and as trainers for heavy aircraft pilots.

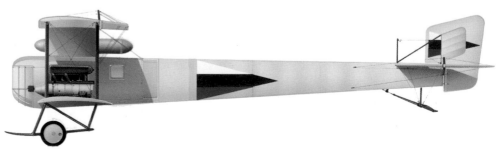

EARLY CAPRONI BOMBERS

AFTER THE SUCCESS of Italian airmen in dropping makeshift bombs during the Italo-Turkish War of 1911, the Italian Army pressed forward with the acquisition of dedicated purpose-designed bombers, turning to Count Gianni Caproni. His newly-formed aircraft firm designed a large three-engined biplane bomber, the Ca 30, its powerplants buried in the central nacelle and driving a pusher airscrew in the back of the nacelle and propellers at the front of each tailboom. The production Ca 31 retained one 100hp Fiat A-10 pusher engine in the nacelle, with similar A-10 tractor engines in the nose of each boom. The first of 164 entered service (with the military designation Ca 2) in July 1915. Caproni bombers were used in the strategic bombing offensive against Austria-Hungary. The Ca 2s flew their first mission on August 20. They were joined by the improved Ca 3 (Ca 33) which together flew long and dangerous missions over the Alps to attack Austrian targets. The bombers were crewed by two pilots, sitting side-by-side, with a front gunner in front of them and a rear gunner in an open cage above the rear engine,

immediately in front of the propeller, projecting above the top wing.

Caproni built a small series of a much bigger Ca 40 (Ca 4) triplane bomber. They were powered by three 270–350hp engines, and carried a 3,900-lb (1,769-kg) bombload. It was slow, vulnerable and mainly restricted to night raids. Caproni's final wartime bomber was the Ca 5 (manufacturers designation Ca 44 to Ca 47). It was a biplane of similar configuration to the Ca 3 but slightly smaller. Some 255 were built by Caproni and other Italian firms, with further production in France and the United States (by Standard and the Fisher Body division of General Motors). These aircraft brought Caproni's wartime bomber output to more than 740 aircraft. His work kept Italy at the forefront of aeronautical technology.

Right: *The Ca 5, Caproni's final World War I bomber. The Caproni company cemented its reputation as the producer of advanced, long-range bombers with the development of this aircraft.*
Below: *This Caproni Ca 3 of XI° Gruppo at Padua shows the squared off lines of the earlier Caproni bombers to advantage.*

THE GERMAN GIANTS

THE FIRST GERMAN attempts to drop bombs were ad-hoc affairs, in which individual officers made generally futile attempts to hand-drop tiny bombs and grenades from small scouts. The first was probably Lt Franz von Hiddeson who dropped two light bombs on Paris from his Etrich Taube monoplane on August 13, 1914, while another German airman dropped the first bomb on British soil (in a garden in Dover, southeast England) on Christmas Eve, 1914.

By comparison with the marginal load-carrying capability of the first aeroplanes, the German Zeppelin airships, were potentially much more dangerous weapons as they were able to carry much heavier bombloads. But although the lumbering airships could carry bombloads of up to 600lb (272.1kg)—far larger than could be carried by contemporary bomber aeroplanes—they proved very vulnerable. They were withdrawn from the campaign against London in the Fall of 1916, and later from the campaign against other British targets.

The Imperial German Military Aviation Service formed its first bomber units in mid-1915, although these original Kampfstaffeln were originally equipped with relatively light aircraft like the AEG KI and GI, carrying small bombloads. Codenamed Brieftauben Abteilungen (Carrier Pigeon Units), these aircraft

Left: *This Friedrichshafen G.III was captured by the British in early 1918. The type was extensively used for bombing duties on and across the Western Front.*

flew nuisance raids against targets on the east coast of England from the Belgian port of Ostend.

The first large, long-range bombers were first tested and deployed on the Eastern Front, where the Siemens-Schuckert Steffen R1 and Zeppelin-Staaken Versuchs Gotha Ost made their debut in 1916. Long-range bomber operations on the Eastern Front were piecemeal, and the emphasis soon shifted to the Western Front and to the campaign against Britain.

The AEG G.IV was introduced operationally at the end of 1916. Due to its combination of comparatively high structural weight and relatively small size for a twin aircraft, the G.IV could only carry a small load when fully fueled. For this reason it was mostly used for short-range tactical bombing behind the lines along the Western Front. By the time the AEG G.IV entered service it was outshone by new Zeppelin Staakens and Gothas, but nevertheless performed useful service.

Gotha produced a succession of bombers, the shorter-range, tactical GII and GIII serving in small numbers, before the introduction of the GIV and GV from early 1917. The Gotha was fast and well-armed. The aircraft's excellent 260hp Mercedes engines enabled it to operate in the region of 15,000ft (4,572m). As the British defenses lacked adequate early warning facilities the Gotha bombers were able to approach and release their bombs before British fighter aircraft could attain the same altitude. Gothas mounted a daylight bombing

campaign against Britain between May 25 and August 22, 1917. These German raids achieved a remarkable degree of success and casualties were surprisingly low. Public outcry in Great Britain forced the withdrawal of operational fighter squadrons from France for home defense duties,

although initially even these found the Gothas a difficult target.

An outstanding feature of the German bomber was the rear gunner's useful field of fire below and above the aircraft. This 'sting in the tail' required the development of new tactics by RFC fighters.

Then, however, the Gothas had to switch to night attacks. These raids continued until May 1918. By the end of its campaign, Bombengeschwader 3 had dropped 84,745kg (186,828lb) of bombs during 22 raids, losing 24 Gotha aircraft to Allied defenses and 37 in accidents.

Left: *A Zeppelin Staaken RVII after crashing en route to the front. The Zeppelin Staaken aircraft manufacturer produced a succession of giant bombers.*
Below: *Gothas like this one formed the backbone of Germany's air assault against Britain during 1917 and 1918. They mounted both daylight and night raids.*

The Zeppelin Staaken VGO I, II and III were one-offs used on the Eastern Front, while the RIV moved from the East to the West. The main production Riesenflugzeug (Giant Aircraft) was the RVI, 18 of which were built, entering service with squadrons near Ghent, western Belgium, in June 1917. Powered by four 200hp or 260hp engines, the RVI could carry 4,409lb (2,000kg) of bombs, including massive 2,204.6-lb (1,000-kg) weapons. The RVIs made their first attack on England on September 17, 1917, and made about 11 more raids plus solo attacks. These included a daring raid in which one RVI scored a direct hit on St Pancras Station, central London, on February 17/18, 1918. No RVIs were lost to Allied defenses, and they dropped 59,943lb (27,190kg) of bombs during their brief career.

On the Western Front, tactical bombing missions were flown by a variety of types, including a succession of Friedrichshafen G-series bombers.

Opposite: *A carefully posed photo of an Albatross Scout and a Gotha G.IV bomber, ostensibly preparing for a bomber/escort mission.* **Right:** *The crew of the Gotha G.Vb were well concentrated in the fuselage nacelle. This enabled them to communicate easily.* **Below:** *A Gotha G.III, a short-range, tactical bomber. Like all Gotha bombers, the G.III was characterized by its long-span, high-aspect ratio three-bay wings.*

SOPWITH 1½ STRUTTER

THE SOPWITH COMPANY became justifiably famous for its family of single-seat Scouts, which served with distinction with both the RFC and RNAS, and became familiar names to every aviation enthusiast. These ranged from the Pup, whose delightful handling and maneuverability allowed it to remain in service long after its performance had ceased to be truly competitive, and the underrated Triplane, to the supremely agile (if dangerously unpredictable) Camel and the Snipe—too late to make much of a difference, but arguably the best fighter of the war.

The company's other fighters and attack aircraft are less well remembered, though some of them were built in enormous numbers, and played a crucial role in World War I. The Sopwith 1½ Strutter is the most obvious of the forgotten Sopwiths, with 1,439 built in Great Britain, and 4,500 more in France!

Named after the unusual W-section struts joining the fuselage and the upper wing, the Sopwith 1½ Strutter was also known as the Sopwith Two Seater and as the Type 9400. The aircraft could fly at 14,993ft (4,570m) and reached a maximum speed of 100mph (161km/h). Armed with a Lewis gun in the rear cockpit and another firing through the airscrew, the 1½ Strutter was intended as a general purpose aircraft, but after entering RNAS service in April 1916 the aircraft was quickly pressed into use in the escort and bomber roles. The Sopwith 1½ Strutter could carry a 60-kg (132.2-lb) bombload.

Although smaller and lighter than the Short Bomber, the Sopwith 1½ Strutter had a long range. The two aircraft together equipped No.3 Wing, RNAS, the first dedicated strategic bombing force, with 15 Shorts augmented by 20 Sopwith 1½ Strutter bombers and 20 Sopwith 1½ Strutter escort fighters. The formation of No.3 Wing was delayed by the offensive on the Somme in 1916, which saw large numbers of Sopwith 1½ Strutters being transferred to the RFC. These were used to make up deficiencies in the Corps' frontline strength.

Despite the Sopwith 1½ Strutter being quickly outclassed by the new generation of German Albatros DI and DII Scouts, it remained in RFC and RNAS use on the Western Front until mid-1917. Thereafter the aircraft was used for home defense and coastal patrol duties. Some were also modified for use on the Royal Navy's first aircraft carriers.

France also employed the Sopwith 1½ Strutter in the bomber role, using the type for a number of historic raids. The first of these was made against the city of Essen, west central Germany, on September 24, 1916, with another solo mission being flown across the Alps on November 17, 1916. But by the time significant numbers of the Sopwith 1½ Strutter were in service, the type was obsolete, and French experience with the aircraft was generally a unhappy one.

Right: *The 1 1/2 Strutter was named after the unusual W-section (when viewed from directly ahead) inter-cabane struts. It proved a useful bomber on the Western Front.*

HANDLEY PAGE HEAVIES

WHEN THE RNAS issued a specification for a long-range bomber capable of hauling six 112-lb (50.8-kg) bombs the requirement was colloquially summarized as being for a 'bloody paralyzer of an aeroplane', although it was modest by comparison with the big Capronis already in service with the Italian Air Force. Frederick Handley Page responded with the Handley Page O/100. This exceeded the Admiralty Specification in every way, with two 250hp engines, a four-man crew, five defensive machine guns and carrying 16 112-lb (50.8-kg) or eight 250-lb (113.4-kg) bombs (all in internal bays). The O/400 entered service with No.5 Wing, RNAS, in November 1916. The aircraft had crew armor and folding wings, allowing the aircraft to fit in a standard canvas Bessoneau hangar. Some 40 O/100s were built with Eagle II engines, and six with 320hp Sunbeam Cossacks. Some were used to equip No.16 Squadron, one of the three units of the RFC's 41st Wing, operating alongside the DH 4s of No.55 Squadron and the FE2bs of No.100 Squadron.

Two were sent to Palestine, supporting General Edmund Allenby's forces, and the Arabs led by Prince Feisal of Hijaz and TE Lawrence. The other went to Mudros in the Aegean, operating against the Turks. The modified Handley Page O/400 (nick-named the Bloody Paralyzer) introduced 360hp Rolls Royce Eagle VIII engines and a

Left: The Handley Page O/400 was nicknamed the 'Bloody Paralyzer'. It formed the backbone of the RAF's heavy bomber force at the end of World War I, and operated in large numbers.

new fuel system. Handley Page delivered more than 400 of the new bombers to the RNAS, RFC and RAF before the Armistice, and 107 more were built by Standard in the United States. The type was probably the most effective strategic heavy bomber of World War I, proving more accurate and less vulnerable to enemy fighters than the day-bombing DH 4s. The O/400 formed the backbone of Hugh Trenchard's Independent Force that was created for the strategic bombing of Germany. Their raids laid the groundwork for the RAF's doctrine throughout the 1920s, 1930s and even World War II.

The aircraft operated in large numbers (including raids of up to 40 aircraft at a time), as singles and pairs. On one occasion, on August 25, 1917, two aircraft from No.215 Squadron attacked the Badische Anilin chemical works at Mannheim in southeast Germany, bombing and strafing the factory from low level.

In September the O/400s began using the 1,650-lb (748.4-kg) bomb, but by then the even larger, more powerful V/1500 was on order, capable of dropping a 3,360-lb (1,524-kg) bomb. The four-engined V/1500 was twice the weight of the 0/400 and carried 28 112-lb (50.8-kg) bombs.

With the amalgamation of the RFC and RNAS to form the Royal Air Force in April 1918, No.3 Wing and the 41st Wing combined to form the Independent Force. This included No.166 Squadron, which received the first V/1500s and which stood ready to bomb Berlin even as the war ended.

The O/400 never received the development it deserved and enjoyed only the briefest postwar career. O/400s

Opposite, top: *The Handley Page 0/100 featured folding wings to allow it to be accomodated in a standard RFC canvas Bessoneau hangar.*

Opposite, bottom: *Despite its size, the Handley Page O/400 proved surprisingly survivable, and few were lost. It featured five defensive machine guns.*

Right: *A No.48 Squadron O/400 overflying the Rhine during 1919. The type served until 1923.*

Below: *One of a batch of Handley Page O/400s built by the Birmingham Carriage Company. D5438 is still factory fresh.*

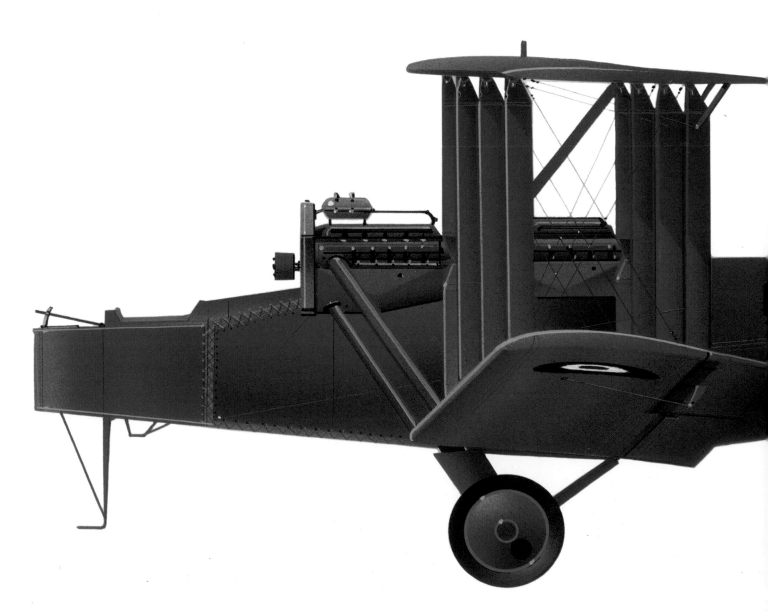

Above: *The V/1500, with its paired pusher/tractor engines, could carry twice the bombload of the earlier O/400.*
Opposite: *With its deep slab sided fuselage, the Handley Page V/1500 was a cumbersome looking machine.*
Below: *A V/1500 of No.274 Squadron, based at RAF Bircham Newton in eastern England.*

were flown with Liberty 12 and Napier Lion engines, either of which would have made the type competitive with aircraft like the DH10 Amiens or the Vickers Vimy. A minor change to the wing section would have had a similarly dramatic effect. But no such development was undertaken, and the

0/400 disappeared from the Royal Air Force by mid-1923. One of about 20 V/1500s completed (of 255 ordered) was used to bomb a rebel stronghold at Kabul, Afghanistan, in 1919, scoring direct hits on Amir Amanullah's arsenal, but the type disappeared from service in 1920.

AIRCO DH 4, DH 9 AND DH 9A

THE DH 4 WAS, in some respects, a more important bomber than the big Handley Page 'Heavies', although it lacked their magnificent size and bombload. It was used in larger numbers and performed strategic and tactical missions with almost equal facility.

The aircraft was of conventional design and its success was largely due to its excellent Rolls Royce Eagle engine, although disruptions to engine production initially limited deliveries of the new day bomber to the RFC. The first DH 4 squadron in France, No.55 Squadron, arrived in March 1917, but the build-up of units was slow. Only four RFC units and two RNAS squadrons were operational by the end of July. They were kept in reserve until the Battle of Arras, northern France, in order to achieve surprise. No.55 flew its first raid on April 6, 1917, bombing railway sidings at Valenciennes. The DH 4 formed the backbone of the Independent Force and 12 squadrons were still equipped with the type in November 1918. The type was also built under license in the United States. It became the only US-built aircraft to see active service, arriving at the front in May 1918. Improved versions equipped the USAAC until the 1930s.

The Airco DH 9 was intended as a modified derivative of the DH 4, and originally promised to offer superior performance, powered by the Siddeley Puma or Fiat A-12 engine. With these engines, the DH 9 would never exceed the DH 4's performance. Many, including Trenchard, then commanding the RFC in France, pressed for the DH 9 to

be abandoned and for production to concentrate on the DH 4. Production was limited and slow, but the DH 9 entered service at the start of 1918. White forces in Russia used the type in 1919, but it was soon retired, apart from some trainers which had been re-engined with Jaguar radial engines.

The limitations of the Puma-engined DH 9 soon became apparent, and Westland were directed to produce a new version of the aircraft, powered by the American 400hp Liberty engine, this becoming the DH 9A or 'Ninack'.

The first 'Ninack' squadron was No.110. This proved to be a revelation when it began operations at the end of August 1918. Only two units had fully converted to the DH 9A by the time the war ended, but this was enough to demonstrate its superiority over the original DH 9, carrying almost double the bombload at a higher ceiling. Some DH 9As were used by the RAF in Russia in 1919. A handful were captured and copied, resulting in Russia's first Shturmovik, the R-1. Planned US production of 4,000 was cancelled after the Armistice, although nine prototypes were completed.

The Airco DH 9A remained in RAF service after the war. It formed the backbone of the Colonial policing squadrons in the Middle East and India. These DH 9As dropped bombs 'in anger' on many occasions, and served until 1930.

Right: *The original Eagle-engined DH 4 was probably the most successful RFC bomber of the World War I. The aircraft first saw action on the Western Front in April 1917.*

BREGUET 14

DESPITE THE RAPID pace of aeronautical development during the World War I and the 1920s, a number of 1914–18 aircraft types enjoyed careers of extraordinary longevity. In Britain, the Avro 504, the Bristol Fighter, the DH 9A, and the Vickers Vimy were the best examples, while in France it was the Breguet 14.

A successful and established 34 year-old aircraft designer when war broke out in 1914, Louis Charles Breguet flew aircraft of his own design during the early months of the conflict, winning a Croix de Guerre for a daring reconnaissance mission during the Battle of the Marne (September 6–9).

Breguet's prewar aircraft had all been tractor biplanes, but his first powerful military aircraft, the U-3. This was a pusher, in order to conform to Armée de l'Air thinking of the time, which demanded an unobstructed front cockpit for the observer.

Breguet returned to the tractor configuration for what was destined to be his most successful design, the Breguet AV Type XIV, with AV standing for 'Avant', indicating the forward location of the engine. By insisting on the use of the 12-cylinder Renault engine, rather than the officially favoured Hispano-Suiza, Breguet harnessed his new design to an engine that was both excellent and at the beginning of its development life. The bomber's power output would soon soar from 220hp to 275hp, and then on to 316hp. Later versions of the engine would produce even more power, going from 350hp to 390hp, and then from 400hp up to 450hp. Slab-sided and square-nosed, the Breguet 14 was an uninspiring aircraft to look at, though its structure, with its extensive use of oxy-welded duralumin was more advanced.

Following the type's maiden flight on November 21, 1916 (in the hands of Breguet himself) the Type XIV soon received massive orders, and a number of factories were pressed into the production program. The new type began replacing Sopwith $1^1/_2$ Strutters from the summer of 1917.

The Breguet 14, as well as equipping the French Army's bomber and reconnaissance squadrons, was also delivered to the Belgian Aviation Militaire. The American Expeditionary Force also received 376.

Production of the Breguet 14 bomber continued until 1926 (by which time some 8,000 had been built) and the type was exported widely. The aircraft was used in a number of French colonial campaigns, and also dropped bombs in anger in China.

Left: *This restored Breguet 14 offers French airshow audiences a fascinating glimpse into their aeronautical heritage.*
Inset: *A Breguet 14 in Armée de l'Air colours. The type made its maiden flight in November 1916.*

DE HAVILLAND DH 10 AMIENS

THE DE HAVILLAND DH 10 Amiens biplane was one of history's great 'might have beens'. Just too late to see significant service in World War I, the DH 10 bomber demonstrated enormous potential, but was ill-suited to peacetime operations. As a result the aircraft quickly faded from the scene.

This aircraft was derived from the DH 3A of 1916. It was built in prototype form and ordered but cancelled in favour of the single-engined DH 4. The same basic twin-engined configuration was resurrected in 1917, to meet a requirement for a medium-range day bomber.

This aircraft would have to haul a 500-lb (226-kg) bombload at a speed of at least 110mph (177km/h) at around a height of 15,000ft (4,572m). The DH 10 was required to have a ceiling of 19,000ft (5,791m). The aircraft was also seen as a potential long distance bomber escort, probably equipped with a $1\frac{1}{2}$ pounder Coventry Ordnance Works COW gun.

The prototype de Havilland DH 10 Amiens even retained the pusher Puma engines of the DH 3. These, however, were soon destined to be replaced by tractor Eagle engines on the type's second prototype.

Production of the de Havilland DH 10 Amiens was delayed by labor problems in Great Britain and a shortage of the internal bracing Rafwires. Once the aircraft was launched it resulted in a plethora of variants. The DH 10A Amiens Mk IIIa had its Eagle engines mounted directly on the lower wing, while the DH 10C had Liberty engines in the same position as on the

A. These later variants of the aircraft did not see any service use.

By the end of October 1918, eight DH 10 aircraft had been delivered, and only two were officially on the strength of the Independent Force, with No.104 Squadron. Captain Ewart Garland flew the De Havilland DH10 Amien's only World War I combat mission, just one day before the Armistice, on November 10, 1918. During this mission Captain Ewart Garland's DH 10 bomber attacked Sarrebourg aerodrome in northeast France.

Small numbers of DH 10s were delivered before production was abandoned and the type briefly equipped No. 60 Squadron (and its predecessor, No. 97 Squadron) in India. The DH 10s performed a Colonial Policing role and dropped bombs 'in anger' during operations against tribesmen in the northwest region of Waziristan. The aircraft was also briefly used by No.216 Squadron in the Middle East. This squadron was responsible for operating the Desert Air Mail service. The DH10s were used by the squadron to transport passengers as well as mail between the Egyptian capital, Cairo, and the Iraqi capital of Baghdad. The de Havilland DH 10 Amiens was finally declared obsolete and withdrawn in April 1923.

Right: *The de Havilland DH 10 Amiens was ill-suited for peacetime duties. The aircraft, however, was too late to see extensive wartime service, and the type quickly faded from the scene.*

VICKERS VIMY

THE VICKERS VIMY is today best remembered for what were really footnotes in its long career—acting as the mount for John Alcock and Arthur Brown's successful non-stop east to west crossing of the Atlantic in 1919, and for Keith and Ross Smith's epic England to Australia journey in the same year. The aircraft was also used for the historic 1920 flight by Pierre van Ryneveld and Christopher Brand from the Egyptian capital of Cairo to Cape Town, South Africa.

This British aircraft was conceived, however, to meet a much more warlike purpose, as a short-range heavy night bomber. The prototype Vickers FB 27 made its maiden flight on November 30, 1917, and quickly demonstrated that it could carry a heavier bombload than the much more powerful Handley Page 0/400. The Vickers Vimy carried a 2,476lb (1,123kg) bombload on external racks.

The Vickers Vimy prototype was powered by two 200hp Hispano-Suiza engines, but early aircraft flew with a bewildering array of powerplants, and wartime contracts placed were for aircraft powered by Fiat A-12bis, BHP and Liberty engines. In the event, however, almost all of those completed (about 200) were delivered with Rolls Royce Eagle engines.

The Eagle-powered Vickers Vimy bomber was something of a revelation. The aircraft proved capable of attaining a maximum speed of 100mph (160.9km/h) with sufficient fuel for an eleven-hour endurance. Its test pilot,

Left: The Vimy followed a similar configuration to that of the big Handley Page bombers, and entered service just as World War I ended.

Squadron Leader Rollo de Haga Haig, even succeeded in looping a Vimy.

Three Vickers Vimys were delivered to the RAF by the end of October 1918, one of these reaching the Independent Force at Nancy in north-eastern France. Two aircraft were sent to experimental units, despite a directive requiring that all aircraft delivered in 1918 should go to anti-submarine squadrons. The Vimy had belatedly (but extremely successfully) been adapted for anti-submarine warfare (ASW) work, and was intended to replace the Blackburn Kangaroo.

Postwar, the Vimy entered service with No.58 Squadron in Egypt in July 1919, replacing the Handley Page O/400s, and two more squadrons in Egypt re-equipped in 1921. Back in Great Britain, No.100 Squadron's D Flight received Vimys in 1922, subsequently splitting away to form No.7 Squadron in July 1923. Two further home-based units re-equipped in April 1924. The type then began to be withdrawn, and after 1925 served only with an Auxiliary unit, No.502 (County of Ulster) Squadron in Northern Ireland. The type remained in use there until 1929.

Even after the Vickers Vimy's withdrawal from the bomber role, the type continued to give useful service as a trainer and as a transport for trainee parachutists. A number of reconditioned Vimys (some with Jupiter or Jaguar radial engines) served until the early 1930s.

The Vickers Vimy also formed the basis of the Vickers Vernon transport. In early 1919 the civilian Vimy Commercial, with a larger diameter fuselage, was produced. This was mainly supplied to foreign purchasers.

MARTIN MB-1 AND MB-2

THE MARTIN MB-2 was derived from the Martin MB-1, the first twin-engined USAAC bomber, only ten of which had been built, four of them as 'Model G' observation aircraft, and one as a 'Model P' transport. There were three delivered as standard 'Model M' day bombers while the 'Model TA' (the GMT) was a long-range bomber intended for a trans-atlantic flight. The 'Model CA' (the GMC) was a 37-mm (1.4-inch) cannon and 3-in (7.62-cm) recoilless rifle-armed ground attack testbed.

The MB-1, while it was numerically unimportant, did break the USAAS's dependence on European designs. Glenn Martin also transformed his firm to build the bomber, charging Lawrence Bell with erecting a new factory at Cleveland, Ohio, while Donald Douglas designed the entirely conventional airframe.

With its Liberty 12 engines, the MB-1 was claimed to offer better performance than the latest Capronis and Handley Page bombers, but this was a rather empty boast. The Army ordered 50 more Martin bombers for the expected 1919 offensive against Germany. Optimists predicted an eventual order for more than 1,500 but this fell to ten aircraft after the Armistice. Orders from the Post Office and the Navy kept Martin in the 'airplane business'. This resulted in six 'Model MP' mailplanes, two torpedo-armed 'Model MBT' torpedo aircraft, and eight 'Model MT' aircraft.

In June 1920 the Army ordered 20 examples of an improved Model MB-2 derivative although the MB-1 had not entered squadron service. They had wider span wings, a larger tail, and did enter squadron service. With a scarcity of military aircraft production work subsequent orders for the MB-2 (later officially known as the NBS-1, but referred to as Martin Bombers) were placed with Lowe, Willard and Fowler (35 aircraft), Curtiss (50), and Aeromarine (25).

The MB-2s were rushed into service in time to participate in 'Billy' Mitchell's controversial July 1921 bombing trials, sinking the captured German battleship *Ostfriesland*. Most were delivered to the 2nd Bomb Group in the United States, units in the Canal Zone, Hawaii and the Philippines. They were replaced by Keystone bombers in 1927–28.

Derivatives of the NBS-1 included the Elias XNBS-3. It was as a replacement for the Martin NBS-1, as was the Curtiss XNBS-4, which closely resembled the NBS-1. Neither the Elias XNBS-3 nor the Curtiss XNBS-4 offered any real advantage over the NBS-1, and they were not ordered.

The XNBS-4 was developed into the XB-2, and flew in September 1927. The XB-2 competed for an order with the Keystone XB-1B, the Keystone XLB-6, the Sikorsky S-37B, and the Atlantic-Fokker XLB-2. It was a clear winner on technical grounds. There were 12 production B-2s ordered and delivered by January 1930.

Right: *Martin MB-2s like this one participated in Billy Mitchell's infamous 1921 bombing trials against captured German ships.*

VICKERS VIRGINIA

THE VICKERS VIRGINIA looked very similar to the World War I heavies, like the Vickers Vimy and Handley Page 0/400. It was, however, a much more modern biplane bomber. The Vickers Virginia had two Napier Lion engines, and, on later variants, it also had sweptback wing, autopilot, Handley-Page slats, and tailwheel.

The aircraft had an all-metal fabric-covered airframe as opposed to wood. Apart from the open cockpit, the positions of the other aircrew members were enclosed in the fuselage.

The prototype Virginia made its maiden flight on November 24, 1922. The Vickers Virginia was intended to replace the Vickers Vimy and served as one of the Royal Air Force's main heavy bombers for most of the period between the two world wars.

The Vickers Virginia entered Royal Air Force service in June 1924 with No.7 Squadron at the Bircham Newton airbase in eastern England. The aircraft, nicknamed Ginnie, eventually went on to serve with ten other RAF squadrons, two of these were auxiliary units.

Some Vickers Virginia bombers enjoyed exceptionally long service lives, at least one serving for 17 years. The Virginia squadrons won the annual Lawrence Minot trophy, the prestigious US bombing competition, on at least eight occasions.

Left: The Vickers Virginia was introduced in 1924 and served until 1938. The aircraft enjoyed a long and productive service career.
Inset: Later Virginias had a swept-back wing, Handley-Page slats, a tailwheel and even a primitive autopilot. The type was regarded as being one of the RAF's main interwar heavy bombers.

There were eight production variants of the Vickers Virginia, although only 124 bombers were delivered to the Royal Air Force. The early versions of the bomber were the dual-control Mk III and the Mk IV, which had dihedral on the lower wing only, and the Mk V, which introduced 486hp Lion II engines. Dihedral on both upper and lower mainplanes was introduced on the Mk VI, while the Mk VII introduced 502hp Lion V engines, sweptback outer wings and a redesigned nose.

The Mk IX had a lengthened nose and a lengthened tail, with a tail gunner's position added for the first time. This finally killed-off the planned gunners nacelles on the trailing edge of the upper wing, flight-tested on the first prototype (which became the sole Mk VIII).

The Mk X introduced the all-metal airframe, and deleted fixed tailfins, retaining rudders only on the tail unit. There were 50 Mk Xs built as such, and 53 aircraft were converted to the later standard.

The Vickers Virginia could fly at 15,501ft (4,725m) and was able to reach a maximum speed of 108mph (174km/h). It could carry a 2,998-lb (1,360-kg) bombload.

A handful of Vickers Virginias remained on Bomber Command charge as heavy night bombers until February 1938. These aircraft served with No.51 Squadron at Driffield in northern England.

These bombers were finally replaced by Armstrong Whitworth Whitleys. The Virginias used by the parachute training school which formed part of the Home Aircraft Depot at Henlow were similarly replaced.

FAIREY FOX

THE FAIREY FOX revolutionized the Royal Air Force's thinking about the day bomber, although only 28 were built for the service. The aircraft was also the first bomber to live up to the oft-claimed ability to be 'faster than fighters of the day'. The Fox was designed as a private venture and replaced undistinguished single-engined bombers like the Fairey Fawn and the Hawker Horsley.

The prototype of this fast biplane was built at the company's own expense. After the aircraft was demonstrated to Hugh Trenchard (the then Chief of the Air Staff), however, it was immediately ordered into production to equip one squadron.

The Fairey Fox was born after Richard Fairey came across the extremely clean and low cross-section Curtiss D-12 engine during a visit to the United States. This was intended to be built in Great Britain as the Fairey Felix. Fairey immediately drew up a new two-seat day bomber design, extremely clean and highly streamlined, with even the gunner's Scarff ring replaced by a new high speed Fairey gun mount.

The prototype flew on January 3, 1925, and the type replaced the then-current day bomber, the Fairey Fawn. It was issued to No.12 Squadron based at Andover in southern England, in June 1926. This squadron became the sole operator of the aircraft. Throughout its service, the Fairey Fox proved virtually invulnerable to fighter interception. The aircraft was also nimble and a joy to fly.

The Fairey Fox had a service ceiling of 17,000ft (5,182m) and the bomber reached a maximum speed of 161mph (260km/h). It was 50mph (80.4km/h) faster than the Fawn. The aircraft was capable of carrying a 458-lb (208-kg) bombload. Some Foxes were subsequently converted to use the Rolls Royce Kestrel IIA engine, these becoming known as Fox Mk IAs.

While the Fairey Fawn had only two and a half years in frontline service, and the Horsley served for four years as a day bomber, the Fairey Fox served until 1931—an exceptionally long frontline career, by the standards of the day. When No.12 Squadron finally relinquished its Foxes for Hawker Harts, its aircraft were still capable of out-running all of the RAF's fighters. The squadron has retained a Fox-head badge to this day, this now appearing on the unit's Panavia Tornados.

Without the Fairey Fox, it is unlikely that there would ever have been a Hawker Hart or Hind. It could also be argued that the success of the type (and that of the Hawker Hart) laid the groundwork for the development of the de Havilland Mosquito and English Electric Canberra. The aircraft demonstrated the advantages and practicality of a bomber which relied on performance to reach its target.

For Fairey, the Fox laid the groundwork for the later, larger and somewhat slower Fairey IIIF, and the further improved Gordon. In Belgium, Avions Fairey progressively developed the Kestrel-engined version of the Fox light-bomber into a two-seat day and night fighter. The type remained in service when Nazi Germany invaded Belgium in 1940.

Right: *When the Curtiss D-12 engined Fox entered service it proved faster than the fighters of the day and revolutionized bomber tactics.*

KEYSTONE BOMBERS

BETWEEN 1924 AND 1932 the Keystone company (originally known as Huff-Daland) delivered more than 150 light bombers to the US Army Air Service and US Army Air Corps. Their designations ranged from LB-1 to LB-14. Individually, the variants were of little significance, but as a family, the Keystone bombers formed the backbone of the USAAC until the advent of the first monoplane bombers. Being conservative they were popular for their low cost, dependability and stability.

The first of the family was the Huff Daland LB-1, which appeared in 1923 as the XLB-1. Powered by a single 800hp Packard 1A-2540 V-12 water-cooled engine, the LB-1 was otherwise extremely conventional, although it did carry its 1,500-lb (680-kg) bombload internally. Nine production LB-1 Pegasus bombers, with an improved 2A-2540 engine were ordered for service tests. These aircraft soon found the single-engined configuration unsatisfactory. A single XHB-1 'Cyclops' was an enlarged and heavier version of the LB-1, which was to have been powered by a single 1,200hp engine, but which actually flew with a single Packard 2A-2540 engine.

The first Huff-Daland aircraft with twin engines was the XB-1. This became the first aircraft in the B-for-bomber designation series, and competed unsuccessfully with the

Left: *The LB-6 Panther differed from the original LB-5 in its engine mounting arrangement and longer span wings.*
Inset: *The LB-5 Pirate was the first of the Huff-Daland/Keystone bomber series to enter service with the United States Army Air Corps.*

Curtiss Condor for orders. This B-prefix was introduced in 1924 along with LB (Light Bomber) and the HB (Heavy Bomber) designation prefixes.

The XB-1 was produced by re-designing the single-engined XHB-1 with twin engines. With two engines, more fin area was required and the new XB-1 also featured twin tailfins. Powered by a pair of 510hp Packard 2A-1530 engines (later 600 hp Curtiss V-1570-5 Conquerors), the XB-1 bomber made its maiden flight during September 1927. Unusually, the XB-1 had two rear-gunners, each in a cockpit in the rear of the engine nacelles, instead of in the tail.

At much the same time, Huff-Daland also produced the twin-engined XLB-3. This one-off experimental bomber planned to be powered by a pair of experimental air-cooled and inverted Liberty V-1410-1 engines, and with triple rudders on the horizontal tailplane. The experimental engines proved unreliable, and the XLB-3 was re-engined with 410hp Pratt & Whitney R-1340-1 radial engines before it flew, re-designated as the XLB-3A. The parallel Huff-Daland XLB-5, used standard water-cooled upright Liberty engines. The aircraft proved more satisfactory, becoming the first of the Huff-Daland/Keystone bomber to enter US Army Air Corps service.

The XLB-5 had excellent handling characteristics and good engine-out performance, and ten were ordered as LB-5 Pirates. The Huff-Daland company was then re-named, becoming Keystone, and as such delivered 25 more refined twin-finned LB-5As to the USAAC.

The LB-6 Panther aircraft was

broadly similar. The bomber, however, had new straight-chord increased span wings and 525hp Wright Cyclone radials suspended between the wings rather than being directly attached to the top surface of the bottom wing. The USAAC received 17 of them during 1929. These proved to be some 10mph (16km/h) faster than the LB-5, with almost twice the climb rate.

When powered by Pratt & Whitney R-1690-3 Hornet radials the LB-6s were known as Keystone LB-7s, 16 of which were produced from scratch. Some LB-6s became LB-7s by conversion, and vice versa!

The penultimate LB-7 aircraft was completed with geared 550hp Pratt & Whitney R-1860-3 radial engines as the Keystone XLB-8, while the final LB-7 had geared 575hp Wright R-1750 Cyclone radial engines, and was designated as the XLB-9.

Other LB-6/7 based testbeds were the XLB-11, with experimental 525hp Wright R-1750-3 Cyclone radials, and the XLB-11A with geared G1R-1750 Cyclones. The LB-12 had direct drive 575hp Pratt & Whitney R-1860-1 radial engines.

The LB-10 originated as another experimental engine test bed. The first was actually the 17th LB-6, hastily fitted with 525hp Wright R-1750-1 Cyclone radial engines. The aircraft also had a single tailfin, and demonstrated sufficient improvement to be ordered into production, and 63 of these improved aircraft were built as LB-10As, powered by Pratt & Whitney R-1690-3 radials.

The LB-10A designation was dropped early on, and the type became the B-3A under the new USAAC designation scheme. They served primarily in the Canal Zone and the Philippines.

The final Keystone bombers were similar, single-finned aircraft like the B-3A. They used a variety of designations according to engine type.

The USAAC ordered seven 525hp Pratt & Whitney GR-1690 radial engined LB-13s. These, however, were

delivered as Y1B-4s with 575hp R-1860-7 engines, or Y1B-6s with 575hp R-1820-1 engines. Three aircraft with 525hp Pratt & Whitney GR-1860 radial engines were also ordered as LB-14s, but these were completed as Y1B-5s with 525hp Wright R-1750-3 engines.

On April 28, 1931, the US Army ordered 39 more production Y1B-6s under the designation B-6A, and 25 B-4As powered by Pratt & Whitney Hornet engines, and these were delivered during 1931–32. There were 27 production B-5's produced through the re-engining of existing B-3As with Wright R-1750-3 Cyclone engines. A handful of B-6As remained in service even as late as Pearl Harbor, but none saw action.

Opposite, top: *The XLB-3 featured triple rudders, and was a one-off experimental bomber flown with a variety of engines.*
Opposite, middle: *The USAAC received 63 LB-10As. These aircraft were later re-designated as B-3As.*
Opposite, bottom: *Keystone switched to a single tailfin with the experimental LB-10. The aircraft was years behind its rivals in Europe.*
Above: *Many of the USAAC's Keystone bombers were based overseas, and this one was pictured over Luzon, in the Philippines.*
Below: *A squadron of Keystone LB-6s position themselves for an attack against a line of US Navy cruisers.*

WITTEMAN-LEWIS NBL-1 'BARLING BOMBER'

THE SIX-ENGINED WITTEMAN-LEWIS XNBL-1 triplane, weighing more than three World War I Handley Page O/400s, was a giant by the standards of the time. The aircraft was designed by the US Army's Engineering Division at McCook Field in Dayton, Ohio, under the direction of Walter Barling who had experience with aircraft design in England.

The Barling bomber had a crew of eight, and carried seven defensive machine guns. The aeroplane was intended to carry a massive 5,000-lb (2,268-kg) bombload. The XNBL-1 was manufactured by the Witteman-Lewis Company of Teterboro, which submitted the winning bid in a competitive process. The New Jersey-based manufacturer won the contract to build two flying examples of this remarkable design.

The aircraft was built in parts, due to its size, at Teterboro. It was then assembled and tested at Wilbur Wright Field (now part of Wright-Patterson Air Force Base). The main test facilities and flying field at nearby McCook Field were too small for the aircraft to take off and land safely.

An unattractive and exceptionally ungainly triplane, the Barling Bomber was powered by six 420hp Liberty

Left: The six-engined triplane NBL-1 was an ungainly and under-performing colossus, and only a single prototype was completed. The Barling Bomber carried an eight-man crew and had seven defensive machine guns.

12A liquid cooled engines, "and flew like it needed all eight," according to one service pilot. Four of the engines were tractors, hung below the the middle wing on struts, with two pusher engines placed immediately behind the inboard tractors.

The Barling bomber had three wings and the main landing gear had no less than 10 wheels. The most significant feature of the aircraft was its wing span of 120ft (36.5m).

Only the first prototype was completed, flying for the first time on August 22, 1923, but its performance proved so disappointing that the second was simply cancelled. The NBL-1 concept had been enthusiastically supported by Colonel Billy Mitchell, but the type's slow speed and poor ceiling rendered it militarily unusable.

The maximum speed of the Barling bomber was well below 100mph (160.9km/h). Its range with a bombload of 5,000lbs (2,268kg) was only 170 miles (273.5km), not a very useful distance.

The operational ceiling of the Barling bomber was so low that it could not safely cross the mountains to reach either coast. The XNBL-1 prototype aircraft did, however, manage to set some new world records. This included flying to an altitude of 6,722ft (2,240m) with a 4,400-lb (1,995-kg) payload. The Barling Bomber was finally broken up in 1928. The US Army did not attempt to produce anything as large until 1937.

BOULTON AND PAUL SIDESTRAND AND OVERSTRAND

BOULTON AND PAUL Limited produced the experimental Bourges and Bugle bombers, but did not put one of its bomber designs into production until its Sidestrand was ordered to meet the RAF's Specification 9/24 for a twin-engined day bomber. A single prototype, which flew in 1926, was followed by 18 production aircraft, which equipped No.101 Squadron from March 1929 until January 1935. The first six Mk IIs were powered by Jupiter VI engines, while the remainder had geared Jupiter VIIIFs and were known as Sidestrand IIIs.

The Sidestrand displayed excellent handling characteristics. It combined the speed and agility of single-engined day bombers with some of the range and load-carrying capability of the heavyweight night bombers.

The aircraft could be rolled, looped and spun like a smaller aircraft. It often out-manoeuvred attacking fighters during exercises.

The bomber had a top speed of 140mph (225km/h) and could carry a bombload of 1,050lb (476-kg). It had a range of 500 miles (804km).

One Sidestrand was modified with supercharged Jupiter XF engines in Townend ring cowlings, to become the prototype Overstrand. Planned as the Sidestrand V, the prototype was re-fitted with 555hp Pegasus IM3 engines, and 24 similar aircraft were built as Overstrands with 580hp Pegasus IIM3 engines. These had an enclosed cockpit, and a power-operated enclosed

gun turret in the nose containing a single Lewis gun. The turret was powered by compressed air bottles, and a compressor that was driven from one of the engines. This was the first aircraft in the world to have such a turret.

The Overstrand had a large protective windscreen for the mid-upper gunners and could carry a 1,600-lb (725-kg) bombload. The gun turret and windscreen brought with them a dramatic improvement in gunnery accuracy, and Overstrands were always regarded as being a difficult target for contemporary fighters.

The aircraft could fly at 6,680m (21,915ft) and reached a maximum speed of 246km/h (152mph). It had a range of 880km (546 miles).

The Boulton and Paul Overstrand was used to re-equip No.101 Squadron until the arrival of the Bristol Blenheim, but some were then used as gunnery trainers until 1940. A few Overstrand bombers were briefly allocated to No.144 Squadron. Plans for an advanced derivative of the aircraft with a retractable undercarriage, provisionally named Superstrand, were cancelled.

Right: *Five of No.101 Squadron's Overstrands put on a show for the cameraman. The aircraft's power-operated turret was a first.*
Following page: *Three No.101 Squadron Sidestrands cruise serenely over the clouds during an air defense exercise. Sidestrands had fine handling characteristics.*

HAWKER HART/HIND FAMILY

HAWKER'S FIRST DAY bomber, the Horsley, doubled as a torpedo bomber, and was large and ungainly, thanks to its square-cowled Condor engine. As such, it presented a marked contrast with the beautifully proportioned and compact Hawker Hart, selected to meet RAF Specification 12/26 for a new day bomber. The Hart prototype made its maiden flight in June 1928, and the type entered service with No.33 Squadron in January 1930. Hawker eventually built 459 Hart bombers for the RAF. The type formed the backbone of the squadrons founded during the initial part of the RAF's interwar expansion. A further 473 more Harts were produced with dual controls as advanced trainers and the type was widely exported.

The Hart also formed the basis of a two-seat fighter, the Demon (234 built for the RAF), a dedicated army co-operation aircraft, the Audax (650 built for the RAF), and the similar Hardy (47 built for RAF service in the Middle East). The Audax and Hardy were bombers in all but name, though operating in a close support role rather than in an independent capacity.

More distant relatives of the Hart included the Fury single-seat interceptor fighter, and the carrier-borne Nimrod (single-seat) and the Osprey (two-seat) carrierborne fighters.

The Hawker Hind was a minimum-change interim replacement for the

Left: This Hind served with No.83 Squadron at Turnhouse in Scotland. Hawker Harts and Hinds formed the backbone of the RAF's interwar expansion.

Hart in the home-based bomber role, with a 640hp Kestrel engine replacing the Hart's 525hp Kestrel IIS or 585hp Kestrel V(DR). Some 508 Hawker Hart bombers and 20 dual control trainers were built, the first entering service with No.21 Squadron in December 1935.

The Hind eventually equipped a peak total of 26 frontline bomber squadrons, plus thirteen Auxiliary units, and formed the basis of the Army Co-operation Hector. This was the only family member to give up the Kestrel engine for the unusual 'H'-section Napier Dagger, and the only 'bomber' version to use the 'straight' top wing of the Fury fighter. There were 178 were built for the RAF.

The Hart and Hind were replaced in home-based bomber squadrons by the Battle, Blenheim and Hampden 1938, and in overseas squadrons by March 1939, though they continued as advanced trainers into the war years. The Audax was replaced in home-based squadrons by May 1938, but remained in use in the Middle East long enough to see active service in the East African campaign, the Iraqi rebellion of 1941 and the Japanese attack on Burma. Hardys were also used in East Africa until March 1941, while Hectors remained in use with Auxiliary squadrons until June 1940, and those of No.613 made the RAF's last biplane bomber attack, dive-bombing German gun emplacements at Calais, northern France, on May 26, 1940. The Hector then gained a new lease of life as a glider tug, remaining in service until 1943.

Left: *Harts of No.12 Squadron take off in formation from a grass runway in Andover, southern England, where they replaced the unit's Foxes.*
Right: *Long exhaust pipes identify this No.30 Squadron aircraft as a Hawker Hardy, an army co-operation aircraft.*
Below: *The Hawker Hart's sleek lines and cleanly cowled Kestrel owed much to the example of the Fairey Fox.*

Right: *The hook below the fuselage of this Audax was intended for snatching messages from a wire rigged by soldiers on the ground. The Army Co-operation role involved a variety of tasks, but close air support was a vital one, and the bombing capability of the Audax was highly prized.*

Below: *This Hawker Hind (masquerading as No.XV Squadron's K5414) is a present day airworthy survivor, operated by the Shuttleworth Trust.*

CURTISS A-8/A-10/A-12 SHRIKE

THE CURTISS COMPANY had been one of the earliest producers of military aircraft in the United States. After World War I the company produced the O-1 Falcon two-seat observation aircraft for the US Army Air Service. This was as a replacement for the ageing DH-4Bs and DH-4Ms then in service.

The A-3 (Model 44) was an attack version of the O-1B, and 144 were ordered, the first flying on October 31, 1927. These aircraft equipped all four of the Air Corps' ground attack squadrons, the 8th, 13th, and 19th Squadrons of the 3rd Attack Group at Fort Crockett, Texas, and the 26th Attack Squadron based in Hawaii.

The A-3s of the USAAC's 3rd Attack Group were destined to be replaced by another Curtiss aircraft, the A-8 Shrike. This was the first Curtiss tactical monoplane built for the US Army, all previous designs having been biplanes. The A-8 was the first of a new generation of all-metal, low-winged monoplane attack aircraft, and had trailing edge flaps, full span leading-edge slats, and enclosed cockpits for its crew. This bomber was the first USAAC aircraft with such features. The A-8's wings were externally braced with struts and wires, however, and the bombload was a modest 400lb (181kg). It could fly at 18,100ft (5,516m) and reached a maximum speed of 183mph (294.5km/h)

The first XA-8 flew in June 1931. It was powered by a single 600hp Curtiss V-1570C Conqueror water-cooled V-12 engine, and five further aircraft (powered by Prestone-cooled V-1570-31 engines) were ordered as YA-8s, and eight as Y1A-8s. All were redesignated as A-8s when testing was complete. In 1932, 11 were issued to the 3rd Attack Group based at Fort Crockett, Texas.

At this time, the 3rd Attack Group was the Army's only group devoted solely to attack. A further 46 production variants were ordered as A-8Bs, although these were never delivered.

Instead, after testing of a YA-8 re-engined with a 625hp Pratt & Whitney R-1690D Hornet 9-cylinder air-cooled radial engine (which transformed it into the sole YA-10) the USAAC ordered that the remaining Shrikes should be delivered with Hornet engines. These became A-12s. The A-12's gunner's cockpit was moved forward to immediately behind the pilot's, and both were covered by a single canopy, thereby improving communication between the crew.

The 3rd Attack Group at Fort Crockett received 43 of the 48 A-12s built. In February 1934, the US Army took over flying air mail services, and 41 A-12s from the 3rd Attack Group were assigned to air mail duties.

There were 20 export versions supplied to China, fitted with a more powerful Wright SR-1820F-52 radial engine. The name Shrike was commonly applied to the A-8 and A-12, but was a company name, and was not officially adopted by the US Army.

Right: *A ski-equipped Curtiss A-8 Shrike of the 13th Attack Squadron seen during winter exercises in February 1936. This squadron had first been issued with A-3s.*

TUPOLEV TB-3 ANT-6

THE TB-3, ALTHOUGH it was in some respects little more than a scaled up derivative of the TB-1 (ANT-4) with four instead of two engines, went down in history as the USSR's most important interwar bomber. Soviet sources often claimed that the TB-1 was the world's first all-metal monoplane bomber, though in fact that honor belonged to the Junkers K 30 (a derivative of the G 23 transport) of 1925, which was delivered to the Soviet, Chilean, Spanish and Yugoslav air forces. The ANT-4 was, in fact, an improved copy of the Junkers aircraft, and the German company brought an unsuccessful action against TsAGI, AGOS and personnel for infringing Junkers patents.

Some 216 TB-1s were built, many of them bombers, before production switched to the TB-3. The aircraft could carry a bombload of almost 3,000lb (1,360kg), but for all its innovative all-metal construction and cantilever monoplane configuration, the TB-1 was slower and less agile than the fabric-covered, biplane Heyford, or the Sidestrand.

The TB-3 in its initial production form was just as slow, though it did carry a bombload of up to 11,000lb (5,000kg). This was a formidable bombload, and one which was not rivalled for some time. More than 800 TB-3 aircraft were built, in a number of successively more capable variants.

Large numbers of TB-3s were used in the border fighting against Japanese forces in Manchuria in 1938–39, and against Finland in 1939–40. From the mid-1930s, the type was also used extensively in the para-dropping role, helping the USSR to pioneer the use of airborne forces.

By the time Germany invaded in June 1941, most had been withdrawn from frontline duties, though some continued to mount long-range attacks against Berlin until mid-1942.

There were a number of specialized sub-variants of the TB-3 bomber. They included one experimental aircraft which carried no fewer than five 'parasite' fighters, and a limited series of aircraft which carried a pair of SPB dive bombers underwing. These, operated by the 63rd Brigade, carried 32nd Regiment dive bombers close to their targets in Romania, and flew many operational missions during the late summer of 1941.

Left: *The Tupolev TB-3 was used by Aeroflot as well as the Red Air Forces, but civilian aircraft retained a glazed bomb-aimers nose.*

Below: *The TB-3 was formidably armed, but was slower and less agile than many of its biplane contemporaries.*

HANDLEY PAGE HEYFORD

HANDLEY PAGE HAD dominated the production of heavy bombers during World War I, and early post war bomber designs for the Royal Air Force. These included the Hyderabad (which equipped four squadrons, entering service from 1925) and the improved Hinaidi, with Jupiter engines and increased use of metal airframe components (which equipped three squadrons, entering service in 1929). The Hyderabad and Hinaidi were little more than military versions of the pioneering W.8 airliner, and owed much to the wartime Handley Page 'Heavies'. Their replacement, the Handley Page Heyford, was a very much more radical aeroplane, despite going down in the history books as the last of the RAF's biplane 'heavies'.

Unusually, the Heyford's fuselage was attached to the upper wing, with the lower wing having a thickened centre section containing bays for up to ten bombs, side-by-side, virtually on the centre of gravity and thus giving no pitch change when dropped. Further bombs could be carried outboard under the outer wing panels.

The maximum load of the Handley Page Heyford was a respectable ten 250-lb (113-kg) bombs, plus a further eight 20-lb (9-kg) bombs. The aircraft's ten 250-lb (113.4-kg) bombs could, however, be replaced by four 500-lb (226-kg) bombs or 16 112-lb (50.8-kg) bombs.

The Handley Page Heyford's low lower wing made for rapid turnarounds and easy ground handling, and gave the crew a superb all-round view, although the pilot sat 17ft (5.1m) off the ground, making landings a tricky business to judge!

For self defense, the Heyford bomber had Lewis guns in the nose and 'mid-upper' positions, together with a retractable ventral 'dustbin' turret. The aircraft was also surprisingly agile, and could be looped with ease.

The Heyford prototype flew on June 12, 1930, and 124 were delivered to the RAF, the first of them entering service with No.99 Squadron on November 20, 1933. The first 15 were Heyford Is, with 23 575hp Kestrel IIIS engined Mk IAs following and introducing four-bladed propellers. 16 Mk IIs were delivered with 640hp Kestrel VI engines, and the remainder had further minor refinements and were designated as Mk IIIs.

The Heyford bomber equipped eleven RAF squadrons, and proved popular for its rugged dependability and pleasant handling characteristics, although its service life was relatively short. Most of the Heyfords were replaced by Wellingtons and Whitleys in late 1938 and early 1939, and the last Bomber Command Heyfords were finally retired from No.166 Squadron (operating as an air observer's school) the day before war broke out. A handful then continued in use with bombing and gunnery schools into 1940, and one survived as a glider tug until April 1941.

Right: *The Heyford's innovative configuration placed the bottom wing close to the ground, allowing the aircraft to be rapidly rearmed.*

MARTIN B-10

THE MARTIN B-10 became the first all-metal monoplane bomber to be produced in large numbers for the USAAC who claimed its performance could 'exceed that of contemporary pursuit aircraft'. Derived from the private venture Martin Model 123 (which first flew on February 16, 1932), the B-10 was characterized by a deep belly containing a capacious internal bomb bay. The Model 123 was bailed to the Army for testing as the XB-907, demonstrating a top speed of 197mph (317km/h).

The XB-907, after being refitted with an enclosed front gun turret and new engine cowlings, and with increased-span wings, demonstrated a 207mph (333km/h) top speed (despite 25 per cent) increase in gross weight). The US Army purchased the aircraft, and re-designated it as the XB-10. The 14 pre-production YB-10s were powered by 675hp Wright R-1820-25 engines. The aircraft had sliding transparencies over the pilot's and gunner/navigator cockpits.

The YB-10 could carry two 1,130-lb (512-kg) bombs or five 300-lb (136-kg) bombs internally or a single 2,000-lb (907-kg) bomb under the starboard wing.

The first YB-10 was delivered in 1933. Most YB-10s went to the 7th Bomb Group at March Field, later being transferred to another unit after being replaced by B-12s.

The USAAC ordered 48 versions of the YB-10. These included the 14 YB-10s, seven R-1690-11 Hornet-engined YB-12s, 25 similar B-12As with increased fuel capacity, and single experimental models.

The main production version was the B-10B, 103 of which were ordered in FY 1934 and 1935. These entered service from July 1935, and equipped five Bomb Groups in the Canal Zone, the Philippines, and at Langley, Mitchell Field, and March Field, until replaced by the B-17 and B-18 in the late 1930s. Some were then relegated to target towing and training duties.

The type was also built for Siam (which took 6), China (6, used against the Japanese), the Dutch East Indies (126, used against the Japanese), Argentina (39), and Turkey (20). A single Model 139 was sold to the Soviet Union for evaluation. The final 78 Dutch aircraft were Model 166s.

The Glenn L Martin company won the 1932 Collier Trophy for producing this 'wonderplane'. In retrospect, it was considerably less impressive than near contemporaries like the Do 17.

Left: *The B-10's deep belly contained a capacious internal bomb bay. Other modern features included a powered nose turret.*
Below: *The Martin B-10. The USAAC ordered 48 different versions of the YB-10.*

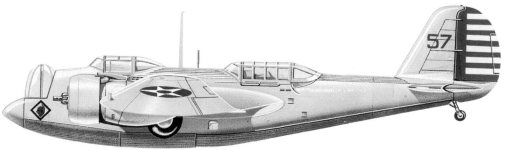

JUNKERS JU 52/3M

THE JUNKERS Ju 52/3m was designed as an airliner, and is best remembered as a civil and military transport aircraft, although it also served as a bomber. Junkers were ordered by the to convert the three-engined Ju 52 into a makeshift bomber during the testing of the infant Luftwaffe's first standard bomber, the Do 23G in 1934.

Some members of the Junker's uniquely ugly and box-like family of 'corrugated-skinned' transports had already been adapted to the bomber role. The civil W 34 was developed into the K 43, converted to military standards by AB Flygindustri in Sweden and exported to Argentina, Bolivia, Chile, Finland, and Portugal, and used by the Luftwaffe during the Spanish Civil War. The G.24b was developed into the military K 30, a tri-motor bomber exported principally to the USSR, and also delivered to Chile, Spain and Yugoslavia. The K 39 was a single-engined bomber design, one of which was produced by Junkers' Swedish subsidiary, AB Flygindustri.

The twin-engined Junkers K 37 (developed from the civil S 36) was not adopted by the Luftwaffe, but 219 enlarged derivatives of the design were built for Japan as Mitsubishi Ki-1 heavy bombers from 1933, and 187 lighter versions as the Ki-2. The G 38 was developed into the K 51 heavy bomber, five of which were built by Mitsubishi as the Ki-20 from 1930.

During early development of the original single-engined Ju 52, Junkers considered military applications, using the designation K 45, and the tri-motor military version was originally known as the K 45/3m. Mass-produced from mid-1934, the Ju 52/3m bomber had a dorsal gun position and a retractable ventral 'dustbin' gun turret, and could carry a 1,500-kg (3,306-lb) bombload.

The type initially equipped the Auxiliary Bomber Group 1, formed in 1934, with three Do 11s and 24 Ju 52s, and went on to equip three bomber Geschwaderen. Between 1935 and the introduction of the Heinkel He 111 and Ju 86, two thirds of the Luftwaffe's bombers were Junkers tri-motors. The type was used operationally in both the bomber and transport roles with the Condor Legion. Most surviving Ju 52s had been converted to transport configuration, with their retractable lower gun turrets removed, by the time war broke out.

Right: *The Ju 52/3m was the world's best known trimotor.*
Below: *The Ju 52/3m enjoyed great success in the transport role and also served as a bomber during the Spanish Civil War.*

SAVOIA MARCHETTI SM 81

THE SM 73 TRI-MOTOR transport formed the basis of the SM 81 Pipistrello, an interim bomber/transport put into production to allow a rapid build-up of the Regia Aeronautica even before the definitive SM 79 was ready for service. The SM 81 resembled the Ju 52/3m, with similar fixed and spatted mainwheels, but was rather more streamlined than the Ju 52, and married wooden wings to a steel tube and aluminum/fabric skinned fuselage. The aircraft had modern trailing edge flaps, and semi-retractable, hydraulically operated dorsal and ventral turrets. These, however, accommodated only single 7.7-mm machine guns (or sometimes two guns). With the nose accommodating the third engine, the bomb-aimer lay in a glazed gondola below the cockpit.

In order to maximize output of the new bomber, it was built by Savoia Marchetti and by Piaggio and CMASA. Other companies produced parts, components and sub-assemblies. The aircraft was built in a number of versions, with a variety of powerplant options. Some used the 650hp Alfa Romeo 125 RC.35, or the Gnome-Rhone K.14. Others used the 670-hp Piaggio P.X RC.35, and some the more powerful 680hp Alfa Romeo 126 RC.34. These were fitted with a variety of cowling rings, some broad chord, some narrow, some straight

Left: *The Regia Aeronautica's Pipistrellos entered service in 1935. It played a vital part in Italy's early campaigns in Africa, and against Allied shipping.*

and others tapered. Early Piaggio engined aircraft even used four-bladed propellers, though most used three-bladed airscrews.

The SM 81 entered service in 1935, and was rapidly committed to action in Ethiopia, where it was used in both the bomber and transport roles, augmenting larger numbers of older Capronis. From July 1936, twelve SM 81s of the 24° and 25° Gruppi were committed to action in Spain, seeing extensive service as bombers, and again being used as troop transports.

Mussolini's personal aircraft was an SM 81, drawn from the 9° Stormo. This was fitted with a new Lanciani gun turret, with a 12.7-mm machine gun. Although regarded as obsolete by 1938, SM 81s remained in widespread service, with Alfa-engined aircraft equipping Italian-based units, K-14 engined aircraft in Libya, and Piaggio engined aircraft in East Africa. Some 312 SM 81s were still in service with five Stormi at the end of 1939. The type played a key part in Italy's early wartime actions, especially in Africa, and attacks against Allied shipping. The type's low speed made it extremely vulnerable, and resulted in the SM 81 being nicknamed Lumaca (slug). Relegated to the transport role SM 81s even served on the Eastern Front, and four survived to fly with the Co-Belligerent Forces in southern Italy following the armistice.

The SM 81bis was a one-off twin-engined derivative. This aircraft had a glazed bomb-aimers nose and was powered by two 840-hp Isotta Fraschini Asso XI inline engines.

DORNIER DO 17, DO 215 AND DO 217

THE DORNIER Do 17 was originally designed as a 'high-speed passenger and mail transport' or as a 'freight aircraft for German State Railways'. The Do 17, however, was never suitable for such a role, its fuselage demanding almost acrobatic agility from any passengers who wished to enter the separate cabins fore and aft of the wing. The prototype aircraft, which first flew in the Fall of 1934, was an exceptionally slender aircraft, earning the type its Flying Pencil nickname—a name which stuck even to the later, fatter versions.

The prototypes were actually placed in storage after testing, but were rediscovered by a Lufthansa test pilot temporarily attached to the Reichs Luftministerium. He immediately flight tested one of them and realised its potential as a 'Schnellbomber'. Three further prototypes were ordered with twin fins and other improvements, and these proved able to show a 'clean pair of heels' to most fighters. The aircraft was ordered into production as the Do 17E, powered by 750hp BMW VI 7.3 inline engines. The Do 17F was a similar version, optimized for reconnaissance duties. Both of these early Do 17 models saw action with the Condor Legion in Spain, and proved able to use their high speed to evade enemy fighters.

Exports were helped by the appearance of the Do 17MV-1 (actually the Do 17V8) which was a specially built high speed demonstrator, specifically finished and powered by a pair of 1,000hp DB 600A engines. At the 1937 Zurich Competition this aircraft astonished onlookers by demonstrating a top speed of 284mph (457km/h).

The next Do 17 variants were the radial-engined Do 17M and the reconnaissance Do 17P, which used 865hp BMW 132N engines. These variants retained the slender nose of the Do 17E and F, with the same heavily glazed area on the starboard side, as did the export Do 17Kb-1 bomber and Ka-1 and Ka-2 reconnaissance aircraft for Yugoslavia, though these export aircraft used 980hp Gnome Rhone 14 radial engines.

Subsequent Do 17 variants had a new, re-shaped nose, bulged below to accommodate a prone gunner, firing aft below the belly, and with a large number of flat panels making up the domed 'front'. This new nose looked much more like the nose of the Ju 88.

The Do 17S was the first variant with the new nose, but only a handful of test aircraft were built. A batch of 15 Do 17U-0 and U-1 aircraft were built as specialized pathfinders for use by KG 100, with the new nose. These later led the infamous attack on Coventry in November 1940.

The first major production model with the new nose was the Do 17Z. This aircraft formed the backbone of the Luftwaffe's bomber squadrons (together with the Ju 88 and He 111) during the Battle of Britain in 1940. The Do 17Ps remained in use in the reconnaissance role, but the Do 17M had largely been replaced.

Right: *The Do 17P was the last member of the family to use the original nose-shape of the design.*

Left: *A Dornier Do 217 cavorts during a pre-delivery test flight. The Do 217 was used mainly in the night bomber role.*
Below: *A Dornier Do 17 bomb aimer poses for the photographer, while his pilot looks on 'heroically'.*

The Do 215 was an export derivative of the Do 17Z-0, powered by 1,075hp DB 601 inline engines. The new type was ordered for the Swedish and Yugolsav air forces, but the aircraft were not delivered. They were instead taken over for use by the Luftwaffe. The type was used

Left: *The Dornier 17Z formed the backbone of the Luftwaffe's bomber force during the Battle of Britain, along with the Junkers Ju 88 and Heinkel He 111.*

Below: *Inline engines identify this aircraft as a Do 215. This type was originally designed as an export aircraft for Sweden.*

only in the reconnaissance role by the Luftwaffe, and not as a bomber. A handful of Do 17s and Do 215s remained in service until early 1943.

The related Do 217 used 1,559hp BMW 801 radial engines (and later DB 601 and even DB 603 inline engines) and replaced the earlier Dorniers between 1941 and 1943. Many were used as torpedo bombers and as carriers for glide-bombs, but most were standard night bombers. These aircraft formed the backbone of the force which mounted Adolf Hitler's infamous 1942 'Baedeker raids'. This offensive targeted cities

in Britain that were considered to be of special historic and architectural interest.

The Do 217K and Do 217M introduced a new, unstepped forward fuselage, and these flew the Steinbok raids against London and other British cities in early 1944. The last Do 217 was delivered in May 1944, and the type then rapidly disappeared from service.

A handful of Do 17s remained active on the Eastern Front. These served until April 1945, when 12 made an attack on crossings over the River Oder, using Hs 293 missiles.

Opposite: *The Dornier Do 217 proved inferior to the Ju 88, which supplanted the original Do 17 as the Luftwaffe's main bomber type.*

Right: *This Do 217, wearing temporary night camouflage, was one of those used during the Steinbok raids on London in early 1944.*

Below: *The DB601-engined Do 215, although ordered by Sweden and Yugoslavia, was not delivered to these customers. Instead the aircraft were diverted to the Luftwaffe.*

CAPRONI CA 133 AND CA 135BIS

THE CAPRONI-BERGAMASCHI Ca 133 monoplane, first flown in 1935, was specifically designed for the colonial policing role. As such it was a multi-role bomber, transport and reconnaissance tri-motor aircraft. The aircraft was developed from the Ca 101 and Ca 111, but was heavier and aerodynamically more refined.

The Caproni Ca 133 had a high wing and fixed landing gear, powered by three Piaggio Stella P.VII C16 engines. The pilot and co-pilot (who acted as bomb aimer) were seated side-by-side in an enclosed cabin. The aircraft could fly at 5,500m (18,044ft) and had a range of 280km (174 miles).

The aircraft achieved a maximum speed of 280km/h (173mph) and carried a modest 500-kg (1,102-lb) bombload externally. It was also armed with 4 7.7mm machine guns. The aircraft, known as Caprona, served in the later stages of the Ethiopian invasion. In June 1940 the aircraft equipped 14 bomber Squadriglie in East Africa and performed well against light air opposition but suffered heavy losses against the British in 1940 and 1941. The Caproni Ca 133 soon became obsolete as a bomber, although the Ca 133 did remain popular in the transport role, and some 525 were built.

Caproni's next bomber project was a more modern and effective bomber. This new aircraft, the twin-engined

Left: *The CA 135bis, though seen here in Regia Aeronautica markings, was principally used by the Hungarian air force on the Eastern front.*

Caproni Ca 135, was built in rather smaller numbers.

The Caproni Ca 135 had a low wing and a retractable undercarriage. The aircraft also had a notably broad chord wing, together with retractable dorsal and ventral gun turrets. Broadly similar to the United States' Lockheed Hudson in configuration, the Caproni's twin fins were closer-spaced, being mounted closer in towards the tailplane roots. The aircraft's fuselage was of 'squarer' cross section.

The Spanish ordered 14 Ca 135 tipo Spagna aircraft. These were fitted with 836hp Asso XI RC 40 engines. These aircraft, however, were not delivered. They were used instead by Mussolini's Regia Aeronautica as Ca 135/A.80 trainers, having been re-engined with 1,000hp Fiat A80 RC 41 engines. Around 32 Ca 135 tipo Peru bombers (with 900hp Asso XI RC 40 engines) were delivered.

Production then switched to the improved Caproni Ca 135bis. This aircraft was powered by Piaggio P.XI RC 40 radial engines. The Ca 135bis had a lengthened, more extensively glazed nose, and a manually operated dorsal turret. The aircraft's new version had a bombload of 1,600kg (3,527lb), and improved defensive armament.

About 100 Caproni Ca 135bis were delivered to the Hungarian Air Force. These aircraft were then used by Hungary in the Axis campaign against the Soviet Union on the Eastern Front. A total of about 150 Caproni Ca 135bis aircraft were built.

JUNKERS JU 86

THE JUNKERS JU 86 was nominally designed to meet a Lufthansa requirement for a fast passenger aircraft carrying ten passengers, and the first prototype flew on November 4, 1934. Poor control responses led to the aircraft being modified, and when it re-emerged, the first prototype had been re-fitted with dorsal and ventral gun positions, while the third prototype had a glazed 'bomber' nose and forward-firing machine gun. The first production batch of Ju 86s included seven transports for the Luftwaffe, and no fewer than 13 Ju 86A-0 bombers that arrived in February 1936. The production Ju 86A-1 entered service that summer, while Junkers began work on the aerodynamically improved Ju 86D.

The Ju 86D, carrying 16 SC50 110-lb (50-kg) bombs, proved capable of a maximum speed of 200mph (321km/h). Four were dispatched to Spain for combat trials. The Jumo 205D diesel engine proved prone to over-heating and piston-seizing in military use—though it had been economic and durable when used in civil roles, at constant speeds and rpm.

Junkers therefore hastily designed a new bomber version with fuel-injected BMW 132 radial engines, this becoming the Ju 86E-1 and E-2, which entered service in 1938. A more extensive redesign resulted in the Junkers Ju 86G-1, produced by conversion of older versions and through new production. The BMW-engined Ju 86G introduced a more streamlined domed and glazed nose.

The Junkers Ju 86D and G variants saw fairly limited service in the tactical bomber role during World War II, but

were used extensively for training and other second line duties. A more developed high altitude version also saw more significant use during the war.

Developed to meet a 1939 requirement, the Ju 86P was built as a dedicated high altitude reconnaissance bomber. It was built on experience gained with the two-seat Ju 49a research aircraft, and two Ju EF 61s, which were of similar configuration to the Ju 86.

The aircraft was powered by two 907hp Jumo 207 engines, and featured extended span wings and a redesigned nose, with a new pressurized cabin. About 40 were produced, mainly through conversion of Ju 86Gs, and these equipped a handful of specialized reconnaissance units.

Initially unarmed, the Ju 86Ps were at first used mainly in the reconnaissance role, occasionally carrying a load of four 550-lb (250-kg) bombs. They remained virtually immune to interception for two years. Specialized high altitude Spitfires were eventually developed which were able to reach the high-flying Ju 86Ps, and several were lost, though not until April 1942. The further improved Ju 86R introduced nitrous oxide for improved high altitude performance, but even these proved vulnerable to the specialized Spitfire VI and Spitfire VII. The Ju 86s introduced defensive armament, and were thereafter used more on the Eastern and Mediterranean Fronts after late 1942, remaining in service until 1944.

Right: *The Junkers Ju 86K was used by the Swedish air force in the bomber role. Ju 86s first entered Luftwaffe service in 1936.*

TUPOLEV SB

MORE TUPOLEV SBs were built than any other aircraft produced by Tupolev. The type formed the backbone of the Soviet bomber force at the outbreak of World War II. More than 90 per cent of the Soviet Union's frontline bomber force consisted of Tupolev SBs (Skorostnoi Bombardirovshchik or fast bombers), and over 1,000 of them were destroyed on the ground between June 22 and 25, 1941—the first three days of Operation Barbarossa. Many more were destroyed during the months and years which followed. The Tupolev SB, like the Fairey Battle and Bristol Blenheim, was inadequately armed and poorly protected. Its performance was insufficient to escape even the slowest of Germany's fighters.

The SB was designed by A.A. Arkhangelski under the direction of Nikolaevich Tupolev. It was produced to meet a 1934 requirement, and drew on Tupolev's experience with the ANT-25 long-range aircraft, the innovative ANT-35 (PS-35) fast airliner, and the ANT-37/DB-2 long-range bomber prototype. Some accused Tupolev of copying the Martin bomber, but this was specious—the Soviet aircraft being more advanced in several key respects.

Mis-designated as the SB-2 by Western 'experts' (the full designation of individual variants included the number and type of engines, eg SB-2M-100A), the prototype SB made its maiden flight on October 7, 1934.

Left: *The SB was Tupolev's most successful and widely built bombers. The aircraft, however, proved inadequate and very vulnerable to Luftwaffe fighters.*

The aircraft was powered by a pair of 710hp Wright Cyclones.

Production Tupolev SBs used 750hp M-100 engines (license-built Hispano Suiza 12Ys) or modified 860hp Klimov M-100As, the latter driving variable pitch propellers. The SB reached a top speed of 393km/h (244mph) and had a range of 1,450km (901 miles). The aircraft was defended by two nose guns, and single dorsal and ventral guns which were later replaced by turrets.

In 1937 some Tupolev SB-2M-100As were dispatched to fight on the Republican side in the Spanish Civil War. The aircraft enjoyed superiority in speed for a while and proved able to outrun biplane fighters like the Italian Fiat CR 32. The situation was less happy the next year, when General Francisco Franco's Nationalists began operating Bf 109 fighters. The tendency of the Tupolev SB's fuel tanks to ignite and its demanding maintenance in the field further exacerbated the aircraft's problems.

Prewar exports included 292 to China, and 60 to Czechoslovakia—some of the latter eventually finding their way into Luftwaffe service! The Chinese aircraft were used in the Sino-Japanese War. These aircraft proved ominously vulnerable.

Successive variants of the Tupolev SB introduced a number of improvements, the SBbis-2M-103 having flush-rivetted structure and a new low-drag radiator installation. These improvements, however, were insufficient to lift the performance of the Tupolev SB to an acceptable level, and the aircraft suffered disastrous losses until it was replaced.

ILYUSHIN IL-4 (DB-3)

THE ILYUSHIN DB-3 (re-designated as the Il-4 in March 1942) was destined to form the backbone of the Soviet Union's bomber forces for most of World War II. The type remained in production until 1945, by which time 6,784 had been built.

The DB-3 was designed around the 800hp Gnome-Rhone Mistral Major (produced in the Soviet Union as the M-85, rated at 760hp). It was a conventional-looking twin-engined monoplane, although the pilot's cockpit was located well aft, above the wing and behind the propellers. The navigator's position in the nose was notably 'blunt'.

The aircraft had a well-proportioned, relatively wide-chord wing, and the engines were positioned close in to the fuselage. The small internal bomb bay of the DB-3 accommodated only 10 100-kg (220-lb) bombs, although further weapons could be carried under the fuselage. The Ilyushin DB-3 was armed with three 7.62-mm machine guns.

The first prototype made its maiden flight on March 31, 1936, and the type was immediately ordered into production. The Ilyushin DB-3 entered service during 1937. The type became the first operational aircraft to bear the name Ilyushin.

The Ilyushin DB-3's high speed, long range and maneuverability ensured its widespread use. Some of the bombers were delivered to China in June 1939 where they saw active service against the Japanese. The type also served during the Soviet invasion of Finland that began in November 1939. The Finns captured five DB-3s. These aircraft were augmented by warplanes captured by the Germans and passed to the Finnish Air Force).

More powerful 800hp M-86 engines soon replaced the original M-85s, and other improvements were also incorporated. A dedicated torpedo bomber version was also produced for the AV-MF from 1937. There were 1,528 aircraft of the basic version made before production ended in 1940.

The prototype of the much-improved DB-3F first flew on May 21, 1939. This was powered by 950hp M-87B engines, although production aircraft had the 1,100hp M-88.

The aircraft had a revised structure, improved defensive armament, increased fuel capacity and a new, more streamlined and heavily-glazed nose. Performance improved significantly and the type entered large scale production. The DB3-F bomber had a maximum speed of 420km/h (261mph) and could fly at 9,400m (30,840ft). Only a handful of DB-3Fs had been delivered by the time Nazi Germany attacked the Soviet Union in June 1941. The DB-3s and DB-3Fs, based further back from the border on the DBA's long-range bases, escaped the slaughter of the opening days of Operation Barbarossa. The Ilyushin DB-3s and DB-3Fs made the Soviet Union's first air attacks on Berlin, before they retreating eastwards.

Some wartime series had wooden outer wing sections and front fuselage. Gunner positions got armoring after combat operations revealed the Ilyushin's Il-4's vulnerability.

Right: *The DB-3 proved versatile, and production included a dedicated torpedo bomber variant for the AV-MF, seen here.*

FIAT BR 20

THERE WERE HIGH hopes that the Fiat BR 20 would be a truly modern replacement for the SM 81. The aircraft, however, was destined to be disappointing in service. Italy had led the world in the employment of bomber aeroplanes. The Caproni company had produced some of the outstanding bomber designs of World War I. General Douhet's theories had greatly influenced air power doctrine. Despite these credentials, the country had lost any lead it had once enjoyed by the 1930s.

Italy was too feeble, industrially and economically, to keep up with Germany and Britain. Consequently, its aircraft lagged behind developments elsewhere.

The Cicogna (Stork) prototype was first flown on February 10, 1936. Production was authorized almost immediately, so that the first production deliveries to the Regia Aeronautica were made in September 1936. Mussolini's propagandists made extravagant claims for the BR 20. In reality the aircraft was far inferior to contemporaries such as the Ju 88 and Wellington. The BR 20 carried a modest 1,600-kg (3,527-lb) bombload over a 2,735-km (1,700-mile) range.

The first production version was powered by 1,000hp Fiat A.80 RC 41 engines. There were 320 were built, including 85 for Japan. Some six BR 20s were despatched to Spain during the summer of 1937. These (and six further aircraft) proved extremely effective in the high altitude bombing and reconnaissance roles. The aircraft proved to be immune to interception by Republican I-15 fighters.

The BR 20M had a new, longer more streamlined nose and improved defensive armament. It also had a strengthened wing, and became the standard version as Italy entered World War II. There were 264 BR 20Ms built, with more being produced through conversion of the original version. The type was prized for its rugged strength. Most were based in the north of Italy, where they could cope with the turbulent air over the Alps and other high ground.

The BR 20Ms were heavily committed to the French campaign. In October 1940, some 80 aircraft were despatched to Belgium for operations over Britain, between October 25, 1940 and January 1941. About 20 were lost during this brief campaign, achieving little in the process. The BR 20 saw service against British forces again in late 1940, being committed to operations in Greece, and from March 1941, operating in North Africa. The type was also heavily used during the attack on Malta, and some were used on the Eastern Front from August 1942.

Some 15 examples of the Fiat BR 20bis were delivered to the Regia Aeronautica in late 1943. These aircraft had 1,250hp Fiat A.82 RC 42S engines and an entirely redesigned, heavily glazed nose section, a power-operated dorsal turret and lateral gun barbettes. Only about 70 BR 20s of all types were operational when Italy signed an Armistice. Most BR 20s were then retired, although one was used by the Co-Belligerent Air Force for liaison duties.

Right: *Fiat BR 20s flying over Spain during the Civil War. The type enjoyed a glorious (but brief) moment of superiority against Republican forces.*

HEINKEL HE 111

THE HE 111, ALTHOUGH it was arguably the most successful tactical bomber of its day, was symptomatic of the inadequacy and weakness of Germany's bomber arm. Superbly well-suited to the needs of the Blitzkrieg, the He 111 was inadequate for the bomber campaigns which followed—vulnerable, short-ranged and carrying an inadequate bombload.

Even as early as the Battle of Britain, the He 111 was showing its age, outnumbered and out-performed by the newer Ju 88, and less effective than the contemporary Do 17. It could, however, carry a heavier bombload than any other Luftwaffe bomber, and was highly prized for this capability. When the first He 111 prototype made its maiden flight on February 24, 1935, it was notably fast, and was well armed by the standards of the day.

The Heinkel 111 was ostensibly designed as a high-speed passenger transport and mailplane. The bomber role, however, was always the real design driver. Thus the first prototype (which flew in early 1935) had three provisional gun positions and provision for a 2,200-lb (997-kg) bombload. The second and fourth prototype aircraft, however, which were the aircraft displayed in public, were to all appearances 'innocent' ten-seat airliners, with a 'smoking compartment' in place of the bomb bay! In standard He 111 bombers, the bombs were accommodated in four vertical cells. Each of these could carry a single 550-lb (250-kg) bomb on each side of a central gangway.

Even these aircraft, however, were not quite what they seemed. The second prototype, for example, was ostentatiously decked out in Lufthansa colours and used for what the airline called 'route proving'. It later transpired that the He 111V-2 was in fact a well-equipped photo-reconnaissance aircraft, manned by military crews and heavily used for target photography in preparation for the Blitzkrieg.

After producing a small number of He 111As, Heinkel switched to He 111B, powered by the 850-925hp DB 600 engine, which in turn gave way to the He 111E, with 999hp Jumo 211 engines. Both types saw service with the Condor Legion in Spain. For ease of production, the elliptical wing of the original He 111 gave way to a wing with a straight leading edge on the He 111F and subsequent variants. An even more obvious visual difference was introduced with the He 111P. This had a new trapezoidal wing planform, a shorter, more heavily glazed, assymetric nose section which incorporated the pilot's cockpit (previously higher on the fuselage and stepped back from the glazed nose). It also had a neatly faired ventral gondola in place of the original retractable belly turret.

The pilot sat offset to port, with the forward-firing nose cannon to starboard, where it could be operated by the navigator. The streamlined and heavily glazed nose offered superb all-round visibility (apart from the heavy framing) but because it was some 6ft (1.8m) feet ahead of the pilots eyes it was somewhat prone to reflections at night. For landing in such conditions, the pilot could slide back a roof panel,

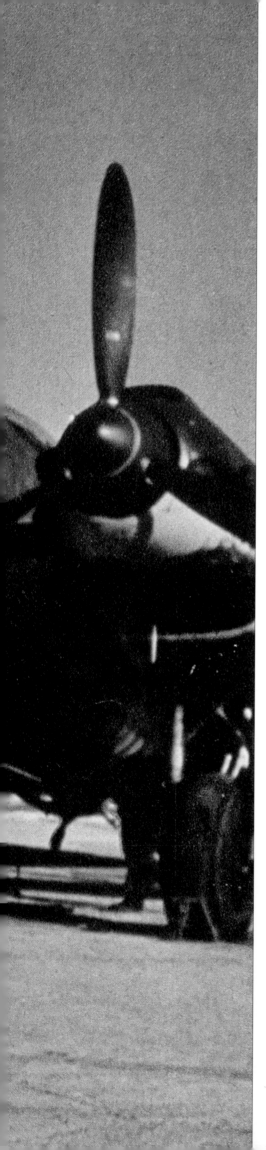

Left: Air and groundcrew haul on a rope as they winch bombs into a waiting He 111H on the Eastern Front. This was the type's definitive variant.

Above: *A pair of He 111H bombers in flight. The He 111H was the mainstay of the Heinkel Geschwaderen during the Battle of Britain.*

Right: *Heinkels continued to give useful service on the Eastern Front long after the aircraft was obsolete. He 111s were finally replaced by Ju 88s*

elevate his seat and sit higher, with his head projecting above the normal nose glazing. The pilot was also protected from the slipstream by a small retractable windscreen.

The DB 601-powered He 111P gave way to the He 111H, with 1,000hp Jumo 211A-1 engines. This definitive variant entered service just too late to see extensive use until after the attack on Poland in September 1939, but which played a vital part in the Battle of Britain in 1940. By then, even the latest He 111 variants were recognized as being well past their prime, and the type was rapidly being replaced by the Ju 88. Only four Kampfgeschwader remained fully-equipped with He 111s

Left: *The glazed nose of the Heinkel He 111 afforded the bomb-aimer an excellent all-round view, although internal reflections could make things worse for the pilot, sitting further aft.*
Below: *A formation of Heinkel He 111s en route to the target. The type suffered heavy losses during the Battle of Britain in 1940, and thereafter served primarily on the Eastern Front or in secondary roles.*
Opposite: *The Luftwaffe's concentration on twin-engined tactical bombers like the He 111, Dornier Do 17 and Ju 88 left it ill-prepared for strategic bombing campaigns.*

by Adlertag (August 10, 1940). These suffered alarmingly high loss rates.

The He 111 was remarkably robust, and during the Battle of Britain many aircraft limped home with severe damage. This was a mixed blessing, since the Heinkels often crash landed on or near their French airfields, beyond repair and laden with dead or dying aircrew on board.

The He 111 was forced to 'soldier on' in a variety of roles for the remainder of the war. Improved variants were introduced following the Battle of Britain, some carried increased bombloads, others had new weapons. The He-111 operated extensively on the Eastern Front, flying close air support, transport and bomber missions. Postwar, Spain produced some 236 Heinkel 111s as the CASA C.2111, about 100 of which were powered by Rolls Royce Merlin engines. These He 111s remained in service long enough to be used in the filming of the Battle of Britain movie in the mid-1960s!

JAPANESE BOMBERS

THE IMPERIAL JAPANESE Army Air Force followed much the same doctrine as the Luftwaffe. Their bomber arm was primarily tactical, mostly equipped with relatively lightweight, short-ranged twin engined bombers which carried small bombloads. It began World War II with a collection of modern and anachronistic aircraft types. Among the latter was the Mitsubishi Ki-30, 704 of which were built between 1938 and 1941. The Ki-30, though radial engined and equipped with a fixed, spatted undercarriage, was similar in concept and configuration to Britain's Fairey Battle. It proved equally vulnerable. Some survived long enough to be used in the Kamikaze role at the end of the war.

The prototype Mitsubishi Ka-15 first flew in July 1935, preceded by an aerodynamic long-range bomber prototype known as the Ka-9, the previous year. In production form for the Imperial Japanese Navy, the Ka-15 became the G3M ('Nell'). After combat evaluation in China from 1937 it was used as a land-based, long-range fleet support bomber, optimized for attacking enemy surface vessels. This capability was demonstrated in December 1941, when G3Ms sank the British battleship *Prince of Wales* and battlecruiser *Repulse* .

The Mitsubishi G3M had a maximum speed of 230mph (368km/h) and a range of 1,615 miles (2,600km). There were 1,048 G3Ms built, but the type was relegated to patrol, transport, training and glider-towing duties from 1942.

The Army's Mitsubishi Ki-21 (code-named 'Sally' by the Allies) first flew in November 1936 and entered service in 1938. The Ki-21 was built in several versions, and 2,064 were built by Mitsubishi and Nakajima before production ended. Nominally replaced by the Ki-49 from 1941, small numbers remained in service throughout the war, though the type was obsolescent by 1943.

The Kawasaki Ki-48 'Lily' was heavily influenced by the Russian Tupolev SB-2, encountered by Japanese forces during the Sino-Japanese War. The prototype first flew in July 1939, and the type entered service in China in late 1940. The type was built in large numbers (1,977) and remained in production until 1944, though by then it was thoroughly obsolete.

The Nakajima Ki-49 Donryu (Storm Dragon), although intended as a replacement for the Ki-21, offered little improvement over the earlier aircraft, and never fully replaced it. Only 819 Ki-49s were built, and the type was dubbed 'Helen' by the Allies. The Ki-49 made its combat debut in China, and attacked the Australian port of Darwin in February 1942, but it was soon relegated to the anti-submarine, transport and even night fighter roles.

The G3M's replacement with the Imperial Japanese Navy was the G4M, code-named 'Betty' by the Allies. The 'Betty' became the most widely-built Japanese bomber of the war, with 2,446 being produced. First flown on October 23, 1939, the 'Betty' served on all fronts. It was successively improved, remaining in production

Right: *Mitsubishi G3Ms like these accounted for the British warships* HMS Repulse *and* Prince of Wales *in December 1941.*

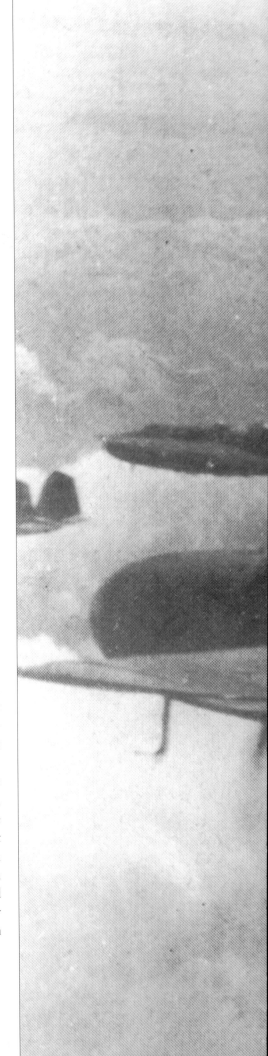

until August 1945. Initially unarmored, the G4M had a tendency to burn when hit, leading to a variety of unflattering epithets among Allied and Japanese pilots. The type remained in service throughout the war, however, and was used to ferry the Japanese surrender delegation to Io Shima on August 19, 1945.

The 698 Mitsubishi Ki-67s built were designated as heavy bombers by the Japanese, though with a maximum bombload of less than 2,000lb (907kg) they were light- or medium-bombers by Allied standards. The Ki-67, named Hiryu (Flying Dragon) and code-named 'Peggy' by the Allies, made its combat debut in October 1944. It had a maximum speed of 335mph (540km/h) and a range of 2,361 miles (3,800km).

The aircraft proved relatively successful, though by that stage of the war, skilled and experienced bomber aircrew were in short supply. Most surviving bomber types were then used in pointless suicide attacks which

entirely failed to halt the inexorable Allied advance.

Japan's equivalent to Britain's Mosquito was the Yokosuka P1Y Ginga (Milky Way, code-named 'Frances' by the Allies). This first flew in August 1943, and which was also pressed into use as a night fighter and torpedo bomber. The Japanese built 1,098, but teething troubles reduced their impact in service.

The final Japanese bomber type worthy of note was Nakajima's G8N, a four-engined machine with an 8,800lb (3,991-kg) bombload, which was flown in prototype form in October 1944. The Nakajima G8N, however failed to enter service.

Opposite: *This disarmed Mitsubishi G4M 'Betty' is seen after capture by Allied forces. The aircraft wears full USAAF markings.*
Below: *This Mitsubishi Ki-67 wears the markings of the Imperial Japanese Army's 61st Sentai. The aircraft were named Hiryu (Flying Dragon). There were 698 Mitsubishi Ki-67s built.*

JUNKERS JU 87

THE JUNKERS JU 87 has the distinction of being one of the most immediately recognizable bombers in history, and one of the best known to the general public. When it first went to war, it was a weapon which inspired enormous terror, yet was quickly found to be vulnerable and of limited operational effectiveness.

Despite the Ju 87's shortcomings and a catastrophic level of losses in the Battle of Britain, the aircraft remained in widespread service for the whole of World War II. It was confined, however, to operating by night, or in theaters where it was less likely to be caught by high performance fighters.

The aircraft was designed to meet a requirement drawn up by Ernst Udet for a Sturzkampfflugzeug (dive bomber). This title was commonly abbreviated as Stuka. A total of 5,700 aircraft of all Junkers Ju 87 versions were produced.

The first prototype Ju 87, derived from Junkers Swedish-built K.47 of 1928, was powered by a 640hp Rolls Royce Kestrel V engine. It had a Do 17 type tail unit, with endplate fins and rudders. The second prototype introduced a more conventional tail unit, which was then made larger and more angular on successive prototypes. The Ju 87 was evaluated against three competitors. It was only selected for production after Udet crashed the other leading contender, the He 118, due to his unfamiliarity with its propeller pitch controls!

The first production Ju 87As had a

Left: *The Junkers Ju 87B-1 formed the backbone of the Stukageschwaderen during the assault on Poland. The version first saw actice service in the Spanish Civil War.*

less powerful 635hp Jumo 210 Da engine, and had a straight, unswept leading edge, with taper only on the trailing edge to ease production. The type entered service in early 1937, with Stukageschwader 163, who deployed three aircraft to Spain, where they served as Jolanthe Kette within the Condor Legion. They were later joined by some Ju 87Bs, which had a 900hp Jumo 211 A engine.

Despite the Stuka's extremely successful performance in the attacks on Poland, the Low Countries and France, they suffered heavy losses when enemy fighters did break through their screen of fighter escorts. Others fell to rapid-firing, light anti-aircraft guns. During operations over Dunkirk in May 1940, for example, the Stukas suffered very heavy losses, and this was to be a precursor of even worse slaughter during the Battle of Britain. The Ju 87B-2 had a 1,100hp Jumo 211 Da engine, and this was in service in time to participate in the Battle of Britain. The Ju 87R was similar to the B, but with provision for long-range fuel tanks.

In conditions of air superiority on the Eastern Front, the Ju 87 performed with great success, again, especially in its later Ju 87D form, with a 1,700hp Jumo 213A engine. Wastage in North Africa, however, was heavy. As the Soviet air forces improved in quality, losses began to mount on the Eastern Front. After some success as a tank-killer, ditching dive attacks for strafe attacks using new underwing 37-mm (1.45-inch) cannon, the aircraft was increasingly used in the Nachtschlacht (night ground attack) role. Many Ju 87Ds were re-engined with 1,500hp Jumo 211 P engines. By opening the

dive brakes, the Junkers Ju 87 pilot put the aircraft into a fully automatic vertical dive, in which the aircraft could easily be pointed at the target. The Ju 87's fixed undercarriage and draggy airframe meant that speed did not build up too quickly in the dive, while the automatic 6 g pull-out was not too uncomfortable for the crew.

Above: *A Luftwaffe technician examines the swing-down crutch on which the 250-kg (551-kg) bomb is mounted.*

Left: *The Ju 87D combined a more powerful engine with a cleaned up airframe, and entered service in late 1941. This version performed especially well on the Eastern Front.*

Opposite, top: *These Ju 87Bs wear the Eagle badge of Stukageschwader 51's III Gruppe, later redesignated as II Gruppe of Stukageschwader 1.*

Opposite, bottom: *The Ju 87R introduced provision for underwing fuel tanks. A total of 5,700 aircraft of all Junkers Ju 87 versions were produced.*

HANDLEY PAGE HARROW

THE HANDLEY PAGE Harrow was one of the Royal Air Force's first monoplane bombers. Despite its frontline service life being extremely short, it enjoyed a much longer and more distinguished career in the transport role. The Harrow was derived from the HP.51 troop carrier (which first flew on May 8, 1935). This competed with the Bristol 130 and the Armstrong Whitworth AW 23 to be selected to meet an RAF requirement for a bomber transport. The Bristol 130 was selected to meet the transport requirement, and 50 were built, equipping three squadrons at home and overseas. These saw extensive service in the bomber role in Eritrea and North Africa, but was always best known as a troop transport.

The unsuccessful contenders were both also destined for production. The AW 23 formed the basis of the Armstrong Whitworth Whitley, while the Handley Page Harrow was also ordered as a bomber, its prototype flying on October 10, 1936.

The Handley Page Harrow was never viewed as being a great bomber, although it did represent a rapidly available monoplane. As such it was regarded as being a useful stop-gap replacement for the Vickers Virginia and the Handley Page Heyford.

The Harrow could reach a maximum speed of 200mph (322km/h). The aircraft could carry a 3,000-lb (1,361-kg) bombload. It had a maximum range of 1,840 miles (2,961km).

Handley Page employed an innovative system of split-assembly construction. This system allowed the entire production run of 100 Handley Page Harrows to be built in less than two years. This was three months ahead of the optimistic contract deadline!

The Harrow was of broadly similar configuration to the Bombay, with a high wing, twin tailfins mounted inboard on the tailplanes, and with a heavily braced fixed undercarriage. The Royal Air Force received 100 Harrows, the first 38 being Harrow Mk Is powered by 830hp Bristol Pegasus X radial engines, the remainder being Mk IIs with 925hp Pegasus XXs. (Interestingly, the Bombay transport used 1,010hp Pegasus XXIIs).

The Handley Page Harrow entered service with No.214 Squadron in January 1937. The type went on to equip five frontline Royal Air Force bomber squadrons, the last re-equipping with more modern aircraft in December 1939.

The last frontline Handley Page Harrows served with Fighter Command. These equipped one flight of No.93 Squadron and were used to drop mines in the path of approaching enemy night bombers. This tactic proved to be of marginal utility.

Some Harrows were then used in the training role, but most reverted to the transport role for which the HP.51 had originally been designed. These equipped No.271 Squadron until February 1945, when they were finally replaced by Dakotas.

Right: *A Harrow of No.214 Squadron in flight. Designed as a transport, the Harrow was pressed into service as a bomber for the RAF's expansion.*

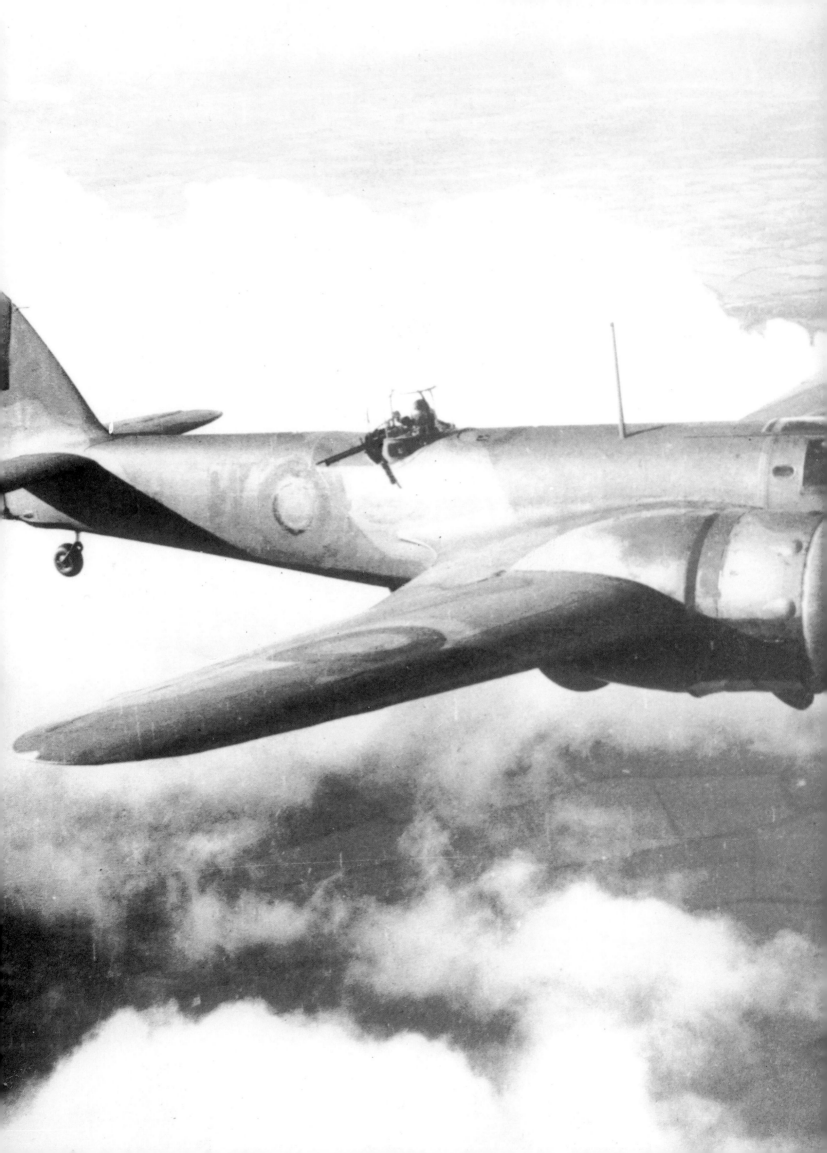

BRISTOL BLENHEIM

THE BRISTOL BLENHEIM marked a major improvement over the Hart biplanes it replaced. Its performance, however, was insufficient to save it from heavy losses once tested in the crucible of war. When it was first conceived, however, the Bristol 142 (as the Blenheim was then still known) looked like a great idea. It would be an up-to-date equivalent to the Fairey Fox and able to out-pace the fighters of the day. Unfortunately, the 'fighters of the day' against which the aircraft was compared were the last of the biplanes, and not the first of the new monoplane fighters. Even here, however, the Blenheim was less impressive than it initially appeared. Although it could attain a speed of 260mph (418km/h), it cruised at only 200mph (321km/h) (less when fully laden, or flying to achieve its best range). A 200mph (321km/h) bomber was only 14mph (22.5km/h) faster than the Hawker Hind, and a 180mph (289km/h) bomber (as the Blenheim often was) was simply inadequate.

The Blenheim was born when Viscount Rothermere, proprietor of the *Daily Mail*, commissioned Bristol to produce the fastest commercial aircraft in Europe for his personal use. It was first flown on April 12, 1935. Rothermere presented this Mercury-engined Model 142, named 'Britain First', to the Air Ministry for trials.

The results were sufficiently impressive to prompt the Royal Air Force to order a derivative of the type as the Bristol 142M, later named Blenheim.

Left: *The best thing that could be said for the Blenheim was probably that it was marginally less useless than the Fairey Battle.*

The Blenheim prototype made its maiden flight on June 25, 1936, and the type entered service with No.114 Squadron in March 1937.

The Bristol Blenheim was of almost unimaginable modernity by the standards of the day. The Blenheim, however, still had a crew of three, and was defended by a single, inadequate 0.303-in machine gun. The aircraft had to be light enough to operate from grass aerodromes in Great Britain like Andover, Bicester and Netheravon.

Many senior Royal Air Force officers still seriously favored open cockpits ('for their better field of view'), and distrusted 'fripperies' such as retractable undercarriages and power-operated gun turrets. Often flying aboard bombers as umpires during peacetime exercises, they were impressed by cross-cover seemingly provided by their neat box formations. They had no reason to disbelieve the extravagant claims of bomber crews, while they tended to dismiss the claims of attacking fighter pilots. They assumed that any bombs dropped would have hit their targets, and would have caused massive destruction, so that a 1,000-lb (453-kg) load of tiny bombs seemed viable. The Blenheim was, in the end, an unsatisfactory compromise. Heavier, faster medium bombers such as the Ju 88 or the Boston needed longer runways but could deliver a meaningful bombload with a greater chance of survival. At the other end of the scale, fighter bombers (such as the Whirlwind) could attack targets in the face of heavier defenses, and still survive to fight another day.

Bristol Blenheims formed the backbone of Bomber Command's interwar

expansion, equipping 17 squadrons by September 1938. By the time war broke out, some Blenheim Is had been passed on to Fighter Command as night fighters, or to overseas squadrons, having been replaced by improved Blenheim IVs in Bomber Command units. The Blenheim IV had an extended forward fuselage with a prone bomb-aiming position. The aircraft also had improved accommodation for the navigator.

A Blenheim IV of No.139 Squadron flew the RAF's first sortie of the war. The type was involved in many of the operations conducted during the so-called Phoney War. They proved extremely vulnerable to enemy defenses, but also gained some successes, including the sinking of a U-Boat. These successes were, however, achieved at enormous cost in aircraft

and aircrew. Matters would only get worse when the Germans attacked the Low Countries and France.

The BEF (British Expeditionary Force) in France had been accompanied by four Blenheim squadrons, and two more had joined the AASF (Advanced Air Striking Force) when British forces were first deployed to the Continent. More Blenheims were committed to the fighting, flying from British bases, and while these suffered lighter losses than the Fairey Battles of the AASF, the loss rate was still unsustainable. These included the destruction of 11 out of 12 No.82 Squadron aircraft during a single mission on May 17.

Despite heavy losses, the Blenheim was the only RAF bomber fast and survivable enough to operate by day at all, when all other RAF bombers were

forced to take advantage of the cover of darkness. The political imperative of continuing to take offensive action 'around the clock' dictated that No.2 Group would continue to make fruitless and costly daylight attacks against Continental targets.

Bomber Command's Blenheims were replaced by Bostons, Venturas and Mitchells during 1942, and flew their last sorties on August 17/18, 1942. Coastal Command retired the type the following month.

The Blenheim fared no better in the Mediterranean and the Far East, although they did remain in service a little longer. The Blenheim V (originally designed for Army Co-operation Command) was used during Operation Torch (the Anglo-American invasion of Vichy French North Africa) giving more opportunities for ultimately pointless heroics as the obsolete aircraft were hacked from the sky by enemy fighters. The Blenheim was withdrawn from frontline use in North Africa in December 1943.

In India, the Bristol Blenheim V was retired from frontline service in October 1943. In May the following year, however, the Beaufighter-equipped No.176 Squadron found a long-abandoned Blenheim V. The squadron used the aircraft for two bombing missions against the Japanese on May 9 and 11, 1944.

Blenheims were used until the end of the war for training and other second-line duties. They had also been built in Canada (as the Bolingbroke) and some of these aircraft continued in use in the training role for a brief period after the war.

Some Blenheims had been used by the Finns. The last of these served on in second line roles into the 1950s.

Top, left: *Blenheim IVs of No. 139 Squadron flying a border reconnaissance patrol during the Phoney War.*
Left: *This Blenheim I of No. 211 Squadron was photographed during the ill-fated Greek campaign in 1941.*

BOEING B-17 FLYING FORTRESS

THE B-17 FLYING Fortress was the best known of the USAAF's wartime bombers. The plane has captured the imagination of the American public. Many of them would be surprised to learn that fewer B-17s were built than B-24s. The public also believe the Flying Fortress was a better all-round aircraft. But while the B-17 may have been less militarily important than the B-24 and the B-29, and while it was built in smaller numbers than the Liberator, it was of huge symbolic importance. The B-17 grew to represent the entire USAAF bomber effort (at least in Europe). Moreover, it preceded the B-24 by some four years. Thus it was in regular USAAF service even before Pearl Harbor, whereas the B-24 had been supplied only to the RAF, and then only from May 1941.

When Japan attacked Pearl Harbor, the B-17 was still heavily out-numbered by the older, smaller, twin-engined bombers that had been designed to meet the country's interwar requirements. It was to the B-17, however, that the USAAF turned to form the basis of its new strategic bomber arm. The B-17 was to open a fight which would be very different to the bomber war envisaged during the 1920s and 1930s.

At the height of American interwar isolationism, many believed that the only possible use for USAAC bombers was against an enemy invasion fleet. No credible enemy could reach the United States. Similarly, USAAC bombers of the period could not reach credible targets. A directive at the time urged the USAAC to concentrate on: "That class of aviation designed for the close-in support of ground troops". Despite this prevailing outlook, coupled with financial constraints, the country did begin looking at developing a much longer-range 'strategic bomber'. This would eventually result in the fielding of the Boeing B-17 and later the B-29.

Boeing began work on another four-engined, long-range bomber even before the emergence of these two historic aircraft. This was the Model 294 or XBLR-1 (later re-designated as the XB-15), made in response to an Army

Right: *The bulk of the B-17πs crew were clustered closely together in the forward fuselage, with a high degree of comfort by comparison with British bombers.*
Below: *A Boeing B-17F of the 303rd Bomb Group that was based in Molesworth, eastern England.*

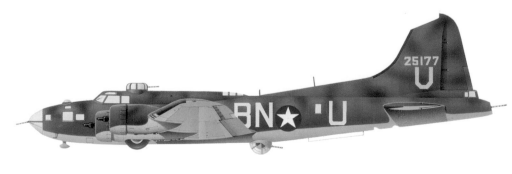

Opposite: *Boeing B-17s based in England with the USAF Eighth Air Force. They participated in the 'precision daylight bombing' of targets in the Third Reich from August 1942.*
Right: *The B-17 was beautifully streamlined and enjoyed superb performance characteristics, but was less successful than the more angular B-24 Liberator.*
Below: *This B-17D of the Philippines-based 19th Bomb Group shows the Fortress' original tail shape to advantage. It wears prewar neutrality stripes on the rudder.*

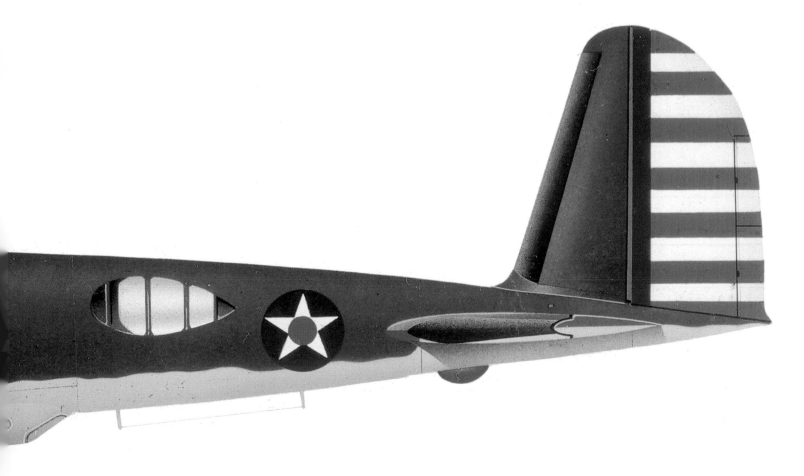

Air Corps requirement issued on April 14, 1934. This called for a 5,000 mile (8,046km) range carrying a 2,000-lb (907-kg) bombload. The Boeing Model 294 was selected in preference to the Glenn L. Martin Company's even larger and unconventional Model 145. This twin-finned 105,000-lb (47,630-kg) monster had a 173-ft (52-m) wingspan. It was to have been powered by six Allison V-1710-2 engines, four of them operating as tractors and two as pushers.

On June 29, 1935, Boeing were contracted to build a single XBLR-1. This was as a massive four-engined all metal monoplane. The XBLR-1 was powered by four 1,000hp Pratt & Whitney R-1830 twin-row, air-cooled radial engines, although it had originally been intended to fit four Allison V-1710 liquid cooled inline engines.

The XBLR-1 had a crew of ten, with what then seemed like a vast arsenal of six defensive machine guns. It was soundproofed, heated, and had ventilated crew accommodation (including bunk beds, a galley, and a lavatory).

The XB-15, although started long before the Model 299 (later the B-17), made its maiden flight two years later, on October 15, 1937. The aircraft was chronically underpowered, and was not ordered into production.

What would become the B-17 was a smaller and slightly more modest aircraft. The original Model 299 design, however, with its 750hp Pratt & Whitney Hornet engines, made it significantly bigger than the USAAC bombers of the time. The prototype first flew on July 28, 1935, and it was evaluated against the B-18 in October, crashing fatally during the evaluation. The Model 299's size, cost and complexity led to its being passed over by the inferior (but more familiar) B-18 Bolo in 1934. Interestingly, the B-17's power and size were not used to haul a heavier bombload (the aircraft carried a similar bombload to the B-18). Instead, they were used to carry that bombload higher, and faster, and in a better-protected aircraft. Soon after

rejecting the Model 299 in favour of the B-18 Bolo, however, the USAAC did order a batch of 13 Wright Cyclone-engined Y1B-17s. These were service tested by the 2nd Bomb Group at Langley Field. They received 12 of the aircraft during March–December 1937. These were used for a succession of long-range and record-breaking flights. The 13th aircraft, a testbed for the turbo-supercharged R-1820-51 engines, became the forerunner of the B-17B. It was also the hot-rod of the B-17 family, the B-17C. The final 'first generation' B-17 was the D model, 42 of which were ordered in 1940.

Some 90 B-17s were in service when the Japanese attacked Pearl Harbor.

Right: *'A Bit O' Lace' was a well-worn B-17G from the 447th Bombardment Group, it's bomb log recording 83 missions when photographed.*

Below: *B-17Gs of the 447th Bomb Group form up over East Anglia as they begin a mission to Germany. One aircraft retains the original olive drab colour scheme.*

Opposite, top: *This modern B-17 warbird shows off its open bomb-bay doors during an airshow appearance. The Fortress was always handicapped by its small bombload.*

Opposite, bottom: *Boeing B-17s take off from RAF Binbrook, eastern England, during the filming of the motion picture 'Memphis Belle'.*

The type, however, had already seen combat service as 20 B-17Cs had been delivered to the RAF as Fortress Mk. Is. These proved extremely disappointing in service. The Fortress Mk. Is suffered a succession of technical problems and their armament was inadequate. Luckily, the RAF's reports on the inadequacies of the Fortress were used by Boeing to design the B-17E. This version introduced new powered gun turrets, a new enlarged tailfin and tailplane to give better directional stability at high altitude.

The B-17E was the variant used to launch the Eighth Air Force's 'precision daylight bombing' campaign against the Third Reich in August 1942. In fact, in most weather conditions, the accuracy of the B-17s was no better than that achieved by Bomber Command at night. It remains unproven as to whether either air arm achieved the results claimed for them. Destruction was very limited until the last year-and-a-half of the war, while the cost in men and aircraft was horrifying. Industrial production in Nazi Germany continued, and civilian morale did not collapse, although large numbers of troops, guns and fighters were diverted from the front for the defense of the Reich.

The best B-17 variant of the war was the B-17G, which had an extra chin turret and other improvements. This formed the basis of the RAF Fortress III which enjoyed limited success in the bomber and ECM roles.

The B-17 was easier to fly than the B-24 (especially in formation), and could fly at rather higher altitude. The Flying Fortress, however, was slower than the Liberator, and carried a smaller load over a shorter range. This was one reason that the B-17 formed the backbone of the Eighth Air Force operating from British bases, since only the Liberators could cope with the very long range missions required in some other theaters. In other roles, the capacious long-range Liberator enjoyed even more of an advantage, yet it is the Flying Fortress that has entered the history books as the USAAF's most legendary bomber.

Below: *'Yankee Doodle' was a B-17D operated by the 97th Bomb Group at Grafton Underwood in September 1942.* **Opposite:** *Several examples of the Boeing B-17 survive in airworthy condition today, most earning their keep on the US airshow circuit.*

VICKERS WELLESLEY

THE VICKERS WELLESLEY, despite its anachronistic appearance, was actually a surprisingly efficient and effective bomber. It was only 10kts slower than the ostensibly 'modern' Blenheim, but carrying double the bombload. Its geodetic structure made it remarkably robust and much more resilient to battle damage. Moreover, the record-breaking Wellesley achieved all of this on the power of a single 950hp Mercury engine. The Wellesley was almost a biplane, and originated in design studies to meet two RAF requirements for a maritime torpedo bomber to replace the Blackburn Ripon (Specification M.1/30) and a later specification (G.4/31) for a general purpose bomber and torpedo bomber.

The Air Ministry clearly expected to select a biplane design, and Vickers produced its Type 253 to meet the requirement, winning the competition and an order for 150 of these businesslike looking biplanes. Alongside the Type 253, Vickers also drew up a rival monoplane design, the Type 246. This was characterized by a long-span, very high aspect ratio cantilever wing and a fully-developed geodetic structure. It promised to be lighter and more efficient than the biplane, and to carry a heavier load further, faster and higher than aircraft using the same engine power. Vickers built a private venture prototype of the monoplane, which flew on June 19, 1935. This delivered all of the promises predicted by Vickers, and was selected for production in place of the biplane. The Air Ministry's requirements had changed, however, and instead of being a general purpose bomber and torpedo bomber the Type 246 (named Wellesley in tribute to the Duke of Wellington) was now expected to be a long-range medium bomber to meet the new Secification 22/35.

The Wellesley carried its 2,000-lb (907-kg) bombload in two removable underwing panniers, and had two 0.303-in machine guns. Later, some Wellesley's gained a ventral gun and two 0.303-in machine guns in the dorsal position.

An initial order for 79 Type 287 production aircraft was increased to 96. Vickers eventually built 176 Wellesleys for the RAF. The first Wellesley delivered to the RAF was sent to No.76 Squadron in April 1937. The type subsequently equipped five more home-based squadrons and four units based overseas. It also equipped the Long Range Development Unit formed in January 1938 to investigate the problems of very long-range operations. In doing so, the unit broke the world distance record set by the Soviet Union in July 1937, by flying from Ismailia in Egypt to Darwin in Australia. The Wellesley's record was eventually broken by a four-engined Boeing B-29.

The Wellesley's career with home-based Bomber Command units was brief. All had been replaced by April 1939. Even as early as one year before that, the 58 Wellesleys were outnumbered by the 119 aircraft stationed in the Middle East. The type served with distinction in the East African campaign and flew ASW patrols in the Eastern Mediterranean until March 1943. The type was finally declared obsolete and grounded in August.

Right: *A No.47 Squadron Wellesley is seen en route to Keren, Abyssinia, to attack Italian military targets.*

ARMSTRONG WHITWORTH WHITLEY

THE ARMSTRONG WHITWORTH Whitley was originally designed, as the AW 23, to meet a Royal Air Force requirement for a bomber transport. The aircraft was eventually destined to perform with distinction in the para-dropping and glider-towing roles, but would first operate with equal success in the bomber role.

The low-winged AW 23 prototype made its maiden flight on June 4, 1935, but was passed over in favor of Bristol's more capacious Bombay. With the wing raised to a mid-wing position, the AW 38 lost its unobstructed cabin, but gained a useful bomb bay. After brief tests of the prototype, which had been designed and built in only 18 months, and which flew on March 17, 1936, the type was ordered into production as a bomber.

The Whitley's massive, rather square wing led some to christen it the 'Flying Barn Door'. The type's high incidence wing (which gave an unusual nose-down flying attitude) and jutting chin gave the aircraft an anachronistic air. This was not borne out by the aircraft's construction, with its all-metal monocoque fuselage and metal wing. It was also seen its deliberate use of the smallest possible number of components and standardized components to aid and streamline production.

The aircraft was destined to be ordered in large numbers, and formed the backbone of the expansion of

Left: The Armstrong Whitworth Whitley was an anachronistic looking aircraft. The Whitley, however, proved to be an extremely effective bomber.

Bomber Command's heavy bomber units in the 1930s. Armstrong Whitworth's facilities in Coventry, in central England, were hard-pressed, and production of the Ensign airliner had to be transferred to Hamble, near the south coast.

The first Armstrong Whitworth Whitleys entered service with No.10 Squadron in March 1937 and the early Mk Is were soon joined by a plethora of improved variants. Production eventually totalled 1,814. Later aircraft within the batch of Whitley Mk Is gained dihedral on the outer wing panels. The Whitley Mk II variant used 845hp Tiger VIII engines (instead of the Mk Is 795hp Tiger IXs) with the Royal Air Force's first two-stage superchargers.

The Mk III introduced a power-operated nose turret and a retractable ventral dustbin turret, while the Mk IV introduced 1,030hp Merlin engines and a power-operated four-gun tail turret. The Mk V had an extended tailcone giving the rear gunner a greater field of fire, as well as de-icing boots on the wing and re-shaped tailfins and rudders. The Whitley VII was essentially similar, but equipped for ASV duties with radar and increased fuel tankage.

Examples of all Whitley variants had entered service before war broke out. The type was heavily involved in what has become known as the Phoney War, operating principally by night. Whitleys went 'leaflet-dropping' on the first night of the war—an activity which would continue for many months, ranging as far as Berlin. In the

following weeks Whitleys also attacked coastal targets. This included a raid on the seaplane base at Hornum, on the North Sea coast, on May 11/12, 1940—the first time that the RAF dropped bombs on German soil. The next month, Whitleys flew over the Alps to attack Italian targets, bombing Genoa and Turin only a few hours after Mussolini's declaration of war. In August 1940, Whitleys flew on the first raid against Berlin.

The Whitleys finally retired from Bomber Command in 1942, but continued in use in a number of other roles. Whitley glider tugs continued to fly occasional leaflet dropping missions over enemy-occupied Belgium as late as the spring of 1943.

Left: *This black-painted Whitley served with No.78 Squadron in the night-bombing role, this unit taking part in Operation Colossus, a daring operation against the Italian water supply network.*

Below: *The Whitley was optimized for ease of production, and the type was built in large numbers, equipping nine prewar bomber squadrons and more units during World War II.*

FAIREY BATTLE

THE FAIREY BATTLE, when first conceived, was extremely modern, and had it been rushed into service, might have been regarded as a useful peacetime stop-gap. But by the time war broke out in 1939, the Battle had been left behind. It was a poorly-armed, under-powered liability, which achieved little, and allowed the slaughter of the cream of the prewar RAF personnel.

The Battle, designed to replace the Hawker Hart, originated in Fairey's response to an Air Ministry specification of April 1933. It was intended to carry a 1,000-lb (453-kg) bombload over a 1,000-mile (1,609-km) range, at a cruising speed of 200mph (321km/h). The Battle was the first service aircraft to be powered by the Rolls Royce Merlin engine. The type was exceptionally clean by the standards of the day. It had a three-bladed variable pitch propeller, and a semi-retractable undercarriage which retracted into underwing fairings, leaving the tyre exposed. The three-man crew sat in tandem under a long continuous 'greenhouse'. The radio-operator also doubled as gunner, with a 0.303-in (7.62-mm) Vickers gun augmenting the fixed forward-firing Browning in the starboard wing. The normal bombload of four 250-lb (113-kg) bombs was accommodated in four wing cells outboard of the undercarriage. This could be augmented by two further bombs carried on external racks.

The prototype Battle made its maiden flight on March 10, 1936, and the type entered service with No.63 Squadron in May 1937. To procure the Battle at all was a disastrous mistake, and represented a squandering of production capacity, valuable Merlin engines and variable pitch propellers. To make matters worse, Battles were built in huge numbers. Their production absorbed the resources of the Austin Motor Company, as well as those of Fairey itself.

About 1,000 Battles were in service when war was declared, equipping 17 squadrons, 10 of these were deployed to France the day before war was declared. The Battles suffered heavy losses even during routine reconnaissance missions over the Siegfried Line. After Germany invaded France, the Battles suffered even heavier losses in action. On May 12, 1940, No.12 Squadron lost all five of the aircraft it sent out against bridges over the Albert Canal in Belgium. The formation leader and his navigator won posthumous Victoria Crosses.

After the withdrawal from France, the Battle continued in service. They mainly flew night attacks against Dutch and French ports, where Hitler's invasion fleet was massing, and against coastal airfields. The last Battle operational bombing missions were flown in mid-October 1940.

The Fairey Battle as a pilot and gunnery trainer, and as a target tug, was useful and competent. The type was effective enough as a patrol aircraft in areas which might be guaranteed to be free from enemy fighters (such as Iceland). Relatively large numbers of Battles served in these roles until July 1944, when the type was finally declared obsolete.

Right: *The Fairey Battle proved disastrously vulnerable to enemy flak and fighters. Large numbers of Fairey Battles were lost in action during World War II.*

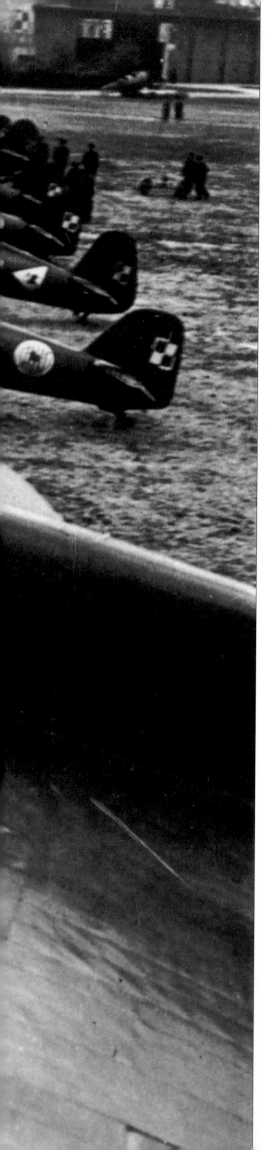

PZL P.37 Los

THE PZL P.37 was exceptionally compact and streamlined, and enjoyed an excellent performance, yet its twin-wheel main undercarriage allowed it to operate from soft grass strips. The first prototype flew in December 1936, and a second prototype followed in November 1937. The second aircraft featured a redesigned cockpit interior, and was fitted with twin endplate fins and rudders, as well as the characteristic twin-wheel main gear units.

The two prototypes were followed by ten P.37As and 20 P.37Abis aircraft. The first ten PZL P.37 aircraft retained the original single vertical tailfin, and all were powered by the interim Pegasus XII engine. One of the later aircraft was fitted with 1,020hp Gnôme-Rhône 14N-01 engines, and served as the export P.37C prototype. The planned production P.37C, with 970hp 14N-07 engines, was intended for Bulgaria and Yugoslavia. Romania and Turkey ordered the P.37D with 1,050hp 14N-20/21 engines.

The definitive Polish Air Force aircraft was the P.37B with 920hp Skoda-built Bristol Pegasus XX engines. The first of these were delivered in August 1938. The aircraft carried a 2,580kg (5,6987-lb) of bombs in the fuselage and centre-section bomb bays, the latter being required because of the slender cross section and limited volume of the fuselage.

Only 90 of the 124 aircraft built had been delivered to the Polish Air Force

by September 1, 1939, and only 36 P.37Bs had been delivered to the frontline. Another nine or 10 aircraft were delivered as attrition replacements. The remainder stayed with training units and at Malaszewicze air base in eastern Poland, where a second bomber wing was being formed. These, however, were destroyed on the ground, or captured.

The P.37s performed well, hitting German armor with determination and great effect. They were credited with holding up several enemy columns for some days, although the outcome of the one-sided fight was never in doubt. At least two PZL P.37 gunners shot down Bf 109Es, but 12 were shot down by the enemy, and one by Polish anti-aircraft guns. Four P.37s landed in the Soviet Union, which evaluated them with great interest.

About 39 examples of the PZL P.37 Los withdrew to Romania when Russia attacked from the east on September 17. It had been hoped that the Polish Air Force would be reborn to fly and fight again in Romania. Instead the Romanians promptly interned the new bombers. These went on to fight the Russians as part of the German Luftflotte 4. They may have been reinforced by complete but unarmed P.37s captured intact by the Germans at the factory airfield.

In September 1944 most of the remaining P.37s of the Romanian Air Force were destroyed in a Hungarian air attack against Cimpia Turzii airfield. Some P.37s survived, however, and one or two of them remained in use as target tugs during the early 1950s. These aircraft were finally scrapped in Romania.

Left: *A P.37 Los heads a line of Polish Air Force aircraft, mostly P.11 fighters. The P.37 performed with distinction but there were too few to make a difference.*

DOUGLAS B-18 BOLO

THE DOUGLAS B-18 Bolo (originally known as the DB1) was a bomber derivative of the DC-2 airliner, marrying DC-2 wings (with extended rounded tips) and tail to a new deeper fuselage, with a glazed nose. The B-18 was designed as a replacement for the Martin Bomber. It was designed to meet a USAAC requirement for a multi-engined bomber capable of carrying a 1,000-lb (453-kg) bombload over a distance of 2,000 miles (3,218km) at a speed of more than 200mph (321km/h). It was envisaged that the aircraft selected would enjoy a 220-aircraft production run. Several producers were invited to submit bids. The B-18 competed with the Martin 146 (an improved B-10) and the four engined Boeing 299, precursor to the B-17 for the order.

The DB-1 made its first flight in April 1935, and was delivered to Wright Field in August. The aircraft was powered by a pair of 850hp Wright R-1820-G5 air-cooled radial engines giving a maximum speed of 233mph (374km/h). The DB-1 had a cruising speed of 173mph (278km/h). Following B-18 prototype trials in 1936, the Army General Staff ordered 82 production B-18s (later increasing the total to 132).

The first production B-18 was delivered to Wright Field in February 1937. Although production B-18s were powered by the more powerful 930hp Wright R-1820-45 the aircraft's performance was reduced by comparison with the prototype, with a maximum speed of 217mph (436km/h), and a cruising speed of 167mph (268km/h).

The basic Douglas B-18 was augmented from May 1938 by the improved B-18A, with 1,000hp Wright R-1820-53 radial engines driving fully-feathering propellers. Only 217 B-18As were built, the remainder being completed as B-23s. The B-18As featured a new 'shark' nose with the bombardier's position moved forward over the nose gunner's station. In 1940, 22 USAAC B-18s and 17 B-18As were modified to carry larger bombs and were redesignated as B-18M and B-18AM respectively.

The Royal Canadian Air Force (RCAF) ordered 20 B-18As. These aircraft were known locally as Digby Mk 1s, and served with No 10 (BR) Squadron in the ASW role. Before being replaced by Liberator GR. Vs in the anti-submarine role in 1943, the RCAF Digbys were credited with one U-boat kill, sinking the U-520 on October 3, 1942.

The B-18 and B-18A, remained the most important and numerous USAAC bomber type deployed outside the continental United States at the time of Pearl Harbor. This was despite the bomber's deficencies in range, speed and armament. In 1942, 122 surviving B-18As were converted to B-18B standards, for maritime reconnaissance duties to counter the increasing U-boat menace. USAAF B-18Bs were credited with two U-boat kills. Surviving USAAF B-18s ended their lives in training and transport roles. At the end of the war some were sold for civil use. The last second-line RCAF Digby was retired in 1946.

Right: *A USAAC Douglas B-18A in prewar 'neutral' colors. Converted to B-18B standards, some Bolos performed usefully in the ASW role.*

SAVOIA MARCHETTI SM 79

THE SAVOIA MARCHETTI SM 79 Sparviero (Sparrowhawk) was Italy's most famous and widely produced bomber. It had a near-legendary reputation among the Italian population. The aircraft was originally designed as a fast, long-range, eight-seat commercial airliner. The prototype first flew in 1934 and set a succession of records. Given three engines for reliability and safety, the SM 79's Trimotor configuration made conversion to the bomber role tricky. The bomb aimer eventually had to be accommodated in a ventral gondola, located quite well aft.

The second prototype was built in bomber configuration. The SM 79 was well-armed, with a fixed forward firing gun mounted in the fairing above the cockpit, and with a free-mounted gun facing backwards in the rear part of this distinctive dorsal bump. This gave rise to the nickname 'Il Gobbo' (Hunchback). More guns were mounted in the ventral nacelle, with another mounted in the fuselage.

The SM 79 Sparviero carried 12 100-kg (220-lb) bombs vertically in its confined bomb bay, or a pair of 500-kg (1,102-lb) bombs. The first SM 79s were powered by 780hp Alfa Romeo RC34 radials. Some of these aircraft served in the Spanish Civil War. Other foreign users of the type included Yugoslavia which acquired 45 standard SM 79-Is. Iraq and Brazil

Left: The Savoia Marchetti SM 79's distinctive dorsal 'bump' led to it being nicknamed 'Hunchback'. The type was Italy's most successful bomber.

preferred the twin-engined SM 79Bs powered by 1,000hp inline Fiat A80 engines or 930hp Alfa Romeo 128 RC 18 radials. Romania took the SM79Bs and the SM 79JRs with twin 1,220hp Jumo 211Da inline engines.

The Regia Aeronautica stuck with the trimotor SM 79, though this was progressively developed, first gaining 860hp Alfa Romeo 128 RC 18 engines and later 1,000hp Piaggio P.XI RC 40s. The Sparviero formed the backbone of Italy's bomber force, outnumbering all other aircraft types, and was also adapted to the torpedo bomber role. It mainly served in the Africa and the Mediterranean theaters and saw some use in the Balkans.

When Italy finally capitulated on September 8, 1943, some 22 SM 79s flew south to join the Co-Belligerent Air Force. Others were used by the RSI forces who remained allied to the Germans. The RSI even introduced a new version, the SM 79-III (or S.579), into service. This contained aerodynamic improvements and a forward firing 20-mm cannon above the cockpit, but which lacked the normal ventral gondola. Others were seized and pressed into service by the Luftwaffe in the transport role.

The Savoia Marchetti SM 79 enjoyed remarkable longevity, with a handful of survivors remaining in use in Italy in the transport, training and drone-control roles until 1952. The Lebanese Air Force bought 3 SM 79s in 1950, and these soldiered on until at least 1959. During its ten-year production life, 1,330 Sparvieri bombers were built.

FOKKER T.V

THE FOKKER T.V was originally designed as a long-range escort fighter and destroyer, intended to defend a given piece of airspace or an object on the ground over an extended period. The aircraft, a cantilever mid-wing monoplane, had a maximum speed of 415km/h (257mph) and a maximum range of 1,630km (1,012 miles). It had a ceiling of 7,700m (25,262ft). The Fokker T.V was armed with a 20-mm (0.7-inch) cannon in the nose, and four machine guns in dorsal and ventral positions, in the tail and on the side of the fuselage. When the aircraft adopted a bomber role, the side gun was deleted. The Fokker T.V was powered by two 925hp Bristol Pegasus XXVI radial engines.

By the time it entered service, it had soon became clear the Fokker T.V would be outclassed by all enemy fighter aircraft. Consequently, the type was therefore reassigned to the bomber role.

The Fokker T.V's five-man crew consisted of the commander (who also acted as the nose-gunner and bomb aimer), and the first pilot. The aircraft also had a second pilot (who doubled up as the mid-upper gunner), the flight engineer/radio-operator (who also manned the belly gun) and finally the tailgunner. The T.V prototype made its maiden flight on October 16, 1937.

The Fokker company built 15 more T.V bombers for the Netherlands Army Air Service. These aircraft equipped one squadron of the service. These Fokker T.Vs were delivered to the Netherlands during late 1939 and early 1940.

By the spring of 1940, however, only two of the 16 available aircraft were fitted with the proper bomb racks required for accurate bombing, and capable of carrying the full design bombload of 1,000-kg (2,204-lb). The other Fokker T.Vs had only improvised bomb racks carrying 200kg (440lb) of bombs.

There were 9 Fokker T.Vs in service when Nazi Germany launched Fall Gleb (Plan Yellow) against France, the Netherlands and Belgium, on May 10, 1940. The rest of the Fokker T.Vs were awaiting completion or overhaul.

The Luftwaffe deployed 3,634 front line aircraft for the invasion of France and the Low Countries. The Nazi fighter and bomber armada raided towns, airfields and other key sites, and quickly achieved air superiority over the Netherlands.

Two Fokker T.Vs were destroyed on the ground during the surprise raids by the Luftwaffe. Five more Fokker T.V bombers were shot down, although before they were lost, these did account for seven enemy aircraft.

In the bomber role the aircraft was hampered by its bombsights, which required full manual adjustment. At least one aircraft was lost after an engine failure, because of the type's appaling asymmetric handling.

Fokker expected to receive an order for at least 130 aircraft from the Netherlands East Indies Air Force. The latter, however, chose the Martin B-10 instead, although the US bomber was inferior to the Fokker T.V.

Right: *The superb Fokker T.V was in service in only tiny numbers when Germany invaded the Low Countries. Poor asymmetric handling and bombsights hampered the crews.*

HANDLEY PAGE HAMPDEN

THE HANDLEY PAGE Hampden was, with the Whitley and Wellington, one of the most important RAF bombers of the early war years. It was nicknamed the 'Flying Suitcase' thanks to its unusually thin and 'square' upright fuselage pod. The aircraft was designed to meet the same requirement as the rather more conventional Wellington. The Hampden, however, was always intended to be something of a compromise between the Wellington and the Blenheim. It carried double the Blenheim's bombload nearly twice as far, and with greater agility than the Wellington or Whitley.

The Air Staff's insistence that, like the Blenheim, the aircraft should be able to operate off the same grass strips as aircraft such as the Hawker Hind. This made it inevitable that the Hampden would be no Ju 88 or Douglas Boston. It did, however, have a top speed of almost 270mph (434km/h) while still being able to land at only 73mph (117km/h), thanks to its advanced and generously slotted, slatted and flapped wing.

The Hampden was originally designed around a pair of steam-cooled inline Goshawk engines. It was redesigned as a slightly heavier aircraft, using a pair of Perseus or Pegasus radials, when it became clear that this powerplant was failing to live up to expectations. The first of two HP.52 prototypes (with Pegasus PE.5S

Left: The Handley Page Hampden's unusually deep but narrow fuselage led to the type's 'Flying Suitcase' nickname. The type entered service in 1938.

engines) made its maiden flight on June 21, 1936. In August, the Air Ministry ordered 180 production versions (with the 1,000hp Pegasus XVIII). The first of these made its first flight in May 1938. At the same time the Ministry ordered 100 (and eventually 150) more (HP.53s, powered by 955hp inline Napier Daggers) to be built by Short Brothers and Harland in Belfast, Northern Ireland.

The Dagger-engined aircraft were officially named Herefords. Thanks to teething troubles with the noisy, high-revving and temperamental engines, many were immediately converted to Hampden standards. Only one training squadron used the type.

The Pegasus-powered Hampden entered service with No.49 Squadron at Scampton in September 1938. By the time war was declared, ten No.5 Group squadrons were equipped with the type.

The Handly Page Hampden, in the long-range, unescorted daylight bomber role, proved unacceptably vulnerable, with inadequate defensive armament and cramped accommodation for its crew. It was too slow to stand much chance of avoiding the attentions of enemy fighters. This was proven (as if proof were needed) on September 29, 1939, when a formation of five Hampdens was cut to pieces as it searched for enemy shipping in the Heligoland Bight in the North Sea. Thereafter, the Hampden operated mainly at night, joining the Whitley in the largely ineffective bombing campaign against Germany. It dropped the first 2,000-lb (907-kg)

bomb on Germany (the Hampden involved being captained by the then-Flying Officer Guy Gibson later of Dambusters fame). The Hampdens flew their last operational mission with Bomber Command on September 14/15, 1942 but continued in Coastal Command service. Some were used as torpedo bombers—two squadrons operating from an airfield near Murmansk in the northwest Soviet Union before handing their aircraft over to the Soviets. The remaining Coastal Command Hampdens remained operational until December 1943. They were finally replaced by more suitable Beaufighters. Handley Page produced 500 Hampdens, English Electric built 770, and there were 160 built in Canada.

Above: *The Handley Page Hampden was too vulnerable for daylight operations, but performed well with RAF's Coastal Command as torpedo bombers.*

Right: *With their Hampden cockpit canopies slid back, three pilots from No.44 Squadron fly a neat echelon formation for the camera.*

VICKERS WELLINGTON

THE VICKERS WELLINGTON was affectionately known as 'Wimpey' (after Popeye's fat, hamburger-eating friend J. Wellington Wimpey). It served throughout World War II, earning an enviable reputation for rugged dependability. It originated from a 1932 Royal Air Force medium bomber specification. The Type 271 prototype made its maiden flight on June 15, 1936.

The type incorporated the geodetic construction invented by Barnes Wallis, but looked surprisingly old-fashioned, with its slab-sided fuselage and fabric covering. By comparison with theoretically 'modern' German and US contemporaries, the aircraft was lighter, much stronger and easier to repair. The aircraft proved able to absorb staggering punishment from enemy fighters or flak. Moreover, the Vickers Wellington was quick and simple to build. Vickers were able to demonstrate the complete construction of one Wellington aircraft in a single 24-hour period. They were able to do this while being able to employ a high proportion of semi-skilled workers at its factories.

As Nazi Germany flexed its military muscles, the Air Ministry Specification B.9/32 was revised further, increasing the aircraft's range and bombload. By the time the prototype flew, the aircraft was designed to carry a 4,500-lb (2,857-kg) bombload in its capacious bomb bay. It also had simplified nose and tail cupolas, each with a single

Left: With an empty nose turret, this Vickers Wellington III was a training aircraft, used by the Royal Air Force's Central Gunnery School.

0.303-in machine gun.

Re-equipping the RAF's bomber squadrons was accorded the highest priority. Some 180 Wellingtons were ordered even before the final configuration of the production version had been decided.

The first production Wellington flew on December 23, 1937. The type entered service with No.99 Squadron in October 1938.

The production aircraft differed from the prototype in having a mid-set wing (dropped from the 'shoulder' position), a raised tailplane, a re-shaped fin and rudder (borrowed from the Supermarine Stranraer, according to legend), and a deeper fuselage. There were also various other refinements, including Vickers nose and tail turrets and a retractable Nash and Thompson ventral turret, each housing two 0.303-in machine guns. The aircraft also used variable pitch propellers, and had new bag-type tanks in the wings.

By the time war broke out, eight Wellington squadrons had formed, and these were committed to daring daylight raids against German warships and coastal military targets. Unfortunately, the expectation that the aircraft would be able to beat off enemy fighters using the combined crossfire from their turrets proved over-optimistic. Losses were heavy.

The Vickers Wellington was then switched to night bombing duties, operating alongside the Armstrong Whitworth Whitley, which carried a larger bombload of up to 7,000lb (3,175kg) but rather more slowly. The type was also used in the Middle East, North Africa, and Far East from June

1942. Coastal Command also used Wellingtons. They managed to sink 26 enemy submarines with the type.

Successive improved variants of the Wellington included the Merlin-engined Mk II, the Mk IV with Twin Wasps. There was also the Mk III with 1,500hp Bristol Hercules XI engines and the similar Mk X, with 1,675hp Hercules engines. The Mark X reached a maximum speed of 255mph (410km/h) and the aircraft had a range of 1,185 miles (3,034km).

The Vickers Wellington Mk II and Mk IV were built only in small numbers. The Mk III and Mk X formed the backbone of the Wellington force within Bomber Command from its introduction in 1940.

The Wellington flew its last offensive missions with home-based bomber squadrons in October 1943. Even after that time, Wellingtons served in the electronic warfare role within Bomber Command's No.100 Group.

The B.Mk V and B.Mk VI were two dedicated high altitude Wellington variants. These had a cigar-shaped metal pressure cabin in place of the normal cockpit, with the pilot looking out through an absurdly small 'pimple-like' astrodome. Three Mk Vs were built, later gaining extended wing-tips, and these aircraft proved capable of reaching heights of 40,000ft (12,192m). The 63 B.Mk VIs were even more impressive, and some briefly equipped a single flight of No.109 Squadron.

The Vickers Type 285 Warwick, although not a Wellington, was designed as a heavier counterpart of the Wimpey. It was powered by bigger, more powerful engines, but using the same structural design and the same basic configuration. In the event, such powerplants were slow to emerge, and after considering the Rolls Royce

Right: *Groundcrew heave a 4,000-lb (1,814-kg) 'Cookie' towards a waiting No.419 Squadron Wellington. The aircraft had a capacious bomb bay.*

Right: *The Merlin-engined Wellington B.Mk II was built in only modest numbers, but gave useful service.*
Below: *This experimental Wellington was a 'one-off' with twin tailfins and Merlin X engines dramatically altering its appearance.*

Vulture, the Napier Sabre and the Bristol Centaurus, Vickers eventually settled on the Pratt and Whitney Double Wasp (available from cancelled French orders). These gave the type about the same performance as the Wellington, but with a Whitley-sized 7,500-lb (3,402-kg) bombload.

In the event, the Warwick never entered service in the bomber role, having been over-taken by four-engined types. The aircraft did, however, enjoy a long and successful career in the transport, maritime reconnaissance and air-sea rescue roles.

The Wellington served on with Coastal Command, and with RAF bomber squadrons based overseas. Wellingtons based in Italy flew their last bombing mission in March 1945. In the postwar period many Wellingtons found further employment as RAF transports and trainers, especially as 'flying classrooms' for navigator training. The last examples were finally retired in 1953.

Above: *The Vickers Wellington's geodetic structure made it exceptionally robust and rugged, and the type proved popular with its crews. This aircraft is a Merlin-engined Wellington Mk II, and is seen before delivery to the frontline.*
Right: *The Merlin I had a crude Vickers nose turret. This was replaced on the IC by a Nash and Thompson turret. Early operations against German warships and coastal targets by daylight proved unacceptably costly. The Vickers Wellington soon switched to night bombing.*

JUNKERS JU 88

THE JUNKERS Ju 88, although it gained a reputation for multi-role versatility, was single-mindedly designed for a single role—that of a high-speed day bomber. There was no thought, when the aircraft took shape on the drawing board, of adapting it to the night fighter and reconnaissance roles which it would later undertake with such facility.

Many were surprised that the Junkers firm (whose previous products had been the anachronistic Ju 52 and the oddly old-fashioned Ju 87) could come up with an aircraft as forward-looking and modern as the Ju 88. That it could was partly due to the replacement of Hugo Junkers by Heinrich Koppenberg, who moved away from Junkers characteristic reliance on corrugated sheet metal, and who hired US engineers Al Gassner and WH Evers to work on the new Ju 88.

The Junkers Ju 88 was initially designed as a three-man, high-speed level bomber, carrying a 800–1,000-kg (1,763–2,204-lb) bombload. It was redesigned, however, at an early stage as a heavier dive bomber, carrying double the bombload and with an extra crew member.

The first of eight Ju 88 prototypes made its maiden flight on December 21, 1936, though it was lost less than four months later. The Ju 88 design was refined and improved during this period, and the prototypes differed markedly from each other. The first with the Ju 88's characteristic 'blunt' glazed nose was the Ju 88V4. The first to use dive brakes was the sixth aircraft, which was effectively the production prototype for the Ju 88A service model.

The Ju 88A entered service with Erprobungskommando 88 (later re-designated as I/KG 25 and then as I/KG 30) in early 1939, and about 60 had been delivered by the end of the year. The Ju 88 effectively missed the Polish campaign, but large numbers were in service for the Battle of Britain. These included the much-improved Ju 88A-4, with 1,410hp Jumo 211J engines, increased span, improved armor protection, a strengthened landing gear, and a bigger bombload. There was also the interim Ju-88A-5, which had the long-span wing, but lacked other A-4 refinements. There were eventually a plethora of Ju 88A variants, some tropicalized, some with dual controls, and others optimized for ground attack duties. Maritime strike or even torpedo bomber variants emerged, while the derived Ju 88C was a heavy Zerstorer and night fighter. The Ju 88A served on the Eastern Front, in North Africa, the Mediterranean, and in Western Europe. The variant remained in service throughout the war, along with the Ju 88D reconnaissance aircraft. It was augmented from 1942 by the Ju 88S, a cleaned-up derivative with massive BMW 801D radial engines (or Jumo 213s in some sub-types).

The Ju 88B variant did not reach production status. The aircraft, however, introduced the 'Kampfkopf' (Battle Head) cockpit, a streamlined fully glazed unit similar to that fitted

Right: *Many still view the Ju 88 as the Luftwaffe's best and most versatile bomber of World War II, rivalled only by the RAF's Mosquito.*

to the Do 217K, and led directly to the Ju 188. This combined the new nose with the enlarged square-shaped tail unit of the Ju 88G night fighter.

The Ju 188 was supplied to four Kampfgeschwaderen, entering service in late 1943. The Ju 388 was a high altitude version of the Ju 188, but only a handful entered service, mainly in the high altitude reconnaissance role. The further developed Ju 288 had a pressurized 188-type cockpit, a lengthened fuselage, a twin-fin tail unit and more powerful engines. This, however, did not enter service. The Ju 88's speed and agility made it a hard target for Allied fighters. It remained extremely popular with crews. In many respects, the aircraft deserves its reputation as the best bomber of the war.

Opposite, top: *The four man crew of the Ju 88 sat together in the heavily glazed cockpit, making for great crew co-operation.*

Right: *Ju 88 aircrew don their bulky lifejackets prior to a long over-water flight.*

Below, left: *This Ju 88 carries a 250-kg (551-lb) SC 250 bomb under each wing, inboard of the engine nacelle.*

Below, right: *The Ju 88 served on every front, in almost every role. This one was used for operations on the Eastern Front.*

Above: *This Ju 188A-2 of III Gruppe KG 26 was captured at the end of the War, and was evaluated by the RAF, its pilots including Eric 'Winkle' Brown.*
Left: *This Junkers Ju 188D-2 was a photo-reconnaissance version, fitted with FuG200 and FuG214 radars. The Ju 188 enjoyed a better all round view than the original Ju 88.*
Right: *Junkers Ju 188s entered service in late 1943. The following year the aircraft participated in the assault against London known as Operation Steinbock.*

MARTIN MARYLAND

THE MARTIN MODEL 167 was designed as a dual-role 'attack bomber' capable of high level precision bombing and low-level close air support missions over the battlefield. The aircraft was designed by James S. McDonnell. It was powered by a pair of Pratt and Whitney R-1830 engines, and could carry its bombload of 1,250lbs (567-kg) at a speed of up to 260mph (418km/h). The aircraft could also be fitted with special racks and chutes in the bomb bay to hold small fragmentation bombs for attack duties. The Martin 167's bomb aimer, pilot, and radio operator/gunner occupied three separate and unconnected compartments. The bomb aimer could use a set of folding flying controls if the pilot was hit.

In February and March 1939, the Armée de l'Air ordered 100 DB-7s, and 215 Martin 167-F1s and -F2s. In October, the French ordered another 280 Model 167-F3s and -F4s which respectively added extra armor around the fuel tanks and improved engines. All 215 167-F1s and -F2s (known as

Glenns in Armée de l'Air service) had been delivered by April 1940. These were sent to France following the German attack in May. Some of these aircraft later served with Vichy forces in North Africa.

Just before the French surrender in June 1940, all French contracts placed by the Allied Purchasing Commission in New York were transferred to Great Britain. Consequently, the British took over 62 completed and partially-completed Martin 167-F3s still in the United States.

The Royal Air Force also received 22 more aircraft that had been en route to France, or which were brought over to Great Britain by defecting French pilots. These had to be modified with British guns, instruments and radios, becoming Maryland Is, as did the 150 167-F4s, delivered to the RAF as Maryland IIs.

Martin 167s enjoyed the unusual distinction of serving on both sides, with Vichy French units in North Africa and Syria flying their Glenns against the RAF and Free French Maryland units. The RAF and SAAF's Marylands proved especially useful with the Desert Air Force in the high-altitude reconnaissance role, particularly operating from Malta. A Maryland crew operating from Malta even managed to shoot down ten enemy aircraft.

Left: *An RAF Maryland shows off its slender lines during an evaluation flight. The type was principally used in North Africa.*
Below: *The main customer for the Martin 167 (or 'Glenn') was the Armée de l'Air, 215 of which were delivered before the capitulation of France in 1940.*

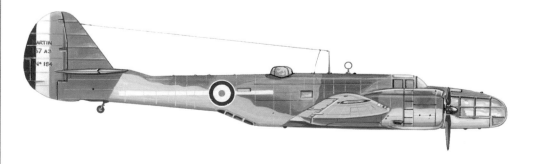

CANT Z.1007 ALCIONE

THE LARGELY WOODEN Cant Z.1007 Alcione (Kingfisher) was arguably the best Italian bomber of World War II. The aircraft had excellent handling qualities, and a relatively fast speed of 290mph (466km/h). This made it quicker than the BR 20 or the SM 79, albeit with a slightly shorter range and a lighter bombload.

The Cantieri Riuniti dell'Adriatico company (abbreviated as Cant or CRDA) produced the Z.1007 as a landplane derivative of the Z.506B reconnaissance-bomber floatplane, following the failure of an earlier landplane version (the Z.508) to attain production status. Another false start came with the CANT Z.1011, a twin-engined medium bomber, five prototypes of which were built before the air force changed its mind and bought the Z.1007. The Z.1011 was then used as a transport.

The Cant Z.1007 Alcione prototype made its maiden flight in May 1937, powered by three Isotta Fraschini Asso XI inline engines. It was followed by a production series of 34 similarly powered aircraft, the first of which joined the Regia Aeronautica in late 1939. The type, however, suffered from major engine problems.

The Z.1007 then underwent a major redesign. The resulting Z.1007B or Z.1007bis emerged with the entire fuselage widened and enlarged to hold a larger bombload, and with improved armament. The Alcione was made of wood rather than metal because of insufficient investment.

The new version of the Cant Z.1007 was powered by three 1,000hp Piaggio P.XIbis RC 40 radial engines. The Z.1007bis was built in nine batches. The last six batches of the aircraft featured a new tail unit, with the conventional central fin replaced by a dihedral tailplane with endplate fins and rudders.

The Alcione had a crew of five. This comprised the pilot, co-pilot, radio operator/bomb aimer and two gunners, one manning the underfuselage gun, and the other the dorsal turret immediately behind the co-pilot. The Z.1007 carried a bombload of 2,000kg (4,410lb) internally, with provision for a further 1,000kg (2,205lb) underwing. Alternatively, the aircraft could carry two 1,000-lb (454-kg) torpedoes. The aircraft could fly at 8,100m (26,575ft) and had a range of 1,280km (800 miles).

Unfortunately, the Cant Z.1007 was not fast enough to be able to rely on speed to outrun enemy fighters. The aircraft's defensive armament was simply inadequate. Even the ultimate Z.1007ter (with 1,150hp Piaggio PXIX radial engines) was capable of only 500km/h (311mph). This speed was still far short of what was required, although production of the type reached 560 aircraft.

The Cant Z.1007s were included in at least one raid on Great Britain during 1940. These aircraft, however, were generally confined to the Mediterranean, Balkan and North African theaters. The Z.1007s performed adequately, although the wooden structure gave some problems in extreme climatic conditions.

Right: *Later examples of the Cant Z.1007bis like this were fitted with a dihedral tailplane with endplate fins and rudders.*

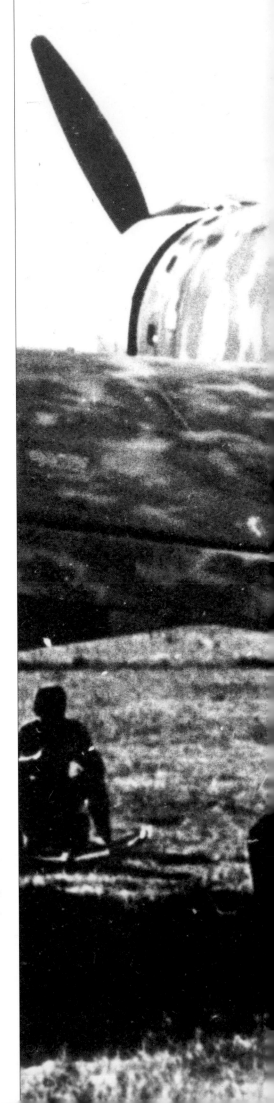

DOUGLAS A-20 BOSTON

THE DESIGN OF the Douglas Model 7A Attack Bomber began before any USAAC requirement was formulated for such a type. To compete in the USAAC's 1938 competitive evaluation of attack bomber designs, the design was refined to become the Model 7B, a prototype of which first flew on October 26, 1938.

The first customer for the Model 7B was the French Armée de l'Air. They had ordered 370 aircraft by the time of the German invasion in May 1940, and shortly thereafter ordered 480 more DB-7Cs, re-designated as DB-73s at French insistence. The British authorities had ordered another 300 and the USAAC had ordered the type as the A-20.

Confusingly, the French aircraft were designated as DB-7s (with 1,200hp Pratt and Whitney Twin Wasp S3C4-G engines) or DB-7As (with Wright Double Cyclones). The DB-7B aircraft ordered by the RAF were similar to the USAAC's A-20As, structurally improved, fitted with an enlarged tailfin, and powered by 1,600hp Double Cyclones but with British armament.

With the collapse of France, the RAF received about 200 of the French DB-7s (some which had not been delivered, others flown by defecting crews) and all 100 of the undelivered DB-7As. These respectively became Havoc I night fighters and Boston I

Left: Apart from some vulnerability to attack from below, the A-20 was a superb light bomber and a joy to fly. They served in Europe, Africa and the Pacific.

trainers, while the DB-7As became Havoc IIs. Some Havocs retained glazed noses and were used as intruders, while others had AI radar and solid noses mounting eight 0.303-in machine guns. Some were even fitted with nose-mounted searchlights as 'Turbinlite Havocs', operating in conjunction with Hurricane night fighters. The first Havocs entered service in October 1940.

The Royal Air Force's intended DB-7Bs (and the French DB-73s, which were delivered to the same standards) were known as Douglas Boston IIIs, and were used as day bombers by Bomber Command's No.2 Group. These replaced Blenheims from August 1941. The Bostons proved fast and was 80mph (128km/h) quicker than a Blenheim. The aircraft was rugged, and was used for a number of highly successful high profile attacks on targets in Occupied Europe. These included the Philips Radio factory at Eindhoven in southern Holland, the Matford works at Poissy, near Paris, and numerous enemy airfields. They were also used in North Africa, the Mediterranean and Italy.

The RAF also took delivery of Boston IVs (A-20Gs) and Boston Vs (A-20Js), taking the total number of Bostons and Havocs to more than 1,000. Some of these served in Europe until April 1945, and elsewhere the type remained in service a little longer. Russia received about 3,600 DB-7s, while the USAAF used 1,962 aircraft. These served in Europe and the Pacific, winning a reputation for toughness and dependability.

PETYAKLOV PE-8/ TUPOLEV ANT-47/ TB-7

THE PE-8, ALTHOUGH it eventually bore the name of its senior designer Petyaklov, began life as the Tupolev ANT-42, and was known to the Soviet air forces as the TB-7. The type's redesignation came in mid-1942, following the January death of Petyaklov.

It was designed as a heavy bomber to replace the TB-3. Work on the ANT-42 began in 1934, and the prototype made its maiden flight on December 27, 1936. Tupolev was arrested and tried (from October 21, 1937) as part of Stalin's purges, under which most Soviet designers and factory managers were arrested (including Myasischev, Polikarpov, Petyaklov and Bartini) and imprisoned. From August 1938, Tupolev returned to work, although the bureau he now headed (Central Construction Bureau 29) was run by the NKVD (internal security service) from within the prison system. Like the other designers, Tupolev and Petyaklov were officially 'non-persons' referred to only by the name of the guard responsible for them, and not allowed to sign drawings except using a numbered rubber stamp. He and his team were freed following the German invasion.

The ANT-47 was of broadly similar configuration to the early-model B-17 Flying Fortress, though it used inline engines rather than radials, and had a tail gunner's position from the start. The two pilots also sat in tandem, and there were gunners' barbettes in the rear of each inboard engine nacelle. The aircraft could carry 24 100-kg

(220-lb) bombs internally, with 16 more on racks under the inner wings, or eight 250-kg (551-lb) bombs (plus four externally), four 1,102-lb (500-kg) bombs (plus two externally), or two 1000-kg (2,204-lb) bombs (plus two externally). It could alternatively carry a 2,000-kg (4,410-lb) or 5,000-kg (11,023-lb) bomb.

The Tupolev ANT-47 had a 39m (128ft) span, and a length of over 23m (76ft). It could reach a ceiling of 37,000ft (11,277m). The aircraft had an empty weight of 91,155kg (41,348lb), and a maximum take-off weight of 32,000kg (200,960lb).

The first ANT-47s in service reached the 14th TBAP at Kiev-Borispol, north Central Ukraine, in September 1939, but reliability was initially limited by spares shortages. The first operating unit was reorganized and re-designated several times, but as the 412th TBAP, attacked Berlin on August 9, 1941. Production of the type was constrained by engine shortages, and the 93–149 aircraft built (sources differ on the total) were powered by at least six different types of engine!

The Tupolev ANT-47 served with great success and distinction throughout the war. It enjoyed a long postwar career as a rugged and dependable transport, being employed in Aeroflot's Polar Division until 1957!

Right: *This Tupolev ANT-47 visited Britain while carrying the Soviet Union's foreign minister to the United States. The type served with distinction in World War II.*

WESTLAND WHIRLWIND

THE WESTLAND WHIRLWIND was a fighter rather than a bomber, and probably represented what the RAF should have been using for offensive operations during the early years of World War II. The Whirlwind used the same engine power as the Blenheim, and could carry a similar 1,000-lb (453-kg) bombload, but was considerably faster. The aircraft was capable of 303mph (487km/h) at sea level and 351mph (564km/h) at 15,000ft (4,572m). These speeds enabled the Westland Whirlwind to out-run the 283/338-mph (455/543km/h) Bf 109E and the 282/342mph (453/550km/h) Spitfire I). With a range of 720 miles (1,158km), the Whirlwind could reach most of the targets attacked by Blenheims, yet could do so with a sporting chance of returning to base. Moreover, the Whirlwind's concentrated pack of four 20-mm cannon in its nose, could also strafe ground targets with devastating effectiveness. When defending itself against enemy fighters, it could destroy any enemy aircraft with a single burst.

The first Westland Whirlwind prototype made its maiden flight on October 11, 1938, and was kept a closely guarded secret. The first production aircraft were initially used in the long-range escort fighter role. From September 1942 they found their niche as cross-Channel fighter-bombers, attacking airfields, bridges, railway locomotives, harbor facilities, and shipping with underwing bombs

Left: *The Whirlwind combined a 1,000-lb (453-kg) bombload, a concentrated battery of four 20-mm cannon and Spitfire-like speed performance.*

or the built-in 20-mm cannon. Although it was arguably the most advanced aircraft in RAF service, the Whirlwind was starved of funding, and the unreliability of its Peregrine engines led to poor serviceability and some prejudice against the aircraft in the higher reaches of the Air Staff. Only 112 aircraft were built, and they were withdrawn from service in December 1943.

If the RAF had despatched squadrons of Whirlwinds against targets which cost whole units of Blenheims and their crews, those targets would have been hit more heavily. The RAF would also have suffered minimal casualties, and defending fighters might have suffered heavy losses. Even with the aircraft's under-developed and troublesome Peregrine engines, the Westland Whirlwind was a superbly effective way of carrying the war to the enemy. With Merlins, it could have been even better, and might have been a superb long-range escort fighter. And a Whirlwind cost less to build than a Blenheim, and required only one man to operate, instead of three. Alternatively, over shorter ranges, single-engined fighter-bombers offered a similar 'low-cost' alternative to the twin-engined, multi-crew light bomber. They gradually supplanted them as the backbone of the RAF's close support and light attack force. The RAF's massive force of Typhoons and Tempests operating against the Wehrmacht as the war drew to a close were the successors to the Whirlwind. These aircraft proved the ability of the long-range ground attack fighter to operate with great effectiveness and relative impunity.

Left: *The Whirlwind's spindly gracefulness belied the aircraft's heavyweight punch and bombload, making it broadly equivalent to aircraft like the Blenheim in sheer striking power.*

Far Left: *Even with its troublesome Peregrine engines, the Westland Whirlwind was a superb performer, and with twin Merlins it would have been unbeatable.*

SHORT STIRLING

THE SHORT STIRLING was the RAF's first four-engined bomber. Unlike the Lancaster (which originated from the Manchester) and the Halifax (originally designed around two Vulture engines), it was designed from the outset to be powered by four engines. Heavily influenced by the near-contemporary Sunderland flying boat, the Stirling had a similar wing, with the same Gouge trailing edge flaps. This was limited to a 99ft 1inch (30.17m) wingspan by the Air Ministry's insistence that the type be able to fit in a standard hangar.

With an empty weight 6,300-lb (2,857-kg) heavier than that of the Lancaster, and a similar maximum take off weight, this artificial limit was a major limitation on the Stirling, which had a ceiling of only 17,500ft (5,334m). The Stirling's eventual usefulness was also limited by the 'compartmentalization' of its bomb bay, which limited it to carrying weapons no larger than a 2,000lb (907-kg) bomb. The Manchester, by contrast, had a large unobstructed bomb bay because it was intended to be able to accommodate long torpedoes as well as bombs.

The Short S29 Stirling was preceded by a half-scale proof of concept aircraft, the S31, powered by four Pobjoy Niagara engines, which first flew in 1938. The S29 prototype followed on May 14, 1939, but crashed on landing and was destroyed. Fortunately a second prototype followed it into the air on December 3, 1939.

The Stirling entered service with No.7 Squadron in August 1940, delayed by the loss of ten aircraft in Nazi bombing raids on two factories.

The Stirling flew its first bombing mission on February 10/11, 1941, when three aircraft dropped 56 500-lb (226-kg) bombs on oil storage tanks at Rotterdam, Holland. The Stirling enjoyed some success, even on unescorted daylight raids, during which Stirling gunners managed to shoot down some enemy fighters.

The Short Stirling was the only four-engined heavy bomber in service until the introduction of the Halifax. The aircraft eventually equipped 13 front-line bomber squadrons. The type attacked Berlin on April 17, 1941, flew over the Alps to attack Turin, northern Italy, and later even ranged as far as the Skoda works in Pilsen, Czechoslovakia. The type participated in the first 1,000 bomber raids mounted in 1942. In August 1942, No.7 Squadron, the pioneer Stirling unit, formed No.3 Group's contribution to the newly-formed Pathfinder Force.

The improved Stirling III joined Bomber Command in December 1942. This new version was powered by 1,650hp Hercules XVI engines and improved defensive armament, but was still hampered by its inability to carry heavier bombs, and by its low operational ceiling. It is said that the crews of other aircraft types cheered when they heard that they would be flying with Stirlings, which, as easier targets, would bear the brunt of enemy defensive efforts. Increasingly, Stirlings were side-lined, and used for mine-laying sorties (code-named

Right: *The vast bulk of a Short Stirling dwarfs the female RAF Air Transport Auxiliary ferry pilot standing by the starboard mainwheel.*

Gardening) and for attacks on less heavily defended targets.

Despite its poor performance and lack of flexibility, the Stirling remained in frontline service throughout the war. Even after the type's withdrawal from bomber duties in September 1944, the Stirling remained in use in the radio countermeasures role with No.100 Group, and in the transport and glider-towing roles.

The Stirling IV used the same powerplant as the B.Mk III, but had its nose and dorsal turrets removed, and faired over. It was also fitted with glider-towing and parachute dropping equipment. The Stirling IV played a major part in D-Day, the Arnhem operation, and in the final assault across the Rhine in the spring of 1945.

The Stirling V was a dedicated transport. The variant was unarmed, and with a new, extended and streamlined nose capable of holding freight, and accommodation in the fuselage for 40 passengers or 20 paratroops. It entered service in January 1945, and was finally retired in March 1946.

Top, right: *Paratroops wait to board their gliders, which will be towed into the air by this line of waiting No.620 Squadron Short Stirlings.*

Below: *This No.570 Squadron Stirling carries D-Day stripes on the rear fuselage. These originally encircled the whole fuselage and the wings.*

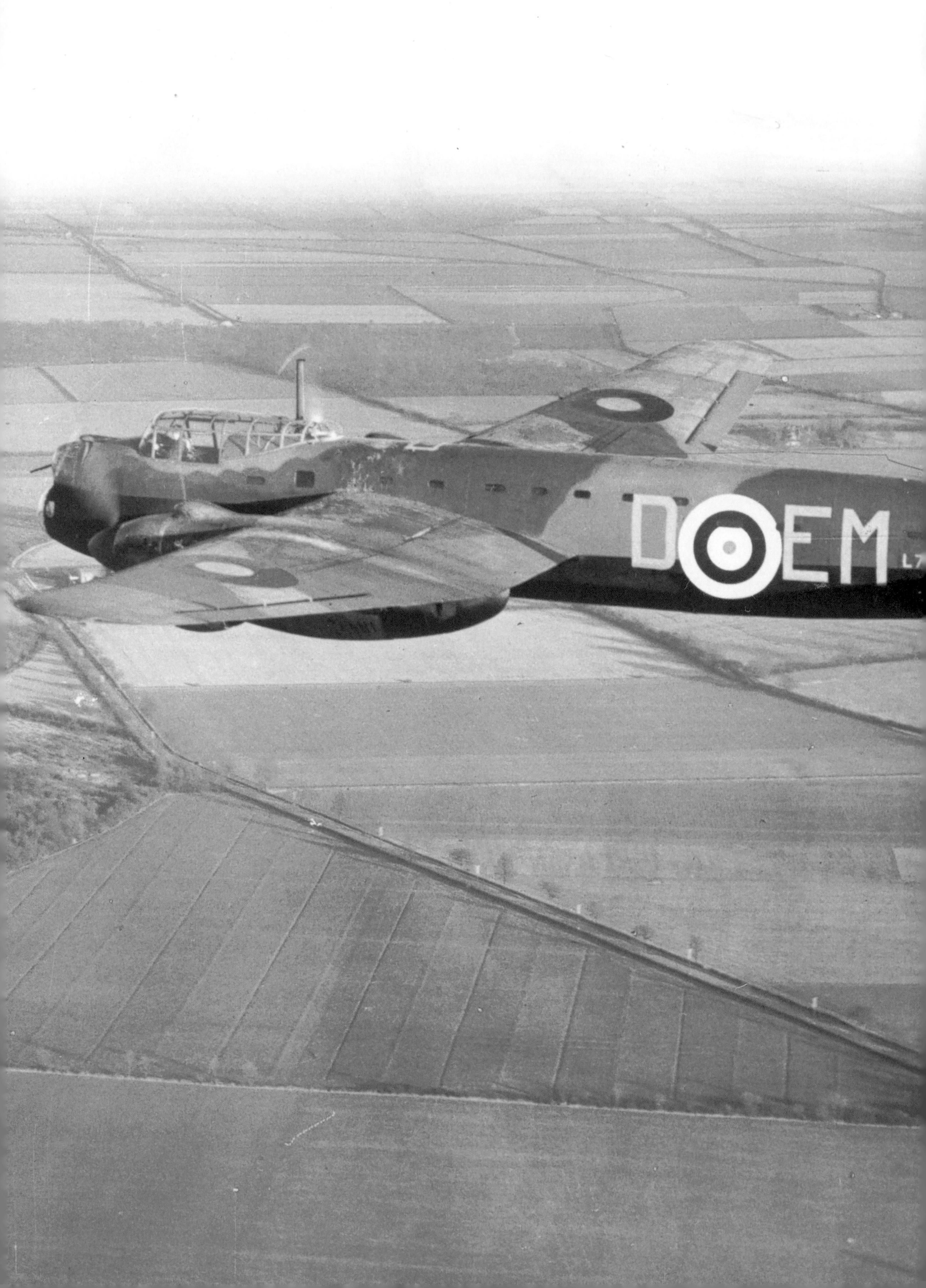
D
EM
L7

AVRO MANCHESTER

THE AVRO MANCHESTER was a twin-engined, medium-range bomber. The aircraft was designed to meet the same requirement as the Handley Page Halifax, and both types were originally to have been powered by a pair of Rolls Royce Vulture engines. It soon became clear that to use the same engines to power both bombers would be impossible, and the HP.56 was redesigned around four Merlins. This was to prove a 'lucky break' for the Halifax, and a grave misfortune for the Avro aircraft. The radical Vulture was under-developed, and would prove to be a liability in service. The engine made the Manchester notable mainly for its unreliability, poor performance and general inadequacy for the task at hand.

Even before the Manchester prototype made its maiden flight on July 25, 1939, Avro had begun work on a four-engined version. This was powered by Merlin X engines, although heavy demands on Merlin production meant that this was not initially accorded a high priority. The British Air Ministry, however, were looking to a future in which four-engined bombers would play a dominant part, even before the shortcomings of the Manchester became apparent. Plans for Avro Manchester production were cut back even before the type entered service.

The Avro Manchester could carry a bombload of 11,200lb (5,080kg) and had a maximum range of 1,630 miles

Left: No.207 Squadron was the first unit equipped with the Avro Manchester, an early version of which is seen here. The type entered service in late 1940.

(2,623km). The aircraft was armed with three 0.303 machine guns. These machine guns were positioned in the aircraft's nose, rear and mid-upper rotating turrets.

Some 200 Manchester bombers were built by Avro and Metropolitan Vickers. These entered service with No.207 Squadron at Boscombe Down, in southwestern England, in late 1940. The Manchester flew its first operation from Waddington, eastern England, to Brest, on the coast of northern France, on February 24/25, 1941. It subsequently equipped six more frontline Royal Air Force squadrons. The Avro Manchesters served until mid-1942, when the type was withdrawn from operations. Thereafter, a handful of Manchesters remained in use in training units for about a year.

Later Avro Manchesters, known as Mk IAs, introduced a wider-span tailplane, with enlarged endplate fins, and without the original central fin. This tail unit would later be used by the Avro Lancaster, which was effectively a four-engined Manchester. The Lancaster's prototype was actually produced by converting an unfinished Manchester airframe.

The Avro Manchester, despite its poor service record, had great potential as a bomber, not least because it had an unobstructed and capacious bombload. This feature was due to the British Air Ministry's initial requirement, which envisaged using the type as a torpedo bomber. The bomb bay would eventually be the main reason for the success of the Avro Lancaster, since it could accommodate even the largest bombs.

HANDLEY PAGE HALIFAX

THE PRODUCTION HALIFAX was introduced to service by the RAF's No.35 Squadron on November 5, 1940, and began flying operations from 11/12 March 1941. Handley Page's last heavy bomber had been the biplane Heyford. This aircraft had given way to Whitleys and Wellesleys, while the contract for the first truly modern heavy bomber went to Shorts for the Stirling.

Handley Page did create the remarkable but badly-used Hampden, but only re-entered the heavy bomber game with the HP.56 type. This aircraft (originally designed around two Rolls Royce Vulture engines) was designed in response to an RAF requirement for an advanced medium bomber, competing with the Avro Type 679 (later the Manchester).

When it became clear that Vulture production would be inadequate to support production of both aircraft, the HP.56 was re-designed around four Merlins. The wingspan was increased to 98ft 8 inches (29.82m). This was 4 inches (10cm) short of the maximum allowed by the stringent specification, which envisaged the aircraft being accommodated in standard RAF hangars. (When Avro came to develop the Lancaster, this limitation had been shelved, since bombers by then sat outdoors. The Avro Lancaster's extra span gave it its superior altitude performance.)

Handley Page favored using radials, but the Air Ministry insisted on the Merlin engine. It was with the latter engine that the HP.56 prototype made its maiden flight on October 25, 1939.

Other Merlin-engined variants included the B.Mk II with increased fuel capacity, and the B.Mk II Series 1 with a power-operated mid-upper turret. The B.Mk II Series 1 Special had the nose turret removed, and the Series 1A, had the turret replaced by a streamlined glazed nose with a single hand-pointed machine gun. The B.Mk V (which also came in Series 1, 1 Special and 1A forms) had a Dowty undercarriage, whose poor quality castings led to the imposition of weight limits.

The Halifax was transformed by the addition of Hercules radial engines. The first radial engined variant, the B.Mk III, entered service in October 1943. The B.Mk IIs and Vs were finally retired from frontline bomber units in July 1944 (but served on with the Airborne Forces, Coastal Command and in support of the SOE until 1945). Meanwhile, the interim Hercules-engined B.Mk VII, which had longer-span wings, entered the fray in June 1944. The superb B.Mk VI, with long-range fuel tanks, more powerful Hercules 100 engines and long-span wings made its operational debut in February 1945. If the B.Mk VI had been given longer to demonstrate its prowess, it would have over-turned most preconceptions about the Halifax. The aircraft it was demonstrably superior to the Lancaster in many key areas. It was expected to

Right: *In B.Mk VI form, the Handley Page Halifax was a superb all-rounder, and suffered a lower loss rate than the rival Avro Lancaster.*

form the backbone of 'Tiger Force' during the expected invasion of Japan. This plan, however, was dropped following the success of the atomic bombs at Hiroshima and Nagasaki.

Halifax aircrew, irked by the media attention lavished on the rival Lancaster, fiercely defended their aircraft's reputation. History has judged the Halifax as second-best, noting its shorter range, lower ceiling and smaller bombload than the Lancaster. There is also the scathing condemnation of the Halifax by the irascible C-in-C of Bomber Command, Arthur Harris, who said, "One Lancaster is to be preferred to four Halifaxes. Halifaxes are an embarrassment...The Halifax suffers four times the casualties for a given bomb tonnage when compared to the Lancaster."

In fact, the Halifax was very much better than its critics admitted. Heavy losses during the dark days of 1942 and 1943 distorted its overall loss rate. In its later radial engined form, the Halifax enjoyed a lower loss rate than did the Lancaster during the same stage of the war. Moreover, its capacious fuselage made it easier to escape from. A higher percentage of Halifax aircrew (29 per cent) survived being shot down than did those flying Lancasters (a miserable 11 per cent). But live bomber aircrew in prison camps mattered little to 'Bomber' Harris. He was similarly unimpressed by the greater versatility and flexibili-

ty of the Halifax, which just made it more likely to be diverted on what he saw as irrelevant and unwelcome 'sideshow' operations.

Some maintain that the Halifax was actually a better bomber than the Lancaster. The Halifax carried its slightly smaller load less far, but bombed with greater accuracy due to its lower ceiling and more comfortable crew accommodation. It has also been asserted that if you wanted to saturate the aim point, the Halifax was the best aircraft for the job. If, however, you wanted to scatter tons of bombs around the general target area, then you needed the Lancaster. Although it dropped far fewer bombs than the Lancaster, the Halifax dropped more

Left: *The Handley Page Halifax C.Mk VIII was a dedicated transport and freighter, which equipped two Polish squadrons.*
Below: *Two No.35 Squadron Handley Page Halifax B.Mk Is in formation. No.35 was the first Halifax unit, flying operations from March 1941. The type served as a bomber, transport, glider tug, and martime and meterological platform.*

bombs than did the Blenheim, Boston, Fortress, Hampden, Manchester, Mitchell, Mosquito, Stirling, Ventura and Wellington combined—an astonishing 224,207 tons, in 36,995 sorties.

The Handley Page Halifax was also a better agent- and supply-dropper than the Lancaster, as well as a better transport and glider tug. The aircraft was also a better maritime and meteorological reconnaissance platform. Within Bomber Command, the Halifax was the aircraft of choice for Sigint (Elint/Comint) and electronic warfare missions. Moreover, the Halifax was better suited to overseas operation than the Lancaster, being less prone to over-heating.

Many expected the Handley Page Halifax to be retained postwar. The numerical dominance of the Avro Lancaster, however, and the emergence of the Avro Lincoln, ensured that the Lancaster served on (even in roles for which it was ill-suited) postwar. The Handley Page Halifax disappeared more quickly.

The last meteorological reconnaissance Halifax was retired in March 1952. Other aircraft remained in use testing parachutes until 1954, when the Pakistan Air Force also finally retired the type from the bomber role. A handful of Halifax bombers may have remained in use in Egypt after that, but this cannot be confirmed.

Right: *Christopher Cheshire (brother of the more famous Leonard) was the Captain of this No.76 Squadron Halifax B.Mk I. The aircraft was shot down on its fifth mission, Cheshire surviving as a PoW.*

Opposite, bottom: *The second Halifax prototype in flight. The production Halifax B.Mk I was basically similar, though black undersides were de rigeur on production bombers.*

Below: *A Halifax B.Mk III over the Ruhr late in the war, when Bomber Command had begun bombing 'round-the-clock'.*

MARTIN B-26 MARAUDER

THE MARTIN B-26 Marauder, known by a variety of unflattering epithets, from 'Widow Maker' to 'Baltimore Whore', had a difficult start. Eventually, however, the aircraft settled down to become a popular and highly effective medium bomber.

The bomber was designed to fulfill the same USAAC requirement as the B-25 Mitchell. Glen L. Martin's Model 179 was ordered into production 'off the drawing board' without first flying and evaluating a prototype.

The B-26 was, in many respects, the complete opposite of British light bombers of the time—which were simple and austere, and which had to be capable of operating from short grass runways. The USAAC requirement set no limits on take off performance, however, and so the Marauder could be optimized for outright performance in the air.

Left: *Dee-Feater was a well-worn Martin B-26B. The aircraft was assigned to the 596th Bomb Squadron of the 397th Bomb Group. Marauders first saw action in the Pacific with 22 Bomb Group in 1942.*
Below: *Like Dee-Feater, Missouri Mule II had the D-Day stripes partially removed from its upper surfaces.*

Martin's Peyton Magruder therefore drew up an extremely streamlined twin-engined bomber. This had a tiny wing and was powered by a pair of Pratt and Whitney R-2800-5 Wasp engines driving colossal Curtiss Electric propellers which were 13.6ft (3.9m) in diameter. The B-26 carried a normal bombload of 2,000lb (907kg) but could take up to 5,800lb (2,631kg) in the tandem bomb bays. It was the only USAAC bomber capable of dropping torpedoes.

By the time the first B-26 made its maiden flight on November 25, 1940, the USAAC had ordered 1,131 of the new bombers, and deliveries began in February 1941. The first 201 were designated B-26, while the next 139 were B-26As, 109 of them A-1s powered by –39 Wasp engines. The RAF took delivery of 51 of the B-26As as the Marauder Mk 1s. Early in its career, Lt. Col. Jimmy Doolittle was ordered to go to training airfields to personally demonstrate that the B-26 could stay aloft on one engine.

The B-26B version retained the original short-span wing, but introduced a longer nosewheel strut. During production improved armament and more powerful engines were introduced.

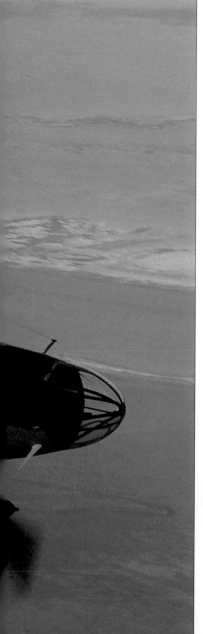

Opposite, top: *Carolyn was the Confederate Air Force's airworthy Martin B-26 Marauder, until it was lost in a fatal accident.*

Opposite, left: *The Martin Marauder is today a very rare bird, and none are airworthy at present.*

Above: *Another view of the Confederate Air Force B-26 Marauder, which was restored to airworthy condition in 1984, having last flown in 1965 as an oil company's executive transport.*

Left: *This B-26 was downed by flak over Italy, none of its crew managing to bail out.*

The crew of seven comprised pilot and co-pilot sitting side-by-side, with a bombardier and radio-operator forward (with a flexibly mounted 0.50-inch machine gun in the nose cone). There was also a tailgunner (who could sit upright, rather than lying prone, as in the B-25) and gunners manning the power-operated dorsal turret and beam guns. The aircraft was able to carry two 2,000-lb (907-kg) bombs on special carriers. Some 19 short-span B-26Bs were delivered to the RAF as Marauder IAs.

The first Marauders in action were those of the 22nd Bomb Group, which moved to Australia in February 1942, and opened operations against Japanese forces on April 5. The Marauders long take off run made it less suitable for the 'island-hopping' campaign than the B-25, and the type was withdrawn from the Pacific theater during 1943. The first RAF Marauders began operations in the Middle East and North Africa during October 1942, No.14 Squadron flying its first operations in support of the Battle of El Alamein.

Despite the B-26s success and popularity in combat, the accident rate in training units was horrific. The USAAF considered cancelling all further production and prematurely withdrawing the B-26 Maraduer from service. Instead, Martin designed a new increased span and increased area wing. These modifications were incorporated into all but the first 641 B-26Bs (starting with 150 B-26B-10-MAs) built at Middle River, Maryland. They were also incorporated in to all of the B-26Cs built at a new plant at Omaha, Nebraska. The

Right: *A Martin B-26 Marauder dropping its bombload. The aircraft carried a normal bombload of 2,000lb (907kg) but could take up to 5,800lb (2,631kg) in the tandem bomb bays.*

Following page: *Aircrew examine the damage to a B-26. The type's good combat record made it a popular aircraft.*

Left: *The B-26 had a radio-operator forward (with a flexibly mounted 0.50-inch machine gun in the nose cone), a tailgunner and gunners manning the power-operated dorsal turret and beam guns.*

Martin B-26 Marauder ended World War II with the lowest loss rate of any Allied bomber.

A single B-26 experimental aircraft was built with exhaust-heated surface de-icing equipment. There was also a single B-26E special stripped version. The B-26F and G were similar to the B-26C, but with increased incidence on the wing. There was also had no provision for carrying a torpedo and carried 11 guns.

Some 105 Martin B-26Cs and 350 B-26Fs and Gs were delivered to the Royal Air Force and SAAF as Marauder IIs and IIIs. A further 5,266 B-26Gs were built. These aircraft could fly at a height of 19,850ft (6,050m) and had a maximum range of 1,150 miles (1,850km).

The later, big-winged, Marauders formed the backbone of the USAAF's tactical bombing campaign in Europe. These aircraft equipped units of the Eighth and Ninth Air Forces from March 1943, and commenced combat operations in May.

Martin Marauder production eventually totalled 5,157 aircraft, and the USAAF had a peak strength of 1,931 aircraft (in March 1944). These equipped 11 Groups.

Some 911 Marauders were lost in combat during 129,943 sorties, in which the type dropped 169,382lb (76,831kg) of bombs. One B-26B, nicknamed 'Flak Bait', flew more missions in Europe (some 202) than any other Allied bomber during World War II.

The Martin B-26 Marauder was retired from service as the war ended, and was replaced by more modern bombers. Some B-26 Marauders were subsequently used as water bombers for fighting fires. Only a handful of museum specimens survive.

NORTH AMERICAN B-25 MITCHELL

WHEN NORTH AMERICAN Aviation built the NA-40B bomber, the aircraft was the company's first large aircraft, and its first foray into the bomber field. The NA-40B was developed in response to the USAAC's 1938 attack bomber requirement, and thus competed against the Douglas DB-7. The aircraft was destroyed in an accident, and the Douglas A-20 won the order as a result.

When the USAAC issued another requirement, for a larger attack bomber, North American scaled up the NA-40B design to produce the NA-62. On September 20, 1939 this was immediately ordered into production (with no prototype or evaluation) as the B-25 Mitchell. A full scale B-25 mock-up was approved on November 9, 1939. By the early summer of 1940 the first B-25 was in final assembly.

The original B-25 made its maiden flight on August 19, 1940, powered by a pair of 1,700hp R-2600-9 Wright Cyclone engines. It was lightly armed, with four flexibly mounted machine guns in the nose, tail and beam. The nose gun had to be moved between three mountings by the bombardier. The aircraft could carry a bombload of 1,360kg (3,000lb). The first B-25 was retained by North American

while two others were sent to Wright Field for testing.

The B-25 was named after the aviation pioneer General Billy Mitchell. It is believed this idea came from Lee Atwood, one of the founders of North American Aviation.

In February 1941 the USAAC approved the aircraft. B-25s were first issued to the 17th Bombardment Group based at McChord Field in Washington state. Some 19 B-25s eventually served with the unit.

The production of 24 B-25 Mitchells were followed by 40 B-25As. These had self-sealing tanks, armor and other improvements, but the first operationally ready version was the B-25B. This aircraft at last introduced

Right: *Anti-ship skip-bombing led to the installation of heavier fixed forward-firing armament on some B-25 Mitchells. This one is a B-25G of the 345th Bomb Group.*
Below: *This North American B-25A was assigned to the 17th Bomb Group's 34th Bomb Squadron—the first unit to fly the Mitchell.*
Following page: *This North American B-25C Mitchell served with the 12th Bomb Group in North Africa. The B-25 Mitchell was used principally in the Mediterranean and the Far East.*

a power-operated dorsal turret (and a remotely operated ventral turret) in place of the beam guns. Some 119 B-25Bs were delivered.

The Mitchell opened its combat career on April 11, when Australian-based USAAF B-25s attacked enemy shipping around the Philippines. The B-25 leapt to fame one week later with one of the most daring and unusual bomber raids of the war. It was mounted by the United States in retaliation for the attack on Pearl Harbor.

This, the Doolittle Raid of April 18, 1942, was also intended to boost morale on the home front in the United States. This was sagging in the wake of a succession of defeats in the Pacific theater. The daring plan involved launching 16 B-25Bs from the deck of the carrier USS *Hornet* to attack Tokyo, after which the aircraft flew on to China. Unfortunately bad weather prevented the raiders from finding their landing fields, and 11 crews had to bail out, four force-landed. One of the aircraft flew on to Vladivostock in southeastern Russia, and internment.

The Soviets examined the B-25 Mitchell and immediately made representations to acquire more of the bombers. These aircraft became so numerous and long-serving in the Soviet Union that they received the postwar code name 'Bank'.

The aircraft used on the raid were each armed with four 500-lb (226-kg) bombs and were laden with fuel, and had their secret Norden bombsights replaced by makeshift low level sights. Dummy tail guns were added to deter enemy fighters. Despite the Doolittle Raid being a military failure (all 16 aircraft were lost, with eight aircrew falling prisoner and three being killed, while inflicting little damage) the US raid was a morale booster and a propaganda success. Its leader, Jimmy Doolittle, was promoted to Brigadier General. Doolittle was awarded the Congressional Medal of Honor. The Doolittle Raid also forced the Japanese to 'hold back' large numbers

of fighters to defend the homeland.

The North American B 25 Mitchell proved to be a tough and versatile aircraft. The bomber, although it had originally been intended for level bombing from medium altitudes, found its true niche in the Pacific. In this theater the aircraft was deployed as a low-level bomber and strafing platform, hitting Japanese airfields from treetop level, and 'skip-bombing' enemy shipping.

The B-25C and B-25D (improved versions with R-2600-13 engines and other refinements) soon spawned dedicated ground attack versions. These had solid noses accommodating up to eight forward-firing 0.50 calibre machine guns. The B-25C version had more fuel capacity and bomb racks. The B-25 Mitchell versions employed in the Pacific theater placed special emphasis upon the use of forward firing guns and bombs for attacking enemy shipping. The B-25G was armed with an Army 75mm gun loaded by hand with 21 rounds. The version also carried two 0.50-inch guns and four 0.50-inch package guns. The B-25H had an Army 75mm gun and 4 0.50-inch guns.

In addition to its service in the Pacific theater, the North American B-25 Mitchell was used by the 12th Air Force in North African and Italian campaigns. The aircraft was also used by a number of Allied nations. These included the Soviet Union, Britain, Holland and Brazil The USAAF did not use the type in Western Europe, leaving the Eighth and Ninth Air Forces operating the B-26.

The Royal Air Force was one of the

Below: *A North American B-25C-20-NA of the 12th Bomb Group's 'fourth' squadron (hence the Roman IV on the fins), the 81st Bomb Squadron, at Gerbini, Sicily, in August 1943. The red-edge to the star and bar lasted only from June until August 1943.*

Following page: *The North American B-25 Mitchell proved adept at both medium and low level bombing.*

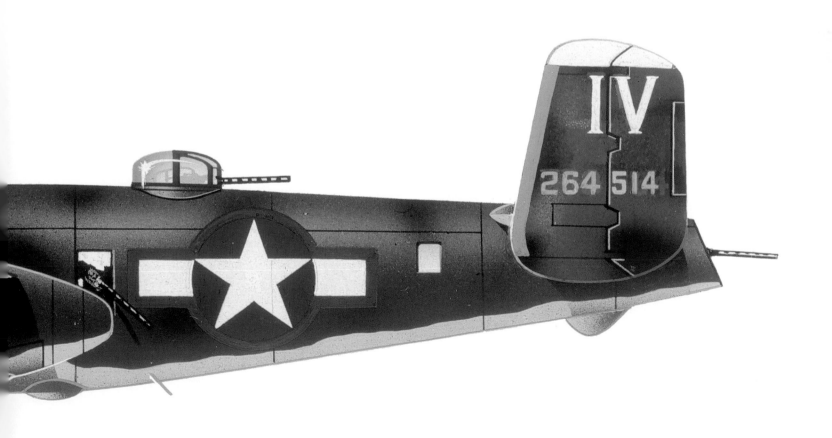

first to order the B-25 through the Lend-Lease scheme. It was the only nation to use Mitchells for raids on Europe from bases in Britain. The type was used as a light day bomber with four squadrons from Bomber Command's No.2 Group. They used a mix of about 800 B-25Bs (which it called Mitchell Is), B-25C/Ds (Mitchell IIs) and B-25Js (Mitchell IIIs) from September 1942 until the end of the war. The first RAF bombing operation using Mitchell IIs was made on January 22, 1943, against oil installations in Ghent, Belgium.

A total of 167 B-25Cs and some 371 B-25Ds were issued to the Royal Air Force. After D-Day in June 1944 these aircraft were transferred to France where they supported the Allied ground campaign. There were also 240 Mitchell Mk IIIs sent to Britain. Many were replacement aircraft for No.2 Group. Some were diverted to the Bahamas for officer training. The B-25 Mitchell also served with second-line RAF units in Britain and overseas. By December 1945 there were 393 Mitchells still serving with the RAF. Some of these aircraft were returned to the United States at the end of the war as part of the Lend-Lease agreement.

The last production variant of the Mitchell, the B-25J, was built in the largest numbers. A total of 4,318 poured off the Kansas City production line (Inglewood having gone over entirely to Mustang production).

The first B-25Js entered service in late 1943. These aircraft replaced earlier versions in service in the Mediterranean theater from April 1944, and in the Southwest Pacific during the summer of 1944.

This aircraft was very similar to the B-25H, but reintroduced the glazed bomb aimer's nose (though some sub-types reverted to a solid eight-gun nose), and the co-pilot's position. The aircraft could carry three instead of two 1,000lb bombs (453kg), or two 1,600-lb (725-kg) armour piercing bombs, while lighter weapons could be carried underwing.

The last B-25J was delivered to the USAAF in August 1945, and the Kansas City plant was closed the day after the war in the Pacific ended. By then, the B-25 Mitchell outnumbered all other USAAF medium bombers.

The B-25 Mitchell did not remain in frontline USAAF service for long. The A-26 Invader equipped the majority of surviving medium bomber units, although large numbers of Mitchells were converted for second line roles. These included training, transport and target towing. The last example stayed with the USAF until January 1959. Overseas, Mitchells remained in frontline service for a longer period. Probably the last serving Mitchells were those of the Uruguayan Air Force. They retired in August 1963.

Below: *This North American B-25C-10-NA Mitchell flew with the 340th Bomb Group's 487th Bomb Squadron at Catania in September 1943.*
Right: *A late-model, gun-nosed B-25 skip-bombs a Japanese gun-boat. The sharkmouth insignia would suggest that it belonged to the 345th Bomb Group.*

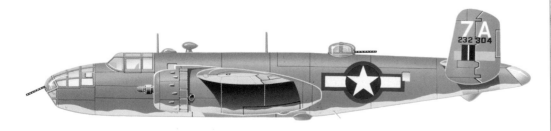

CONSOLIDATED B-24 LIBERATOR

THE CONSOLIDATED B-24 Liberator, was built in much larger numbers than the B-17, and was a better-performing, more versatile and more useful military aircraft. The Liberator, however, failed to grip the popular imagination in the way that the Fortress did and remained less well known. While the Fortress gained the plaudits, the Liberator quietly went about winning the war. US industry built 19,203 Liberators (producing more B-24s than any other aircraft type) in an ambitious program which eventually encompassed Convair at Fort Worth, Ford at Willow Run, Douglas at Tulsa and North American at Dallas.

Consolidated, although it had not produced a successful bomber, had built one of the world's most advanced aeroplanes in the form of the Consolidated 31 flying boat. This featured an exceptionally slender but deep, high aspect ratio Davis Wing. When General 'Hap' Arnold asked Consolidated to design a bomber that could 'fly the skin off any rivals', the company adapted the Model 31 to produce a four-engined landplane bomber derivative, and this Model 32 design became the Liberator.

The aircraft's shoulder-mounted wing housed 1,952 Imperial gallons (8,873 litres) of fuel, and left space below for a massive bomb bay. This was divided by a keel member which

Left: Consolidated B-24Js of the Seventh Air Force en route to their target. The long range of the B-24 was much prized in the Pacific theater.

also doubled as a catwalk to access the rear part of the fuselage. The bay was covered by low-drag flexible doors which worked on the same principal as a roll-top desk. The aircraft had an innovative tricycle undercarriage, and had twin endplate fins and rudders on its tailplane.

The XB-24 prototype made its maiden flight on December 29, 1939, nine months after contract signature. Early orders included seven YB-24s and 36 B-24As for the USAAC and 120 aircraft for France. With the fall of France, the 120 aircraft were taken over by the RAF, who also ordered a further 164 aircraft. All these aircraft were fitted with the same engines as the prototype, but introduced pneumatic de-icing boots for the wing and tail unit leading edges.

In the event, it would be the British who introduced the Liberator to service, taking the first 26 aircraft off the production line as LB-30As and LB-30s. These were used mainly for transatlantic transport duties.

British experience led to the development of the B-24B (Liberator II) with extra defensive armament, armor and other improvements. These entered service with the RAF's Coastal Command in the long-range ASW role in June 1941. The B-24C (Liberator II) had power-operated dorsal and tail turrets, and entered USAAF service in November 1941. In Britain 139 Liberator IIs were used in the bomber role in the Middle East, and in the ASW role.

The B-24D variant had a relocated mid-upper turret, immediately behind

Opposite: *This B-24, christened 'All American', is just one of the hundreds of nicknamed bombers with which aviation enthusiasts have become familiar.*
Left: *A B-24 Liberator being prepared for another mission. The B-24 saw service in Europe with the RAF and USAAF. It also served in the Pacific theater.*

the cockpit, exhaust-driven turbo-superchargers and oil coolers in the nacelles, giving a characteristic oval-shaped nacelle. These improvements boosted the type's performance from 265mph (426km/h) to 310mph (498km/h). They aircraft's ceiling also increased from 22,000ft (6,705m) to 32,000ft (9,753m).

The B-24D was the first mass-produced Liberator (with 2,738 built). This aircraft formed the backbone of the first Liberator units sent to Europe. RAF Coastal Command used the type as the Liberator III and V. The next major improvement came with the B-24G. This variant introduced a power-operated nose turret, also fitted to the B-24H, J, L and M. B-24Gs, Hs and Js were delivered to the RAF as Liberator VIs and VIIIs (according to equipment fit, with all Gs and Hs being VIs, but with the Js being delivered as VIs and VIIIs).

The Consolidated B-24 Liberator equipped several Groups within the Eighth and 15th Air Forces in Europe, and took part in some of the most important USAAF missions of the war, from Schweinfurt to Ploesti. Its very long-range capability, however, meant that many aircraft were delivered to the Pacific, where they had the range to be able to reach targets which lay far beyond the reach of the B-17. Some were even converted to tanker configuration to haul fuel 'over the Hump' from India to China. While the B-17 was exceptionally stable and easy to fly, the B-24 was something of a handful. The aircraft was a pleasure for the 'switched-on' and skilled pilot, but less suitable for hastily-trained wartime pilots, and more difficult to

Left: *'All American', this restored Consolidated B-24 saw active service in the Pacific theater with the RAF. The aircraft was abandoned in India at the end of the war and served as a patrol bomber for the Indian Air Force until 1968.*
Below: *'Black Zombie', a B-24J of the 406th Bomb Group.*

fly in close formation.

A handful of B-24Ns were delivered before the end of the war, with a massive single tailfin replacing the earlier versions' twin fins. This had previously been fitted to a handful of transport versions of the Liberator, including Winston Churchill's personal aircraft, 'Commando'. The US Navy introduced a similar version as the PB4Y-2 Privateer. This version of the aircraft went on to enjoy a brief but exciting role as a Cold War spyplane.

The Consolidated B-24 Liberator remained in frontline service in India until well into the 1960s. A handful of B-24s remain airworthy today.

Left: *The B-24's ball turret gave excellent coverage. Since the gunner was completely enclosed in an aluminum and Plexiglas sphere he probably had the least coveted position in the crew.*

Opposite: *'All American' prepares for take-off. This warbird was initially restored in the United States but then underwent a further name and nose art change in 1999.*

Below: *In the air the B-24's design was a graceful bird which flew faster and further than the B-17.*

Opposite: *B-24 crews in the United States perfected their skills over California's High Sierras and Arizona's canyons.*
Right: *Gunner's positions were remote, cramped and difficult to exit from.*
Below: *Distinctive nose art and nicknames breathed life and individuality into the bombers.*

DE HAVILLAND MOSQUITO

THE DE HAVILLAND Mosquito was, like many of the world's most successful military aircraft, originally designed as a private venture. It represented what the designers thought that the customer needed, and not what an officially stated requirement specified. Design work on the Mosquito began in October 1938, when the company sketched an all-wooden bomber with no defensive armament. This relied entirely on its high speed performance to escape enemy fighters. At one stage, de Havilland were considering a bomber derivative of the beautiful, wooden and highly streamlined (but troubled) Albatross airliner. This idea, however, was short-lived.

This was an even more radical idea than it now seems, since the British Air Ministry had actually banned the use of wood in the primary structure of military aircraft as long before as 1924. Once Britain was at war, however, the lure of producing another bomber type without using up scarce light alloys, and involving new industries (like furniture manufacturers) became too great to resist.

The de Havilland design study inspired great enthusiasm in Air Marshal Sir Wilfred Freeman, an influential member of the Air Council. Freeman pressed for a specification to be written around de Havilland's proposal. He ensured that the company received an official order for a single prototype and 49 production aircraft.

In the wake of the Dunkirk evacuation, aircraft production was concentrated on a core of types. The de Havilland Mosquito program was actually cancelled, before being reinstated some days later, and then stopped again. Despite this, work on the prototype aircraft continued throughout this period.

Even after being reinstated, and even after the prototype made its first flight on November 25, 1940, there was further unhelpful interference in the program. One result was an instruction that 28 of the aircraft on order should be completed as fighters, and 19 as dedicated reconnaissance aircraft, with only 20 remaining as bombers. There were even suggestions that these latter aircraft should receive power-operated gun turrets.

The reconnaissance Mosquito entered service and flew operations first (in September 1941), while the night fighter variant flew its first mission in April 1942. The bomber variant entered service with No.105 Squadron at Swanton Morley, eastern England, in November 1941. The bombers, however, did not begin operational sorties until May 31, 1942, when four aircraft attacked Köln the day after the first 1,000 bomber raid.

During the type's first year of operations, Mosquitos flew more than 100 successful daylight pinpoint bombing raids over Germany and Occupied Europe. These included a daring raid on the Gestapo headquarters in Oslo, Norway. After May 1943, with the growth of the USAAF in Britain, the

Right: *Wearing spurious codes applied for the making of the film '633 Squadron' this Mosquito T.Mk 3 was an active warbird into the 1990s.*

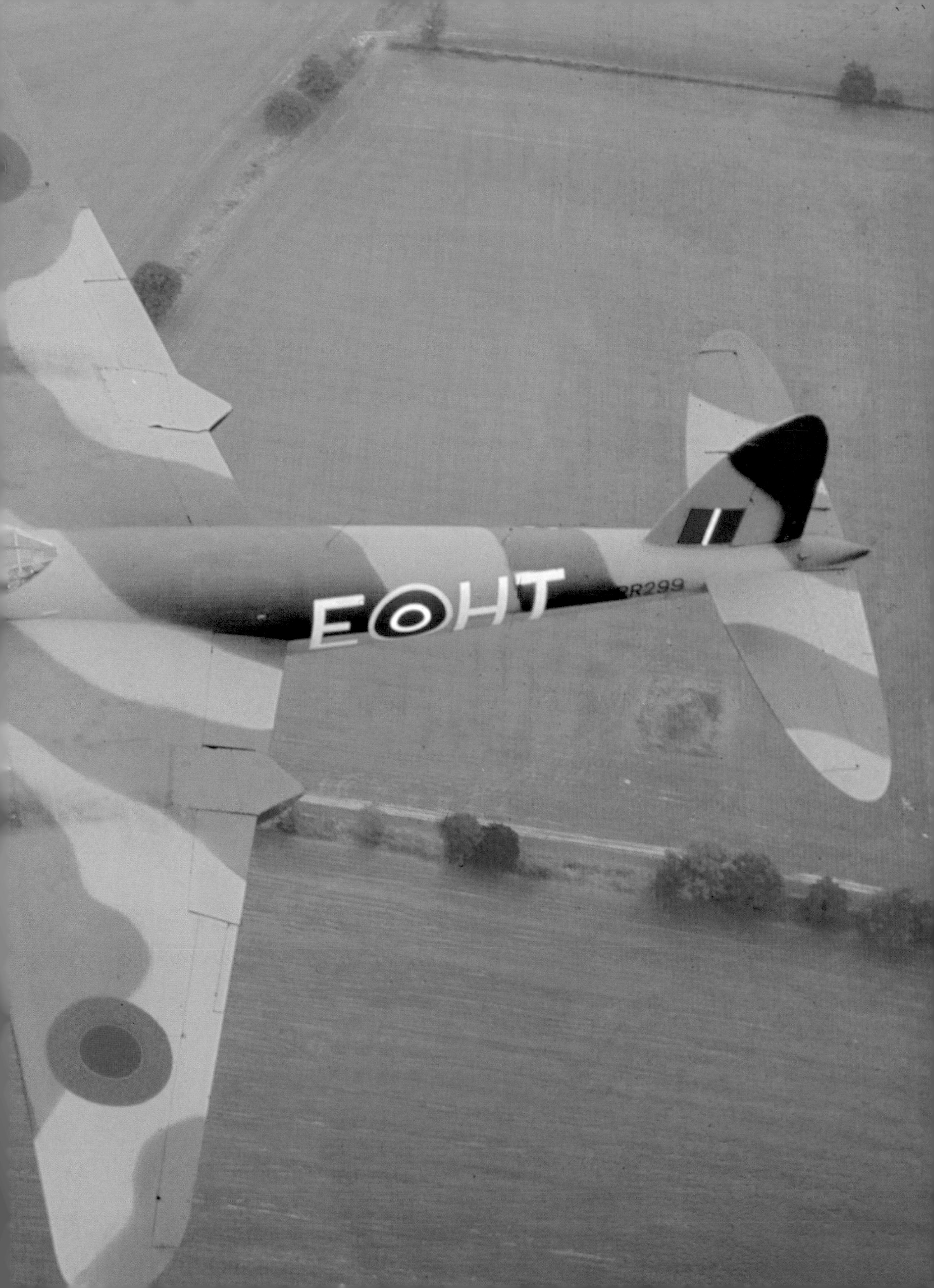
EHT
RR299

Left: *The de Havilland Mosquito T.Mk 3 was a dual control trainer based loosely on the fighter version of the aircraft. The bomber variant entered service in 1941.*

Mosquitos were entirely switched to night attacks. These missions started in December 1942 and the Mosquitoes operated in the Pathfinder role, and also as part of the Night Light Striking Force.

Later versions of the Mosquito had more powerful Merlin engines and bulged bomb-bay doors. These allowed them to carry the 4,000-lb (1,814-kg) HC blast bomb, and moreover to do so at altitudes of up to 40,000ft (1,292m). The Mosquito ranged as far as Berlin, and achieved speeds which rendered them almost invulnerable to interception. The aircraft, for example, could fly at 408mph (656km/h) over the target, and 419mph (260km/h) after dropping their bombs.

The Royal Air Force suffered a loss rate of only one Mosquito in every 2,000 sorties! Mosquitos were widely built, some being brought over from Canada, while Australia also built the type for RAAF use. Meanwhile, the Mosquito fighter-bombers continued to attack pinpoint targets by day. These included the Amiens jail, northern France, where the walls were breached, allowing important Resistance prisoners to escape. Mosquitos also hit the Gestapo HQ in the Hague, Holland, and in Copenhagen, Denmark.

The final bomber version of the Mosquito, the B.Mk 35, first flew on March 12, 1945, and though too late to see wartime service, equipped RAF bomber units until the arrival of the Canberra in 1952–53. Converted B.Mk 35s then served as target tugs into the 1960s. Reconnaissance Mosquitoes remained in frontline service until December 15, 1955, when a No.81 Squadron PR.Mk 34 made the type's last operational sortie over Malaya.

Left: *The de Havilland Mosquito Mk XVIII was a dedicated fighter-bomber used by two Coastal Command squadrons, Nos. 248 and 254.*

Below: *No.418 Squadron was an RCAF-manned unit equipped with Mosquito FB.Mk VI fighter-bombers.*

Above: *Armorers make final preparations to load a No.105 Mosquito B.Mk IV with 500-lb (226-kg) bombs at its Marham home in eastern England.*

Left: *No.105 Squadron was the RAF's first Mosquito bomber squadron, receiving the type in November 1941 and beginning operations on May 31, 1942.*

AVRO LANCASTER

BOMBER COMMAND'S MOST important bomber was the Avro
Lancaster, a four-engined and refined
derivative of the hopeless Manchester.
The Lancaster dropped a higher tonnage of bombs than any other Bomber
Command aircraft. By the end of the
World War II the type equipped the
bulk of the Command's squadrons,
except within the Canadian No.6
Group, and No.4 Group based in
northern England. These were still
dominated by the Halifax. By March
1945, Bomber Command had 745
Avro Lancasters on charge and ready
for operations in 56 squadrons, with
296 more serving with the various
training and conversion units.

The Lancaster carried a heavier
bombload than any of its rivals, and
was able to carry Bomber Command's
largest blast bombs. The average
Lancaster was thus able to carry a
higher tonnage of bombs to Nazi
Germany in its short life than could
the average Halifax or Wellington.
Even the superb Halifax VI could not
carry the larger 12,000-lb (5,443-kg)
bomb, and was best suited to carrying
1,000-lb (453-kg) bombs and smaller
weapons. And in 'Bomber' Harris'
campaign against area targets in the
Reich this alone was enough to ensure
that the Lancaster remained his
'bomber of choice'.

Left: *This Avron Lancaster remains*
airworthy today, and is painted up as the
No.419 Squadron aircraft in which
Andrew Mynarski won a posthumous
Victoria Cross.
Following page: *This No.467 Squadron*
Lancaster survived the war and is today
displayed inside the RAF Museum, London.

The aircraft was less versatile than
the Halifax (whose capacious and
comfortable fuselage allowed it to be
easily adapted for ECM, maritime,
meteorological and transport duties).
They were was less well-suited to
operation in hot climates. But other
roles and theaters were an unwelcome
and irrelevant diversion to Harris. The
Lancaster's shortcomings in these
areas were a matter of supreme indif-
ference for him. More worryingly,
only 11 per cent of crews survived
being shot down in a Lancaster, while
29 per cent of Halifax aircrew baled
out successfully. Live aircrew in the
enemy POW camps were of little use
to Harris, however, and so the
Lancaster remained dominant.

The Lancaster was also very popular
with its crews. Pilots prized the aircraft's superb handling, while other
aircrew were aware that the type had
long enjoyed a lower loss rate than
other Bomber Command heavies. The
Halifax III, VI and VII actually
enjoyed a lower loss rate, but few
Lancaster aircrew were aware of this!

Avro began exploring the possibility
of producing a four-engined version of
the Manchester even before the
Vulture-engined prototype made its
maiden flight. This was lucky, since in
August 1940 the company was asked
to switch from production of the
Manchester to license manufacture of
the rival Halifax, as part of the drive
to move towards a force of four-
engined bombers. Two separate
Manchester production lines were
already in operation. Avro desperately
pleaded that it would be quicker and
more efficient to switch to producing
the then-unnamed four-engined

Left: Three Avro Lancasters of No.207 Squadron, one of the early units to re-equip from the Manchester.

Below: The 'City of Lincoln' was built in 1945 for service in the Far East. This Lancaster was intended to serve with Tiger Force that was supposed to invade Japan and secure the Allied victory in Asia.

Manchester than to go over to producing the rival Halifax.

The Air Ministry accepted this proposal in September 1940. Avro began building the 'Manchester III' prototype. This first flew on January 9, 1941, with a Manchester-style short tailplane and triple fins.

By this time, operational experience had showed that bombers would be kept and serviced in the open, and there was no attempt to force Avro to keep within a particular wingspan limit. Nor did the company have to pay lip-service to using the aircraft in a secondary transport role, and could optimize its design for bombing performance. Finally, while the prototype used the same Merlin X engines as the Halifax, the production Lancaster used Merlin XXs with 135hp more power per engine.

The Avro Lancaster, freed from all of

the constraints imposed on the early Handley Page Halifax, demonstrated superb performance. The Lancaster thus ordered into large-scale production by a group of factories. These included Austin Motors, Armstrong Whitworth, Avro, Metropolitan Vickers and Vickers Armstrong.

No.44 Squadron began conversion to the Lancaster in December 1941, and the type flew its first operation on March 3, 1942. Early operations included a low-level daylight raid on the MAN diesel works at Augsburg, Germany, on April 17, 1942, and another against weapons plants at Le Creusot, France, on October 17. The following year, the Lancasters of No.617 Squadron used the Upkeep 'bouncing bomb' against the Möhne, Eder and Sorpe dams in Germany. Apart from the short time they provided direct support to Allied invasion forces, however, Bomber Command's Lancasters were kept busy flying night bombing missions against Germany's industrial cities. They used progressively larger and more lethal bombs. Lancasters continued to be used for attacks on more pinpoint targets. Some attacked and sank the German battleship *Tirpitz*. Other Lancasters, using 12,000-lb (5,433-kg) Tallboys and 22,000-lb (9,979kg) Grand Slams, hit canals, viaducts, and even U-Boat pens.

There were detail differences between the Lancaster B.Mk I, B.Mk III and the Canadian-built B.Mk X,

while 300 B.Mk IIs were built with 1,650hp Bristol Hercules radial engines. These were intended as an insurance against failure of the Merlin Lancaster, or in case Merlin production could not keep pace with Bomber Command's requirements. In the event, however, production of the engine by Packard in the United States meant that there was never an engine shortage. Operational equipment varied, with the see-sawing of measure and counter-measure in the bomber war. By the end of the war, though, most Lancasters had H2S bombing radar and other refinements.

The Lancaster B.Mk IV became the Lincoln (described separately) while the B.Mk VI was a dedicated high altitude bomber. It only built in small numbers and delivered to just one unit before the war ended. The B.Mk VII was designed for use by Tiger Force. This had a new Martin mid-upper turret, located further forward than the old turret. Avro and its partners

eventually completed some 7,366 Lancasters, a smaller total than that achieved by the less well known Vickers Wellington.

The numerical dominance of the Lancaster, and its close relationship to the new Lincoln, ensured that it was retained postwar rather than the arguably more suitable Halifax. The last Lancaster bombers with the RAF were retired in March 1950. Others served on in the survey role until December 1953, and in the air-sea rescue and maritime reconnaissance roles until October 1956. Elsewhere, maritime Lancasters survived even longer, notably in Canada and France.

Opposite: *The same aircraft as is pictured on pages 236–237 from No. 467 Squadron, with its jubilant crew. The quote on the nose is by Herman Goering.*
Below: *The Avro Lancaster's greatest attribute was its large, unobstructed bomb bay. This enabled the aircraft to carry the largest weapons.*

Opposite: *Lancasters were built by a number of factories, in both Britain and Canada. The aircraft was significantly quicker and cheaper to build than the rival Halifax.*

Above: *The Avro Lancaster had a crew of seven, with a pilot and flight engineer side by side on the flight deck, and with navigator/bomb-aimer, radio operator and three gunners.*

Left: *The Lancaster became the most important aircraft in RAF Bomber Command, supplanting the Halifax.*

CARRIERBORNE BOMBERS 1939–45

WORLD WAR II aircraft carriers were relatively small vessels, by modern standards, and inventions like the steam catapult were still far from being ready for service. These factors limited the size and weight of carrier-borne aircraft, and the Doolittle raid, in which B-25s were launched from the USS *Hornet*, was very much an exception. Most land-based medium bombers could never have fitted on a carrier's deck during routine operations, and even with folding wings could not have used lifts and hangar decks. Most carrierborne bombers were thus relatively small, single-engined aircraft, with limited range and warloads.

As carrierborne aircraft were seen primarily as a means of attacking enemy ships, which were small and relatively agile targets, they had to be capable of great precision and destructive power. This, in turn, placed greater emphasis on weapons accuracy, and most carrierborne attack aircraft were optimized for the delivery of torpedoes or for making dive attacks. Appropriately enough it was Britain (birthplace of carrier aviation) which was the first nation to use aircraft carriers in action during World War II. On the outbreak of war, Royal Navy carriers embarked Blackburn Skua dive bombers and Fairey Swordfish torpedo bombers. The Blackburn Skua was used in Norway, sinking the German cruiser *Königsberg* in April 1940. It enjoyed some success as a two-seat fighter, but the type was relegated to training duties from 1941.

The anachronistic-looking biplane Fairey Swordfish was an extremely effective torpedo bomber, and enjoyed an enviable combat record. They destroyed Mussolini's fleet at Taranto, Italy, in November 1940 (an action which convinced the Japanese that their Pearl Harbor attack plan was feasible). The type also participated in the Channel Dash, the sinking of the *Bismarck*, and remained in production until 1944. The planned successor to the Swordfish was the Fairey

Right: *The Curtiss SB2C Helldiver was designed as a replacement for the Douglas SBD Dauntless but proved mediocre in service.*

Below: *The Grumman TBF/TBM Avenger was probably the best carrierborne bomber of the war. This one served in the Atlantic with VC-58 aboard the USS* Guadalcanal.

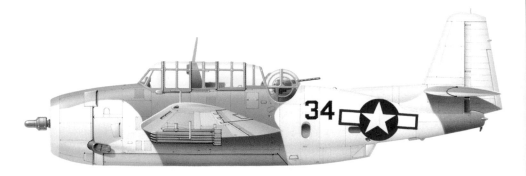

Albacore. This biplane had an enclosed cockpit and more streamlined undercarriage, hydraulic flaps, and a variable pitch prop. Despite these improvements, the Albacore proved less successful than the Swordfish, and never fully replaced the original aircraft.

The Fairey Barracuda was a high-winged monoplane, with a high-set tailplane and retractable undercarriage. This combined the torpedo and dive-bombing roles, and began its operational career during late 1943. Barracudas were responsible for the sinking of the *Tirpitz* in April 1944, scoring 15 direct hits. The Barracuda could carry a 1,500-lb (680-kg)

bombload yet proved remarkably survivable, thanks to the crews' excellent training and tactics.

The attack on Pearl Harbor in December 1941 by Japan's carriers was spearheaded by the Aichi D3A ('Val'). This ancient-looking monoplane with a fixed, spatted undercarriage and prominent dive slats under the wing leading edge.

The aircraft carried a 250-kg (551-lb) bomb under the belly, with single 60-kg (132-lb) bombs underwing. The type remained in service until the end of the war, though they were replaced by Yokosuka D4Ys from 1941.

Some 2,038 examples of the D4Y Suisei ('Judy') were built, and the type

operated in land-based and carrier-borne forms, with inline and radial engines respectively. The type entered service in the dive bomber role in March 1943.

The other vital type at Pearl Harbor was the Nakajima B5N ('Kate') torpedo bomber, 1,149 of which were built up to 1943. The B5N formed the basis of the Nakajima B6N Tenzan ('Jill') which married the same basic airframe with a new more powerful engine. Another 1,266 were built.

The Aichi B7A Ryusei was designed to replace both the D4Y in the dive bomber role and the B6N in the torpedo bomber role. It showed great promise initially, demonstrating that it

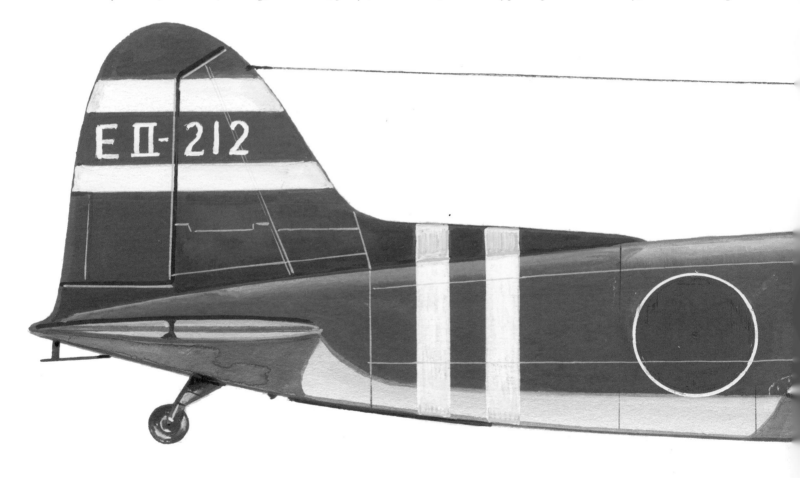

Right: *A modern 'warbird' Avenger displays the type's rearward folding wings— enabling it to be stowed on crowded hangar decks.*
Below: *The Aichi D3A Val dive-bomber played a pivotal role in the Japanese attack on Pearl Harbor, but was replaced by Yokosuka D4Ys from 1941.*

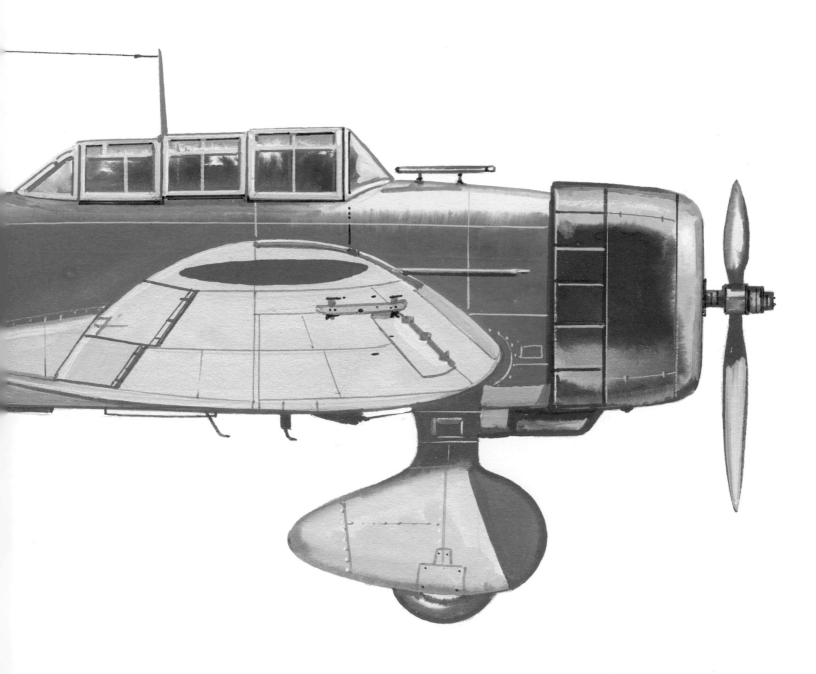

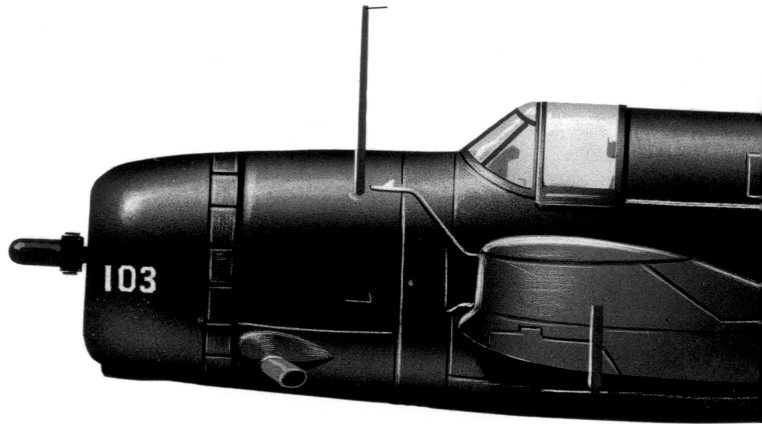

Left: *The Fairey Barracuda proved equally effective in the dive- and torpedo-bombing roles, and was popular and survivable.*
Below: *The Curtiss SB2C Helldiver made its combat debut over Rabaul in the Pacific during late 1943. Early models carried a smaller bombload than the Douglas SBD Dauntlesses they replaced.*

had the speed and agility of the Zero as well as sufficient range and bombload for its intended role. Unfortunately, the program suffered severe teething troubles.

By the time the aircraft entered service, most of Japan's carriers had been sunk. The aircraft industry had also been so disrupted by Allied bombing that production was limited to only 114 aircraft, equipping two land-based squadrons.

In the United States, the Vought SB2U Vindicator was the Navy's first carrierborne monoplane 'scout-bomber', entering service in late 1937. The type was also supplied to the French Armée de l'Air, and some 50 SB2Us destined to France were taken over by the British as Chesapeakes, and used for training. US Navy and US Marine Corps Vindicators saw service during the early stages of the war in the Pacific, but proved excessively vulnerable to enemy fighters.

The later Brewster SB2A Buccaneer and Bermuda saw no combat service, though the 771 built included 468 for the RAF. Those ordered by the Dutch East Indies were diverted to the USN and USMC, which used the type only

Above: *The Aichi D3A Val looked anachronistic, with its open cockpit and fixed, spatted undercarriage. The type attacked Pearl Harbor in 1941.*
Right: *The Blackburn Skua performed with some success as a dive bomber and as a two-seat fighter, but the Roc, with a four-gun turret, was too heavy and cumbersome.*

for training.

The Douglas SBD Dauntless did see frontline service as a dive bomber. Despite being widely viewed as being obsolescent by the time war broke out, it enjoyed an enviable combat record. During 1942, Dauntlesses sank more enemy shipping than any other US weapon. The type flew in the Battle of the Coral Sea—the first major naval battle fought entirely by carrier-based aircraft, with the opposing fleets never directly exchanging gunfire. Surprisingly, the Dauntlesses also took a toll of attacking Zeros. They also fought with distinction at Midway. The type was also used in small numbers by the USAAC as the A-24, and by France, New Zealand and Mexico, which used the type until 1959.

The Curtiss SB2C Helldiver was

designed as a replacement for the Dauntless, and made its combat debut over Rabaul in late 1943, then rapidly re-equipping the Navy's SBD units. Early models carried a smaller bombload than the Dauntlesses they replaced. They were no less vulnerable to enemy defenses, but later models did mark more of an improvement. A handful were delivered to the RAAF and USAAF as A-25 dive-bombers. These, however, were relegated to second-line roles before they could be used in action.

The Douglas TBD-1 Devastator was considered an astonishingly modern aeroplane when it entered service in November 1937. It was also the US Navy's first all-metal low wing monoplane, and the first aircraft with wings that could be power-folded while taxying. Unfortunately, the Douglas TBD-1 Devastator was anything but devastating by the time war broke out, and it was destined to enjoy only a brief combat career. The aircraft was used in the level-bombing and torpedo roles. It enjoyed some success during the opening stages of the war in the Pacific, including the sinking of a Japanese aircraft carrier during the Battle of the Coral Sea. At Midway, however, in June 1942, Devastators suffered heavy losses (38 of 41 aircraft despatched) without inflicting any damage on the enemy. The type was rapidly phased out of service.

The Devastator's replacement, the Grumman TBF/TBM Avenger, was designed as a dedicated torpedo bomber, but proved versatile and adaptable. A handful remain in service to this day, fighting forest fires and spraying budworm! In many respects a scaled-up derivative of Grumman's superb F4F Wildcat, the TBF was simple, rugged, and powerful. The type made an inauspicipus debut at Midway, with VT-8 losing five of its six aircraft. It soon, however, demonstrated its formidable capabilities, scoring successes with bombs, rockets, mines and, of course, torpedoes. The type was heavily used in the Atlantic and Mediterranean as well as the Pacific. Large numbers were used by the USMC, the Royal Navy (who initially called it the Tarpon), the RNZAF and the Canadian Navy.

The Avenger enjoyed a long postwar career. It served with the US Navy until 1954, the RCN, the French Aeronavale, the JMSDF, the Royal Netherlands Navy, the RNZAF (until 1960), the Royal Navy (until 1957) as well as in Uruguay.

THE GERMAN HEAVY BOMBER PROGRAM

HITLER OFFICIALLY INAUGURATED the new Luftwaffe on March 27, 1935, announcing its existence and confirming the appointments of Göring as Commander in Chief, Milch as Secretary of State for Air and Wever as Chief of Staff. Milch and Wever planned to base the next stage of Luftwaffe expansion around the building of a new strategic bomber force. Wever had a tremendous grasp of air power theory, and was also a great organizer. He drew up the so-called Langstrecken-Grossbomber (Long-striking large bomber) or Ural-bomber program. This aimed to produce a bomber with sufficient range to reach targets in the north of Scotland or across the Ural mountains. The program resulted in orders for the Junkers Ju 89 and Dornier Do 19. These four-engined bombers were broadly equivalent to the RAF's Stirling.

The death of General Wever in an air accident in 1937 left the long-range bomber program vulnerable to cancellation. The prevailing culture of short-termism within the highest echelons of the Third Reich discriminated against any project which would not produce near-immediate results. At the same time, Göring and the head of his technical department, Udet, were both ex-fighter pilots, with little understanding of the finer points of bombing.

Wever's replacement as Chief of the Air Staff was Albert Kesselring, a

Left: *This Heinkel He 177 was evaluated by the Royal Air Force after being captured intact by the Maquis fighters inside Occupied France.*

former army officer who had transferred to the Luftwaffe relatively late, and who naturally focused on the needs of the army. Kesselring did not share Wever's enthusiasm for long-range strategic bombers and quickly became a passionate advocate of tactical air operations.

Albert Kesselring pointed out to Göring that three twin-engined bombers would cost the same (and take up the same industrial capacity) as two four-engined bombers. He knew that Hitler would ask how many bombers the Luftwaffe had, and not how many engines they had. The fate of the Dornier Do 19 and Junkers Ju 89 was sealed and the program was cancelled on April 29, 1937. Those who noticed the end of the long-range bomber program were reassured: "Hitler will never let us in for a conflict that might take us outside the confines of the continent."

The two aircraft developed to meet Wever's 'Ural Bomber' program were the Do 19 and the Ju 89. Dornier produced two Do 19 prototypes, the V-1 with 715hp Bramo (Siemens) 323H-2 Fafnir nine-cylinder radial engines and the V-2 with 810hp BMW 132F radials. The aircraft had twin fins and a retractable undercarriage, but their slab-sided fuselage and massive wing were reminiscent of those of the older Do 11 and Do 23. The Do 19V-1 made its maiden flight on October 28, 1936. The aircraft's capabilities were surprisingly modest, carrying a load of four SC 250 250-kg (551-lb) or sixteen 100-kg (220-lb) bombs over a 2,000-km (1,242-mile) range. Some suggest that the planned Do 19A production model would have out-performed the rival Ju 89.

The Junkers Ju 89 was a rather more modern-looking aircraft than the Do 19, although it shared a similar configuration. It was heavier than the Do 19 and had more powerful engines. The first prototype made its maiden flight on April 11, 1937, and a second was completed soon after the program's cancellation. Both Ju 89s were extensively flight tested, and on June 4, 1938, one was used to set a new Payload/Altitude World Record carrying 5,000-kg (11,022-lb) payload to an altitude of 9,312m (30,550ft), and later taking 10,000kg (22,045lb)

to 7,242m (23,759ft). The Ju 89 demonstrated 25 per cent better speed, and ceiling than the Do 19, with 19 per cent longer range, but this was not enough to save it. The two completed aircraft were used as transports by the Luftwaffe. The uncompleted third prototype was used as the prototype for the Ju 90 airliner, marrying a complete new wider fuselage to the wings and tail unit of the original Ju 89.

The later Ju 90 subsequently formed the basis of the Ju 290, a small number of which were used as bombers and anti-ship aircraft. The Ju 290 also formed the basis of the single six-engined Ju 390. This was built and flown in prototype form and intended

as an 'Amerika Bomber' carrying a 10,000 kg (2,204-lb) payload over a range of 8,000km (4,971 miles).

In fact, though the Ju 89 and Do 19 were cancelled, the long-range Heinkel He 177 had already been launched (as the Bomber A) and this had a longer range and a heavier bombload than either of the cancelled aircraft. Technical problems delayed the Heinkel's service entry, however, and for most of the war, the Luftwaffe was left with no heavy, long-range bomber.

The so-called 'Bomber A' requirement called for a 539km/h (335mph) bomber which could carry a 4,400-lb (1,995-kg) bombload out to a radius of 1,609km (1,000 miles). Heinkel

favored a twin-engined configuration, but this would have required an engine producing 2,000hp. In the absence of a suitable powerplant, Heinkel employed the Daimler Benz DB606 double engine—essentially a pair of 12 cylinder DB 601s mounted side by side in a single nacelle, driving a single propeller. Heinkel hoped to use evaporative cooling and remotely controlled gun barbettes to minimize drag, but instead was forced to use conventional radiators and manned gun turrets. The design suffered weight and drag growth, and the flight test program, which began on November 19, 1939, was troubled. From an early stage, the aircraft

proved prone to engine fires and failures. Although some were delivered to I/KG 30 at Bordeaux Merignac in 1942, they were quickly withdrawn. More were briefly used as transports to resupply Stalingrad in late 1942. The type, however, did not enter full operational service until November 1943, when KG 40 started flying anti-shipping operations with He 177s equipped with Hs 293 glide-bombs.

During the first operational mission (against a British convoy) the unit lost three aircraft (with others being badly damaged). The appearance of a lumbering British Liberator proved the type's vulnerability and lack of agility. The Heinkel He 177 was used during

the Luftwaffe's night-bombing campaign against Great Britain in early 1944 (Operation Steinbock), developing tactics which included a withdrawal in a steep dive. This made interception difficult.

The aircraft was also used on the Eastern Front, mainly against tactical targets just behind the frontline. The majority of the He 177s were grounded in late 1944 as a result of fuel shortages, and the heavy bomber Gruppen were disbanded.

Below: *The Heinkel He 177's engines were prone to fires and failures, limiting the aircraft's usefulness, and it was soon withdrawn from use.*

MARTIN BALTIMORE

THE ANGLO-FRENCH PURCHASING Commission ordered the Model 187 Baltimore to follow the French Model 167 Maryland off the Middle River production line. Whereas the French had been happy with the 167s, the British felt that the type would be obsolete by the time it entered service. The new Model 187 was about a third larger than the 167. It had a deeper fuselage, a powered gun turret, a new tail and more powerful Wright R-2600 engines, but had a very similar configuration. In order to fulfill the initial Franco-British order Martin had to get US Government permission to delay planned B-26 Marauder deliveries. This was granted in exchange for Martin providing the Marauders with self-sealing fuel tanks and armor without charge to the US Army Air Corps.

In June 1940 the whole order was reluctantly taken over by Britain, who actually wanted the Marauder. Martin felt that work on the Model 187 had progressed too far, and that cancellation would be costly for the company. Remarkably, the prewar, old-fashioned Model 187 had a contract price of $120,000, whereas B-26s only earned the company $78,000 each! The Model 187 was allocated the RAF name Baltimore. The first Model 187 made its maiden flight in June 1941, but problems caused some difficulties and 52 early B-26 Marauder Is were supplied to the RAF as stop-gaps. The first 50 Baltimore Is were supplied without gun turrets and desert air filters, and had a single Browning .30-caliber machine gun in an open rear cockpit. The next 100 Baltimore IIs were similar, but with twin mounts.

The last 250 aircraft of the original order were designated as Baltimore IIIs, and finally had four-gun Boulton-Paul hydraulic turrets.

It had been planned that many of the Baltimores would be earmarked for service in Singapore, but Japan seized the colony before they arrived. Instead, all 400 Baltimores went to British forces in Egypt. The aircraft suffered heavy losses when used at low altitude and without fighter escort. They were more successful when they adopted medium-altitude bombing with fighter escort. The aircraft were also used for night intruder, maritime patrol, reconnaissance, and target-towing missions. Two dedicated maritime reconnaissance A-30C/Baltimore GR.Mk VI prototypes were built. The A-30C program, however, was cancelled in April 1944. Two Lend-Lease orders of 575 and 600 Baltimore Mk IIIAs (US designation A-30), Mk IVs, and Mk Vs (A-30A) also went to the RAF, the SAAF, and to RAAF, Greek, Free French and Italian Co-Belligerent squadrons operating under Allied command. Some 71 aircraft were supplied to neutral Turkey.

Most Baltimores were scrapped after the war but a single RAF squadron in Kenya used them in aerial mapping and locust control until 1948. A planned XA-23 ordered for the USAAC in 1940 was to have had Wright R-3350 engines, but the program was cancelled. The US Navy, however, used one ex-RAF Baltimore for testing transonic aerofoil sections.

Right: *The Martin Baltimore served principally in the Middle East, and proved useful in the medium bombing role.*

LOCKHEED VENTURA

THE LOCKHEED 14 airliner was developed to form the basis of a family of military variants. The L-214 and L-414 Hudson were primarily used as ASW and maritime patrol aircraft, proving popular and highly successful. The similar-looking V-146 Ventura (also known as the PV-1 and B-34) was a further developed aircraft, derived from the civil Lockheed 18 Lodestar transport. This was in turn a stretched, up-engined version of the Lockheed 14.

The Ventura was powered by a pair of 2,000hp Double Wasp engines (the Hudson had used 900hp or 1,200hp Wright Cyclones, or 1,200hp Twin Wasps). Its mid-upper turret was located further forward, with a stepped rear fuselage incorporating a ventral gun position.

The aircraft was originally designed and manufactured for the British government. It was procured by the Royal Air Force as a replacement for the ageing Bristol Blenheim. The Ventura, however, was never as effective as the Boston or Mosquito, which it partnered within Bomber Command's No.2 Group. While the Ventura marked a great improvement over the Lockheed Hudson, it was late into service. By the time No.21 Squadron received its first Ventura Is in May 1942, and then when it flew combat operations from November, the aircraft was outclassed and vulnerable. The unfortunate bomber was soon derisively nicknamed as 'the Pig'.

Left: *The Ventura was derived from the Lockheed Lodestar. It was used by the USN as the PV-1, by the USAF as the B-34, B-37 and O-56 and by the RAF as the Ventura.*

The Lockheed Ventura II and IIA were powered by 2,000hp R-2800-31 engines. US contracts with Vega for these versions incorporated modifications, mostly in armament and equipment. These aircraft saw service with Bomber Command (under the Lend-Lease Scheme) and had the US designation B-34. The USAAF also flew these aircraft. A few were flown by the US Navy as PV-3s.

Lockheed did begin making Ventura IIIs for the RAF but only delivered 18 aircraft. They received the US designation O-56 and later B-37.

A final version, the Lockheed Ventura PV-1, was mainly issued to the US Navy. This version served as a patrol bomber. Its bomb bay was adapted to carry bombs, depth charges or a torpedo. The aircraft had a maximum speed of 502km/h (312mph) and a range of 2,672km (1,660 miles). The PV-1 could carry a bombload of 1,360kg (3,000lb).

There were 1,600 PV-1s produced. Coastal Command and the RAF received 388 of these aircraft as Ventura IVs or GR. Vs.

Ventura losses were heavy, although crews showed great heroism and commitment. This was typified by Squadron Leader Len Trent. This pilot won a Victoria Cross during a daylight raid by 11 Venturas on a power station in Amsterdam, Holland, in 1943.

The type was phased out of Bomber Command service in September 1943. Venturas, however, continued in use in the maritime role, and with RAF and SAAF bomber Squadrons based in North Africa and the Middle East. The type was also used by the RNZAF and RAAF in the Pacific.

VULTEE VENGEANCE

THE USAAC WAS briefly influenced by the success of the Ju 87 dive bomber during the Spanish Civil War and the Polish invasion. As a result, a number of US dive bomber types were put into production. These included the Vultee Model 72. By the time they entered service, however, the drawbacks of the type were apparent, and none were used in significant numbers by the USAAC or USAAF.

The aircraft was scheduled for production at the Vultee plant in Nashville, Tennessee, and also at a Northrop plant in Hawthorne, California, following the completion of licensing agreements. The V-72 aircraft made its first flight on November 30, 1941.

The Vultee Vengeance was a big and brutal looking low-winged monoplane. The aircraft had a distinctive 'W'-shaped wing in planform. It had unusual forward-swept outer wing panels and was of an all-metal stressed-skin construction.

The USAAF operated 342 examples of the Vultee Vengeance as the A-31, A-35A and V-72. The majority of the aircraft built, however, were exported to Australia, Britain, India (30) and Brazil (29). Export versions included the Vengeance Mks I, II and III (equivalent to the USAAF A-31), also the Mk IV (USAF equivalent A-35).

The A-35B was the first version fully fitted with US equipment. The aircraft was powered by a 1,700hp Wright R-2600-13 engine. It achieved a maximum speed of 449km/h (279mph) and had a cruising speed of 370km/h (230mph). The A-35B had an operational range of 966km (600 miles) and was capable of carrying two 500-lb bombs.

By the time the Royal Air Force's first Vultee Vengeance made its maiden flight in July 1941, it was clear that the type was not required in Europe. Consequently, all frontline Vengeances served in the Far East, equipping four RAF dive-bomber squadrons in Burma from August 1942. Vultee Vengeance bombers were also sent to five RAAF squadrons. After a rather indifferent career the Vengeances were withdrawn from operations by the RAAF in 1944.

The RAF Vengeances served with surprising success, proving extremely adept at attacking pinpoint targets in the dense jungle. The aircraft suffered relatively light losses, although the RAAF aircraft, committed in New Guinea, unaccountably proved rather less successful.

A handful of RAF Vengeances were also participated in the East African campaign. These aircraft saw little action, but were used for chemical warfare experiments and trials.

A total of 1,528 Vultee Vengeances were built before production ended in the Fall of 1944. In Britain, the Vengeance was finally replaced by aircraft such as the Mosquito during 1944. The type flew its last combat operations in July 1944. The Vengeance enjoyed a brief postwar career as high-speed target tug with various air forces. The RAF replaced the last examples of these with redundant Supermarine Spitfires in 1947.

Right: *The majority of Vultee Vengeances built were used by British and Commonwealth air forces in the Far East during World War II.*

TUPOLEV TU-2

THE TUPOLEV TU-2 (not to be confused with the earlier SB-2) was arguably the best Soviet light bomber of World War II. The aircraft's development, however, was protracted. It was less widely used than earlier bombers. This included the similar-looking but rather smaller Petyaklov Pe-2, which it was intended to replace.

This aircraft was Tupolev's first tactical bomber. The Tupolev Tu-2 was also destined to be his most important wartime aircraft. Incredibly, the design of the aircraft was undertaken while Tupolev was in prison (on fabricated charges) and was the work of the unnamed NKVD-run section (Department 103) which he led. Tupolev was to be incarcerated with Department 103 until July 1941.

The aircraft made its first flight in May 1941. It went into serial production in July.

The Tu-2, originally known simply as Aeroplane 103, was designed as a tactical level bomber. From the start it was intended to be capable of being adapted to various roles. These included dive-bombing, reconnaissance, 'shturmovik' (ground attack), torpedo-bombing and even long-range escort roles. The 'Soviet Mosquito', the Tu-2 proved to be almost as fast as contemporary fighters, and was tough and rugged.

The Tupolev Tu-2 was fitted with two 1,850hp ASh-82FNV radial engines. The aircraft had a maximum speed of 550km/h (342mph), a range

of 2,500km (1,553 miles), and was capable of carrying a bombload of 2,270kg (5,004lb). It had a fixed forward firing armament of two 20-mm cannon and two 7.62-mm machine guns. The bomber's radio operator had a single rear-facing ventral machine gun and a rear gunner had a dorsal twin machine gun mounting. Although the aircraft had a glazed underside to the nose, this was to improve the pilot's field of view downwards. The aircraft's navigator/bomb-aimer sat behind the pilot, aiming bombs through his own glazed panels in the floor.

The prototype flew on January 29, 1941, although development was constrained by the shortage of suitable engines. Development was also affected by the relocation of Department 103 from its original prison accommodation after the Nazi invasion. The type entered service in September 1942 but production was initially slow. It was outnumbered by older bomber types for most of the war.

Production of the Tupolev Tu-2 continued until 1948 (totalling just over 3,200 aircraft). The Sukhoi design bureau was assigned the task of manufacturing the aircraft. The type was widely exported to Soviet allies (such as China) and client states (such as Poland), gaining the NATO/ASCC reporting name 'Bat'.

The Tupolev Tu-2 remained in widespread service into the 1950s (with small numbers lingering into the 1960s in second-line roles). The aircraft saw active service in the Korean War. The Tupolev Tu-6, a high-altitude reconnaissance version of the Tupolev Tu-2, was also produced.

Left: The Tupolev Tu-2's glazed nose was provided to improve the pilot's downward/forward view, the bomb aimer sitting behind the pilot.

BOEING B-29 SUPERFORTRESS

THE BOEING B-29 Superfortress was the most sophisticated propeller-driven bomber to serve during World War II. The aircraft was the first to have compressurized compartments for its crew. In addition, the Superfortress was fitted with a range of advanced armament, propulsion and avionics systems.

USAAC attempts to obtain a truly strategic, long-range bomber began during the 1930s, with the XB-15. This aircraft eventually proved to be something of a false start. There were destined to be further 'dead-ends' before the USAAF finally obtained such an aircraft.

The Douglas XB-19 marked another false-start. It originated in a secret requirement (Project D) for an experimental long-range bomber. This was designed to be a proof-of-concept aircraft for advanced technology, rather than the prototype of a production military aircraft.

The aircraft was originally designated XBLR-2, while a competing Sikorsky design was assigned the XBLR-3 designation. Both aircraft were built in mock-up form, after which the Army ordered a flying prototype of the Douglas aircraft. Development was slow due mainly to funding constraints, and the concept became progressively more out-dated. The technology it had promised to pioneer appeared on other aircraft. Douglas even recommended the aircraft's cancellation. In May 1941 the XB-19 was finally completed after being removed from the Army's list of

secret projects in 1940. The aircraft weighed 162,000-lb (73,483-kg) and had a 212-ft (64.6-m) wingspan. It could carry a maximum bombload of 37,100lbs (16,828kg). This included eight 2,000-lb (907-kg) bombs in the internal bomb bay, and a further ten more underwing!

The XB-19's 16-man crew (and if carried, an additional two flight mechanics and six relief crew members) could protect themselves with 13 guns, including two 37-mm cannon and five 0.50 cal machine guns. The aircraft was originally intended to be powered by four 1,600hp Allison XV-3420-1 24-cylinder liquid-cooled engines. These were replaced, however, by four 2,000hp Wright R-3350 air-cooled radials.

The aircraft finally flew on June 27, 1941. It was sold to the Army a year later, for $1,400,064, although it had cost nearly $4,000,000 to build.

The XB-19 was later re-engined with four 2,600hp Allison V-3420-11 turbo-supercharged twenty-four cylinder liquid-cooled engines (the originally intended powerplant). This was converted to cargo configuration as the XB-19A. In this form the aircraft reached a maximum speed of 275mph (442km/h), and provided

Right: *'Fifi' is the world's sole surviving airworthy B-29, and is operated by the US-based Confederate Air Force.*

Following page: *The B-29 was arguably the most modern bomber of the World War II, with its pressurized fuselage and remotely operated gun turrets.*

Left: *Fleets of B-29s pounded the Japanese by day and night, operating from the Marianas, Guam, Tinian and Saipan.*
Below: *B-29s had a tricycle undercarriage rather than the B-17's old-fashioned tailwheel. The B-29 was the most advanced propeller-driven bomber in World War II.*

extremely useful lessons to the B-29 and B-36 design teams. The XB-19A was eventually retired to Davis-Monthan Air Force Base, Arizona, on August 17, 1946, for storage, where it was scrapped three years later. The XB-19 remained the largest US aircraft built until 1946, when the Convair B-36 finally emerged.

By the time the XB-19 made its final landing at Davis-Monthan the USAAF had a fleet of long-range bombers. Two of these had dropped the atomic bombs on Hiroshima and Nagasaki that finally brought the war to a close. This was the culmination of an island-hopping campaign whose primary purpose was to seize bases for the long-range bombers which then battered Japan into submission.

The new bomber resulted from a USAAC specification issued on January 29, 1940. This called for a long-range bomber capable of carrying a 2,000-lb (907-kg) bombload over a range of 5,333 miles

(8,582km). This saw study contracts being placed with Boeing for the XB-29, Consolidated for the XB-32, Douglas for the XB-31 and Lockheed for the XB-30. Two XB-29 and two XB-32 prototypes were ordered in August 1940.

The Boeing B-29 was a considerably smaller aircraft than the XB-19, but was rather more modern. The aircraft represented the practical limit of the technology of the day. This allowed its development to be remarkably swift and relatively trouble free.

The prototype made its maiden flight on September 21, 1942. Pre-production YB-29s were delivered to

GROUND CREW
T/SGT. HARRY L. TEMPLE
SGT. JAMES B. KEITH
SGT. JOE L. BRADLEY
CPL. JAMES T. BRADBERRY
CPL. WILBER V. EGELSTON

ARMORERS

CPL. FRANCIS J. DAMATO
CPL. GEORGE L. STRIEBING
S/SGT. TED S. RUTKOWSKI

BETTY

40K

the USAAF in July 1943, while production aircraft arrived in the Pacific in April 1944. Eventually, Boeing B-29s operated from five bases in the Marianas Islands, two on Guam and Tinian, and one on Saipan. This gave them a 3,000-mile (4,827-km) trip to their Japanese targets, including Tokyo from November 1944. Poor weather forced a change of tactics in March 1945, when B-29s began making maximum effort incendiary raids on enemy cities by night. They attacked from altitudes of only 6,000-8,000ft (1,828–2,438km), and carried much larger bombloads. These reduced Japan's industrial cities to ruins, while suffering remarkably low loss rates.

Vast numbers of B-29s were placed in storage at the end of World War II. The B-29s that remained flying formed part of the Strategic Air Command and were reclassified as medium bombers by 1950.

Some of these aircraft served in the Korean War, using a range of weapons. These included very large 12,000-lb (5,433-kg) Tarzon bombs which were used against bridges and similar targets. The B-29 was rapidly retired from service at the end of the Korean War. The USAF's last B-29 bombers had been replaced by B-47s by 1954. Some aircraft, however, were converted to continue serving in specialized missions. These included flight-refuelling, weather reconnaissance, radar evaluation and towing.

The United States built 3,970 B-29s (2,766 being built by Boeing itself, 668 by Bell and 536 by Martin). Small numbers went to Britain under the designation Boeing Washington B.Mk 1. Larger numbers were illicitly copied (reverse-engineered from aircraft which force-landed in Russia) as the Tupolev Tu-4—the Soviet's first modern strategic bomber.

Left: *'Sentimental Journey' flew with the 330th Bomb Group and ended her days in the Pima Air and Space Museum, Tucson.*

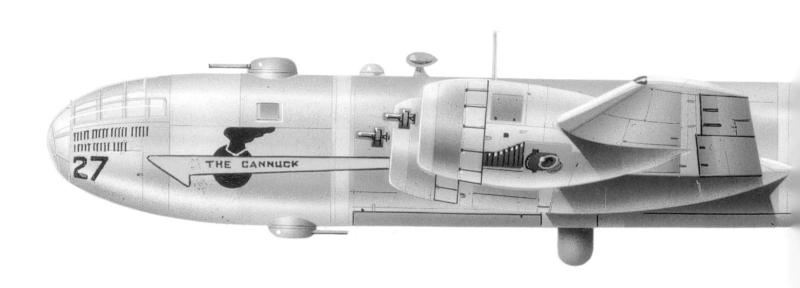

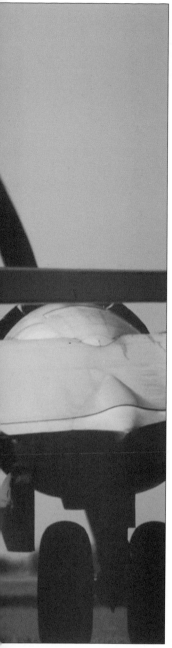

Left and Above: *The Confederate Air Force's B-29 was discovered as a gunnery target at the Naval Weapons Center at China Lake in 1971, and was restored to fly before being ferried to the CAF's Harlingen home in Texas. Full restoration took until 1974.*
Below: *This B-29A flew with the 500th Bomb Group, part of the 73rd Bomb Wing during 1945.*

ARADO AR 234

THE WORLD'S FIRST purpose-built jet bomber was the deceptively modern Arado Ar 234. The aircraft was of broadly conventional configuration. It not only had a pair of axial-flow Jumo 004 jet engines but some also had a pilot's ejection seat. All had a pressurized cabin, and also had a sophisticated bombing computer. The Ar 234 reconnaissance versions also had a primitive three-axis navigation system.

The Arado jet bomber had a simple, unswept wing. The aircraft was fitted with engines that were the same as those which powered the rather smaller and lighter Me 262. The Ar 234 was, nevertheless, extremely clean, aerodynamically, and had breathtaking performance. It also proved simple to produce and relatively easy to fly, with much better single-engine handling than the Me 262.

The Ar 234 was originally developed without an undercarriage, taking off on a jettisonable trolley and landing with the aid of retractable skids. Only two of the 20 prototypes ordered initially between April 1942 and February 1943 were specified with a retractable conventional undercarriage. The resulting 'skidded' Ar 234A was not ordered, however, and a second batch of 20 Ar 234 prototypes with wheeled undercarriages were ordered in June 1943.

The first Ar 234 flew on July 30, 1943, and the first aircraft with a retractable undercarriage followed on March 12, 1944. This was the ninth

Left: *Despite the Arado Ar 234's engine life and reliability being an Achilles heel, the innovative aircraft was an operationally effective jet bomber.*

Ar 234 prototype, and formed the basis of the production Ar 234B. The first pre-production Ar 234 flew on June 8, 1944, and the type was delivered to KG 76 soon afterwards.

The Ar 234B-1 reconnaissance aircraft began flying high altitude missions over Britain and Italy in September 1944. The aircraft's top speed of 764km/h (475mph) and a ceiling of 10,000m (32,810ft), made it virtually immune to interception. It also carried enough fuel to give it a formidable radius of action.

The Ar 234B-1 version, carrying three 500-kg (1,102-lb) bombs, or a single 1400-kg (3,086-lb) weapon, followed in November 1944. This version arrived just in time to take part in the Battle of the Bulge (December 1944–January 1945).

The type was used in a series of successful attacks against Allied advances across the Rhine bridges at Remagen, west central Germany. The aircraft proved almost invulnerable except when returning to its bases to land, when small numbers were successfully 'bounced' by prowling Allied fighters.

A total of 210 production Ar 234B-1s and B-2s were built, before production switched to the four-engined Ar-234C. Fortunately for the Allies, only 14 Ar 234Cs were built. Other advanced derivatives of the Ar 234 taking shape on the drawing board, or in Arado's experimental workshop, remained unbuilt.

Allied pilots who sampled the Arado Ar 234 postwar were astonished by the aircraft, and most rated it very highly indeed. Fortunately it arrived in service too late to make a difference to the course of the war.

DOUGLAS A-26/B-26 INVADER

THE SUCCESS OF the Douglas DB-7 Havoc/Boston prompted the company to develop the larger XA-26 as a potential successor. The prototype contract was placed in June 1941 and the first prototype made its maiden flight on July 10, 1942. This aircraft carried approximately twice the bombload required by the original specification and exceeded all performance guarantees.

The type was ordered into production in two distinct forms. The A-26A had a solid 'cannon nose', while the A-26B had a glazed nose and reduced gun armament.

The Invader first saw active service on November 19, 1944 with the Ninth Air Force in Europe. Invaders later joined the closing stages of the fighting in the Pacific theater. In service, the two variants often operated together, with the A-26Cs (often also equipped with bombing radar) operating as 'lead ships'.

Unfortunately, however, deliveries of the type were very slow, prompting General Henry Arnold, Commanding General USAAF, to exclaim that he wanted the A-26 "for this war, not the next". His wish was not really fulfilled, though, and the type played a relatively minor role in World War II. The aircraft was, however, retained to form the backbone of the USAF's peacetime light bomber squadrons

Once the Marauder was retired after 1945, the Invader was re-designated as the B-26, and saw extensive service in the Korean War. The aircraft was used by the ANG after its withdrawal from regular units. The final B-26B

bombers were withdrawn from the Virginia ANG in 1958, after which the Invader was relegated to transport, target towing and hack duties. Large numbers of Invaders were also exported to Brazil, Chile, Colombia, Cuba, France, Guatemala, Honduras, Indonesia, Laos, Nicaragua, Peru, Portugal, Saudi Arabia and Turkey. They saw active service in Indochina, Algeria, Portugal's African colonies and in the Bay of Pigs fiasco in Cuba.

Invaders remained in use in second-line roles into the 1960s, when the type gained an unexpected new lease of life in a frontline role. The aircraft was finally used by the US Air Force in another war, this time in Vietnam. Small numbers of B-26s were reintroduced into squadron service in 1961. Some of these were used in Project Mill Pond (based in Thailand), ostensibly in Laotian service, but flown by seconded USAF aircrew. Further B-26Bs were used for Project Farm Gate, ostensibly providing training for Vietnamese forces, but actually used against infiltrators from the North. The B-26 was withdrawn from combat in 1964, following a spate of fatigue-related accidents. The aircraft's unique capabilities, however, were soon missed, and the decision was taken to refurbish and upgrade further B-26s to a new standard.

In the United States, a number of B-26s remained in use, the last being

Right: *The Invader played a major role in the Korean War, mainly operating in the night intruder role, for which many were painted black overall.*

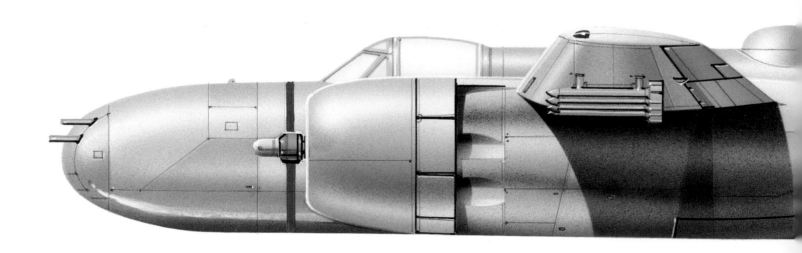

Left: *This A-26B Invader, 'Sugarland Express' spent its working life as a trainer, but now flies with the Scandinavian Historic flight in quasi-wartime Ninth Air Force markings.*

Below: *This A-26 flew with the 319th Bomb Group from Okinawa at the end of World War II. The unit was known as the 'Big Tail Birds', or 'Colonel Randy's Flying Circus'.*

Left: *Invaders served with glazed nosecones, as seen here, and with solid noses containing eight forward firing machine guns. This warbird wears wartime 319th Bomb Group markings.*
Above: *This civilian-owned B-26 was converted to executive transport configuration, but has since been modified to resemble a military aircraft, at least externally.*
Below: *This B-26B flew with the 3rd Bomb Group (Light) during the Korean War, operating mainly from Iwakuni.*

Right, top: *The Invader fought in three major wars—World War II, Korea and Vietnam—and in countless other conflicts.*
Right, below: *The sleek A-26 Invader combined high performance with a heavy warload, and in foreign service several served into the 1970s.*

three VIP-configured aircraft assigned to the ANG headquarters. These were retired between November 1969 and October 1972.

On Mark Engineering eventually converted more than 70 Invaders to B-26K Counter-Invader standards. These had more powerful R-2800-103W engines driving massive paddle blade propellers and wingtip fuel tanks. The aircraft's improved load carrying and short-field performance allowed up to 14 guns to be carried. The first B-26K made its maiden flight in February 1963. The type was subsequently re-designated as the A-26A. The new version had interchangeable solid and glazed noses, allowing the aircraft to be re-configured for particular missions. With its long endurance and heavy warload, the B-26K was well suited to operations in Vietnam. Its piston engined configuration allowed it to operate from primitively equipped bases while appearing not to represent a major escalation by the United States. The aircraft were used mainly for interdiction of enemy vehicles using the Ho Chi Minh Trail, especially at night, until being withdrawn from use in late 1969 and January 1970. Invaders were subsequently used as trainers, transports and drone launchers/controllers. Small numbers of B-26Ks were also used by the CIA in a number of operations, including deployments to the Congo.

Brazil and Peru finally retired their last Invaders in 1975, while Chile (which had relegated the type to second-line duties in 1974) and Nicaragua followed suit in 1979. Portugal retired its last Invaders in 1975, and the type was retired in Indonesia in 1977. The last Invader in military use was probably a sole aircraft used by Honduras until 1982. Invaders remain in use as fire-bombers, and as warbirds.

Left: *The Invader kept being retired from frontline US service and then returned to active duty. It finally retired in 1972.*

AVRO LINCOLN

THE AVRO LINCOLN was originally developed as the Lancaster B.Mk IV (with Rolls Royce built Merlin 85 engines) or the B.Mk V (with US Packard-built Merlin 68s). It was a direct derivative of the Lancaster, with increased span, higher aspect ratio wings, a lengthened fuselage, improved armament, increased fuel capacity and higher take-off weights. Although its high wing, slab-sided fuselage and tailwheel undercarriage gave it an anachronistic air, the Lincoln was in some respects more effective than the sleek, streamlined and pressurized Boeing B-29. The aircraft had more modern armament, also better bombing accuracy, and with only a 15mph (24km/h) difference in cruising speed. The Lincoln, although just too late to see service in World War II, did replace the Lancaster in Bomber Command as planned. It equipped 23 frontline bomber squadrons and a plethora of signals, training and reconnaissance units. Plans for Canadian production of the Lincoln were cancelled at the end of World War II, after the completion of a single aircraft.

The Lincoln prototype made its maiden flight on June 9, 1944. Some were delivered to No.57 Squadron for service trials in August 1945, with full squadron service beginning in early 1946. Some Lincolns were replaced by Washingtons from June 1950, and others by Canberras from May 1951. The Washington proved disappointing in service, and costly and difficult to maintain. It was out-lasted by the Lincoln. Some of the type served well into the jet age, until finally giving way to the Valiant. The Canberra naturally marked a considerable improvement over the ageing Lincoln, but lacked the older type's ability to carry very large and outsize weapons. This included the 12,000-lb (5,443-kg) Tallboy, which equipped a single Lincoln squadron between 1948 and 1950. It was thereafter retained as a 'contingency' capability. The Lincoln also proved ideally suited for deployed, out-of-area operations. It saw extensive use in a latter-day 'Colonial Policing' and anti-insurgency role during Kenya's Mau Mau rebellion, in Malaya and Aden.

The RAF's last Lincoln bombers were phased out of service in 1957. The type remained in service with the RAAF in the bomber role until 1958, and in the maritime patrol/ASW role until 1963. Australia received 73 Lincolns, the first five being locally assembled from kits supplied by Avro. The remainder were manufactured in Australia 'from scratch'. The final 12 were completed as dedicated MR aircraft, with a stretched forward fuselage and relevant mission equipment. The last RAF Lincolns served in the signals role until March 1963, when they were also retired. This did not mark the type's final retirement as Argentina had received 30 Lincolns from 1947. The last of these remained in operational use until January 1968.

Left: *This Avro Lincoln wears the white topsides originally intended for use by 'Tiger Force' aircraft for the planned invasion of Japan.*

Following page: *A RAAF Lincoln B.Mk 30 drops 1,000-lb (453-kg) bombs on terrorist targets in Malaya. The type remained in RAAF service in the bomber role until 1958.*

CONVAIR B-36

WHEN THE XB-36 prototype made its maiden flight on August 8, 1946, it was the world's largest and heaviest aircraft, and was the United States' first truly intercontinental bomber. The aircraft was capable of carrying a 10,000-lb (4,536-kg) bombload from bases in the United States to European targets, and then return home, all without inflight refuelling. Over shorter ranges, the Convair B-36 could carry much heavier loads with a maximum of 84,000lb (38,102kg) in four weapons' bays in later versions.

The YB-36 production prototype first flew on December 4, 1947. The YB-36 was followed by the initial production version, the B-36A. Convair produced 22 of these aircraft, initially without any armament and intended for training and familiarization.

The Convair B-36, quite apart from its sheer size, was an impressive aircraft, with six 3,500hp Pratt and Whitney R-4360-41 engines buried in the wings and driving enormous pusher airscrews. On later versions, these were augmented by four podded underwing J47 turbojet engines. The aircraft could reach a top speed of 381kts, cruising at 340kts and reaching a service ceiling of 39,900ft (12,161m). The forward and aft pressurized cabins of the B-36 were linked by an 80ft (24m) trolley tunnel over the weapons bays. The aircraft had eight remotely controlled gun turrets, six of them retractable.

The aircraft, sometimes known as the 'Peacemaker', was used primarily in the long-range nuclear bombing role. Convair also made a dedicated reconnaissance version known as the RB-36. At one time, it had been planned that the B-36 would be able to carry its own escort fighter in the shape of an XF-85 Goblin, trapeze mounted and semi-recessed into one bomb bay. This project was eventually abandoned, although some GRB-36D and GRB-36J reconnaissance aircraft were equipped to carry a RF-84K Thunderflash reconnaissance fighter. These aircraft entered service with the 99th Strategic Reconnaissance Wing. Use of the RF-84s allowed the USAF to stretch the range of its RB-36 by 2,000 miles (3,218km), or to penetrate more heavily defended airspace.

Convair produced a total of 325 B-36s. Production of the Convair B-36 ended in August 1954 after a service life of 11 years. The last of these aircraft were eventually retired in February 1959, after a career dogged by technical problems, but extended due to delays with the Boeing B-52.

The Convair B-36 formed the basis of the one-off C-99 transport aircraft, and the YB-60. This married a swept wing and tail surfaces (and eight J57 turbojets) to the fuselage of a B-36D. Two YB-60 prototypes were built. The first of these aircraft flew on March 15, 1951, but the type offered no improvement over the Boeing B-52. As a result the YB-60 was not ordered into production.

Right: *The B-36 was the world's first truly intercontinental bomber, with the ability to carry a 10,000-lb (4,536-kg) payload from the United States to Europe and back.*
Following page: *The one off XB-36 prototype had a simple, airliner-type flight deck rather than the production aircraft's raised cockpit.*

Left: *This Peacemaker was built as a B-36A, but was later converted to RB-36E standards, with a strategic reconnaissance fit and underwing jet engines.*
Below: *With Arctic red panels on its tail unit and outer wings, this B-36B shows the massive size and sheer brute power of the type.*

NORTH AMERICAN B-45 TORNADO

THE USAF's FIRST jet bomber, the B-45, was designed to meet a 1944 requirement for a jet bomber. It married an entirely conservative airframe with four 4,000-lb (1,814-kg) st J35 turbojets mounted in pairs in pods below the unswept, plank-like wing. With a relatively 'draggy' airframe, the B-45 was in some respects rather less modern than the wartime Arado Ar 234. The aircraft was capable of carrying a 22,000-lb (9,979-kg) bombload, albeit only over relatively short ranges. It was selected for production in preference to the rival Convair XB-46. The first of three XB-45 prototypes made its maiden flight on March 17, 1945.

Some 96 production B-45As were built, before production switched to the B-45C, ten of which were produced as bombers. A further 33 were produced as reconnaissance aircraft, with a camera bay replacing the usual glazed nose, and with provision for water injection or JATO gear. A proposed B-45B would have introduced new radar and fire-control systems, but never reached production. The C Models introduced 5,200-lb (2,358-kg) J47 engines, and were capable of reaching a speed of 503kts, although the type remained underpowered. All versions could be fitted with large wingtip tanks. Its range

Left: This aircraft was the first of ten B-45Cs, with wingtip fuel tanks and reheated engines. Its radar nose identifies it as an RB-45C reconnaissance aircraft.
Following page: *A B-45 takes off from Edwards Air Force Base, California.*

remained unimpressive, although the Cs also had inflight refuelling capability. All versions had a four-man crew, including a tail gunner.

The B-45 was severely handicapped by its unreliability and unserviceability, with structural problems, and engines which had a seven-and-a-half hour time between overhauls. It also had inadequate bombsights and unreliable radar bombing equipment. Plans to deploy the type to the Far East had to be cancelled due to insufficient range to reach Hawaii (the natural first refuelling stop). They could not practically be transported by sea because of their wingspan. Subsequent plans to deploy the B-45 to Britain for use in the tactical strike role were also frustrated, as the type's bomb bay was too small for the early nuclear bombs.

Some 55 North American B-45s were converted to carry the next generation of atomic bombs under the *Backbreaker* program from May 1952. These aircraft equipped four USAFE squadrons until 1958.

RB-45s were used for a number of important Cold War reconnaissance missions. They included operations flown from RAF Sculthorpe in eastern England. Each of them involved three USAF RB-45s, crewed by RAF officers and painted in British markings. These penetrated Soviet airspace and flew radar reconnaissance profiles against likely targets for USAF and RAF nuclear bombers, preparing radar maps for targeting use. The RB-45, however was never officially used by the RAF. The missions are still surrounded by secrecy.

ILYUSHIN IL-28

THE Il-28 was the Soviet Union's first in-service jet bomber, and was often called the 'Soviet Canberra'. The aircraft was Ilyushin's second jet-bomber, following the company's four-engined Il-22 prototype. The Il-28 was a smaller aircraft, powered by a pair of Rolls Royce Nene engines (or the Soviet-built Klimov VK-1A equivalent). The Soviet Air Force's insistence, however, on having a rear gun turret and 500-kg (1,102-lb) of armor forced Ilyushin to design a larger aircraft than the company might have wished.

The type emerged with an unusual wing, whose straight leading edge and tapered trailing edge made it look almost forward-swept, but with swept tail surfaces. The pilot sat high in the fuselage, and the navigator/bomb-aimer in front in the heavily glazed nose. The tail gunner sat in a separate pressurized rear compartment controlling two NR-23 cannon which augmented the fixed, forward-firing NS-23 23-mm cannon.

The prototype made its maiden flight on July 8, 1948. The type was evaluated (by randomly chosen front-line air force crews) against the rival Tu-73. Stalin ordered 50 Il-28s to be ready to fly in the 1950 May Day parade. Over 1,959 were built by two factories between 1950 and 1955. These included some dual-controlled trainers, dedicated Il-28T torpedo bombers, Il-28R reconnaissance aircraft, Il-28RT, RTR and REB EW/ECM aircraft, and Il-28D nuclear strike aircraft, with all guns removed. The trainer version received the ASCC reporting name 'Mascot', while operational versions were called 'Beagles'.

Conversions included the Il-28ZA meteorological version, the Il-28P transport and the Il-28B target tug. Il-28s were delivered to a number of Soviet allies and client states. China received some 500 Il-28s before the Sino-Soviet split of the early 1960s, and then reverse-engineered the type to produce an unlicensed copy. They went on to build some 2,000 of these Il-28 clones as the Harbin H-5 (B-5 for export) between 1966 and the mid-1980s. Small numbers remain in use as bombers in China, and for reconnaissance and target towing in Romania.

The Il-28 formed the basis of the swept-wing Il-30, and the enlarged Il-46, neither of which entered production. The rival three-engined Tu-73 was not selected for production, but did form the basis of the Tu-14.

Right: *The Il-28 was the first Soviet jet bomber in service, and was powered by Soviet-built Nene engines.*
Below: *The Ilyushin Il-28U 'Mascot' was a dedicated trainer.*

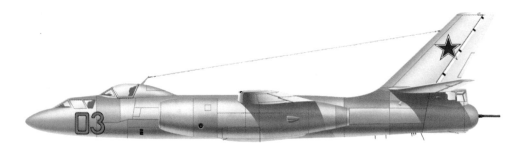

ENGLISH ELECTRIC CANBERRA

THE CANBERRA WAS not the world's first jet bomber, but it was arguably the best of the early jets. Despite the type's conventional appearance, it combined breathtaking performance (few fighters of the day could reach its lofty ceiling, or even catch it), with superb handling, and great reliability.

The Canberra was designed by 'Teddy' Petter, who was previously responsible for the Westland Lysander and Whirlwind, and later for the Lightning and the Folland Gnat. The aircraft was derived from studies for a jet-powered, ground-attack aircraft to succeed aircraft like the Typhoon. It was actually submitted to fulfill an RAF requirement for a new high-speed, high-altitude bomber to replace the Mosquito. Initially conceived as a single-engined aircraft, the English Electric A1 evolved, first with two engines buried in the wing root, and then with wing-mounted nacelles at roughly $1/3$ span. This would allow easy substitution of alternative power-plants, in case Rolls Royce's new Avon failed to live up to expectations.

The Canberra was intended to bomb entirely by radar. The necessary black boxes, however, failed to materialize. Although the four prototypes had solid noses, the production B.Mk 2 reverted to a visual bomb-aiming position in a transparent nose cone.

The prototype made its maiden

Left: *The English Electric Canberra B.Mk 6 introduced integral fuel tanks in the wings and more powerful engines.*

flight on May 13, 1949, and the type entered service with No.101 Squadron at RAF Binbrook, eastern England, in May 1951. The Canberra replaced Lancasters, Lincolns and Mosquitos with RAF Bomber Command, equipping a peak total of 23 home-based squadrons. The last Canberras were withdrawn in September 1961, having played a crucial role in maintaining the deterrent, and deploying for combat operations in Kenya, Malaysia and the Suez operation. The original B.Mk 2 was augmented from 1954 by the B.Mk 6, with more powerful engines and increased fuel capacity. The Canberra's superb high-altitude performance kept it viable for decades, while its aerobatic capabilities and agility made it a joy to fly. It was a difficult target for fighters even at lower altitudes.

A 10-year frontline career was eminently respectable by the standards of the day, but the Canberra's operational life was far from over. As the new V-Bombers were introduced, 'surplus' Canberras were 'freed up' for service overseas. These aircraft served with RAF Germany (where a nuclear strike wing formed in 1954), the Middle East and Far East. For overseas service, the B.Mk 6 formed the basis of the B.Mk 15 and B.Mk 16. This had new avionics and weapons, including rocket pods and Nord AS 30 ASMs. These versions remained in frontline RAF service until 1970.

For service in RAF Germany, English Electric developed a dedicated interdictor/strike version. This had a new fighter-type offset cockpit for the

pilot. There was also provision for a gun pack (containing four 20–mm cannon and 525 rounds per gun— enough for 50 seconds firing!) in the rear part of the bomb bay. This new version, the B(I).Mk 8 equipped three squadrons, with another unit receiving B.Mk 6s converted to a similar armament configuration. These Canberra interdictors served from January 1956 until June 1972, when the RAF finally retired its Canberras from the bomber role. Their cannon armament was little used (except on annual armament practice camps). The aircraft (like

those based on Cyprus) were primarily assigned a nuclear strike role, delivering US nuclear weapons in LABS (toss-bombing) and lay-down profiles.

Canberras were also adapted for a host of second-line roles. Dedicated reconnaissance variants would serve on in the frontline until 1982, and thereafter gradually adopted a primary survey role. In second-line EW, Elint, and target facilities roles, RAF Canberras played an important part in training a pool of pilots. These men had narrowly 'failed to make the grade' for frontline fast jets when they

went through training on the Gnat and Hawk. After a tour on the Canberra, many were able to complete fast jet training, and become productive pilots on the Harrier, Jaguar, Lightning and Tornado.

The Canberra enjoyed considerable export success. New-build and refurbished bomber versions were delivered to Argentina, Australia, Ecuador, Ethiopia, New Zealand, Peru, Rhodesia, South Africa, India, and Venezuela. Other versions went to Chile, France, Germany and Sweden. With these overseas customers, the

Canberra bomber remained operational for many years. They fought with distinction in southern Africa, Latin America (including the Falklands War in 1982) and Vietnam.

License built in Australia, the Canberra also enjoyed the unusual distinction of being operated by the USAF, and built under license (in modified form) as the Martin B-57. The B-57 was used in the tactical light bomber role in Europe during the 1950s and 1960s. It then saw intensive service in Vietnam in the interdictor role, with the USAF and VNAF. The

Left: *The English Electric Canberra PR.Mk 9 remained in service with the RAF's No.39 Squadron well into the new millenium.*
Below: *The Canberra became a useful engine testbed, and some of these testbed aircraft set new world records. The Canberra enjoyed considerable export success across the world.*
Following page: *English Electric Canberra B.Mk 6s of No.s 109 and 139 Squadrons from RAF Hemswell during 1955. The aircraft are fitted with Blue Shadow SLAR.*

Above, left: *This Canberra B.Mk 2 wears the markings of a fighter unit, No.56 Squadron, who used this aircraft for target towing.*

Above, right: *The Canberra B(I).Mk 8 served in the interdictor and strike roles until 1972 with the RAF, and proved popular with export customers.*

Bottom, right *This Argentinian Canberra was a refurbished B.Mk 2. Argentina's Canberras fought against the British in the Falklands War.*

US B-57 served on into the 1980s in second-line and support roles. B-57s were also exported to Pakistan, which ironically used them operationally against India—an operator of the British-built Canberra. NASA retains two long-winged RB-57Fs for upper atmosphere research and trials duties to this day.

Remarkably, the Canberra remains in service today, 53 years after the prototype made its maiden flight. About a dozen remain in service in Peru, still operating in the bomber role. Some 12 more reconnaissance aircraft form the backbone of India's strategic reconnaissance capability. Canberras also remain active in Britain, with five frontline reconnaissance aircraft. These were heavily committed to operations over Afghanistan during 2001-02. A pair of trainers, and two target tug/drone launchers operate with Qinetiq, the former Defence Evaluation Research Agency.

The Royal Air Force's Canberra PR.Mk 9s have been comprehensively modernized and upgraded. Today the Canberras fly with a sophisticated

Opposite, top: *Four United States Air Force Canberras over France. The USAF procured the type as the B-57, built under license by Martin.*
Left: *The General Dynamics-built RB-57F was an extensively redesigned high altitude reconnaissance version.*
Below: *The basic B-57B was extensively used by the United States Air Force in the Vietnam War. The aircraft featured a new tandem cockpit, redesigned airbrakes and a rotating bomb bay.*

electro-optical reconnaissance system similar to that used by USAF U-2s. In operations over Afghanistan, the Canberras proved to be the most useful reconnaissance aircraft available to allied force commanders—quite a tribute to a 53-year-old aircraft! To put this in perspective, to rival the Canberras achievements, the de Havilland Mosquito would have had to have remained in frontline service as a bomber until 1980. It would also have still been in use in the reconnaissance role in 1994!

BOEING B-47

THE BOEING B-47 Stratojet was a six-engined medium bomber. The aircraft, although over-shadowed by the later, larger, longer-serving B-52, was built in much larger numbers (2,042 as against 744 B-52s). In many ways it was a more important aircraft, historically, equipping 36 frontline Bomb Wings.

The aircraft introduced the swept wing and underwing podded engines which characterized Boeing's later bombers and airliners. The B-47 also featured a fighter-type cockpit with pilot and co-pilot in tandem under a 'bubble' canopy (the navigator bombardier sat further forward, in the nose). The type had a tandem 'bicycle-type' undercarriage, and outriggers in the inner nacelles. The aircraft thus ushered in a new era of aerodynamic and airframe design. Interestingly, early XB-47 studies featured a straight wing. A swept wing was added only as a result of studying German research findings that were captured at the end of World War II.

There were two prototypes built with the first making its maiden flight on December 17, 1947. The first production order was then placed in September 1948.

The Boeing B-47 was sized around a massive bomb bay due to the size of early nuclear weapons. This bay could also accommodate conventional weapons of up to 22,000lb (9,979kg) in weight! Furthermore, the aircraft dispensed with manned defensive gun positions. It retained only a pair of machine guns in the tailcone, which could be aimed and fired automatically using a built-in radar, or from the pilot's cockpit.

Production of the Boeing B-47 was accorded a very high priority, and the type was built by Lockheed (395) and Douglas (274). The main production version was the B-47E. This version had 20-mm cannon in the tail instead of 0.50 cal machine guns, more powerful engines with water injection, ejection seats for the crew and strengthened structure to allow operation at higher weights. The B-47E also introduced the 'Chrome Dome' color scheme, with highly reflective glossy white undersides. These were designed to reflect the heat and radiation of a nuclear 'flash'.

Following the switch to low level operations, many B-47E versions were refurbished and modified under Project Milk Bottle. This allowed the aircraft to penetrate at low level, and even to make toss-bombing attacks. They were re-designated as B-47E-IIs and B-47E-IVs.

There were also two dedicated reconnaissance sub-variants of the B-47E built. Some 240 RB-47Es and 15 RB-47Ks were built for long-range photographic reconnaissance duties. These versions augmented and then replaced 91 converted, interim RB-47Bs. A further 35 new-build RB-47Hs were produced for Sigint missions. Additional crew members were housed in a pressurized capsule

Right: *The B-47 was built in massive numbers, and formed the backbone of SAC's Cold War bomber fleet. The last of the bomber versions were withdrawn from use in February 1966.*

Following page: *A B-47B test aircraft carrying four Radioplane (Northrop-Ventura) GAM-67 Crossbow drones.*

Right: *The use of RATOG (Rocket Assisted Take Off Gear) was a routine part of B-47 operations. This improved the aircraft's take off performance significantly.*

in the former bomb-bay.

This small group of aircraft flew among the most dangerous missions of the Cold War. They prowled along the peripheries of the Soviet Union and its client states, recording signals traffic and radar emissions for subsequent analysis. Several were attacked and badly shot up by enemy fighters, and at least one was shot down. Other versions were produced by conversion of existing bombers. These included the EB-47E ECM platform and the weather reconnaissance WB-47E. There were also 35 EB-47L versions produced as radio relay platforms. These versions were intended to form part of any post-attack command and control network.

The Boeing B-47 had a shorter range than the intercontinental B-52. Although the B-47-equipped Bomb Wings were based in the United States, deployed 'Reflex Action' operations from bases in Alaska, Great Britain, Spain, Guam and even French North Africa became a routine part of Stratojet operations. The main B-47E variant had a brake parachute and jettisonable RATOG for improved take-off performance. This increased the range of deployment airfields which could be used by the type.

The Boeing B-47 Stratojet enjoyed only a relatively brief service career, unlike the B-52 that was destined to serve on for decades. The last of the bomber versions were withdrawn from use in February 1966. Even in the Elint role, the aircraft had been entirely replaced by the RC-135 by December 29, 1967. The weather reconnaissance WB-47 version followed during 1970. Two Navy EB-47E electronic aggressor aircraft, and a single RB-47H used for test and trials duties at Eglin AFB were retired during 1977.

TUPOLEV TU-16

THE TUPOLEV Tu-16 was always over-shadowed by the longer-range, more 'glamourous' Tu-95 'Bear'. The 'Badger' (as NATO referred to it), however, was probably a more dangerous threat, and represented a more significant weapon in the Soviet Union's Cold War armory. It was also built in larger numbers and represented a more commercially important program for Tupolev. Not for nothing has the Tu-16 been referred to as the 'Soviet Stratojet'.

The aircraft was derived from systems and technologies copied from those B-29s which fell into Soviet hands during World War II. Although the fuselage bore some similarities to that of the B-29, the aerodynamic configuration of the new medium bomber was all-Soviet. It had a boldly swept wing and tail surfaces, and had the main undercarriage units retracting backwards into drag-reducing 'carrot fairings' on the wing trailing edge. The latter would subsequently become something of a Tupolev OKB trademark. The aircraft's fuselage was 'pinched in' in accordance with Whitcomb's area rule.

Tupolev had initially hoped to build a long-range bomber. It was intended to combine the bombload and range of the Tu-4 (Russia's illicit B-29 clone) with the performance of the new jet-engined light bombers. Even as these studies were underway, Josef Stalin ordered Tupolev to produce just such an aircraft.

Left: *A US Navy F-4 escorts a prowling Soviet Navy Tu-16R 'Badger-E' reconnaissnace aircraft during the Cuban missile crisis.*

It soon became clear, however, that it would be impossible to produce a jet bomber with quite the same payload/range capability. While Tupolev turned to turbo-prop power for his intercontinental bomber project, he produced the Type 88 (later given the Soviet Air Forces (VVS) designation Tu-16). The Type 88 had new axial flow turbojets to meet a more modest VVS requirement.

This outlined an aircraft which could carry a 5,000-kg (11,022-lb) bombload over a radius of 2,500km (1,553 miles), or to carry a single 9000-kg (19,841-lb) FAB-9000 over a shorter range. Tupolev had the Mach 0.9 low-level speed requirement relaxed to 700km/h (434mph) to save weight. The first prototype made its maiden flight on April 27, 1952. In the event, however, the aircraft proved too heavy to meet even the relaxed specification. The second prototype aircraft was then delayed while Tupolev reduced its weight and sought more powerful engines.

The Tu-16 entered service in late 1953. The basic version was soon augmented by the Tu-16A, a dedicated atomic bomber, the maritime Tu-16M, and the reconnaissance Tu-16R. There was also the Tu-16P and Tu-16PP EW platforms, the tanker Tu-16Z and Tu-16N, the SAR-configured Tu-16S and a range of missile carrier versions. These included cruise missile launchers and dedicated anti-shipping strike variants. Some of these had a solid nose, incorporating a massive flattened radome. Others retained the standard glazed nose of the bomber version, with a missile guidance radar in the 'chin' position.

The Tu-16 remained active in the reconnaissance and ECM roles after the Tu-16 bombers and missile carriers were replaced in Soviet service by Tu-22 'Blinders' and Tu-22M 'Backfires'. These were finally retired in the mid-1990s, driven from use by the demands of new arms limitation treaties and the need to save money.

Standard bomber and missile-carrying Tu-16s were exported to Egypt, Indonesia and Iraq. In China the type was put into production as the Xian H-6 (B-6 for export). This added about 200 aircraft to the total of 1,508 aircraft in the Soviet Union. Chinese production included new missile-carrier and tanker versions, and aircraft exported to Iraq. They remain in frontline service in China. A handful of Iraqi B-6s may have survived Operation Desert Storm.

Top: *Phantom and Crusader escort a pair of Tupolev Tu-16s (one a 'Badger-E' the other an '-F' near the USS* Kitty Hawk *in January 1963. The Tu-16 was a significant weapon in the Soviet Union's Cold War armory.*
Right: *The Tupolev Tu-16RM-2 'Badger-F' was a dedicated maritime Elint platform, distinguished by its underwing ESM pods.*

BOEING B-52 STRATOFORTRESS

THERE IS A standard story, told by many Boeing B-52 pilots, that sums up the aircraft, 'The B-52, with its familiar wrinkled fuselage sides, had enough metal to make 10,000 garbage cans. The wiring in the Stratofortress is equivalent to five miles of baling wire. Its engines are as powerful as eight locomotives. And that's the way it flies, like eight locomotives, pulling ten thousand garbage cans with five miles of baling wire!' In fact the Stratofortress is something of a pilot's favorite, with good handling characteristics for such a large aircraft. Its robust and rugged structure has 'taken care' of generations of grateful aircrew.

The B-52 Stratofortress has already notched up an impressive 47-year service career, and the 94 remaining B-52Hs are destined to remain in service for many years to come. Even if the type were retiring tomorrow, this would be an almost unrivalled period of service for a combat aircraft. The B-17, in order to rival it, would needed to have stayed in frontline USAF service until 1967. But the B-52H is expected to serve until 2040, by which time the B-52 will have been in frontline service for 85 years. Individual B-52H airframes will each be between 78 and 79 years old! This is perhaps surprising. When the YB-52 prototype made its maiden flight on April 15, 1952 (before the XB-52, damaged in a ground accident) many expected the aircraft to quickly give way to much more ambitious, supersonic, long-range heavy bombers.

The pre-production B-52A first flew in 1954, and the operational B-52B model entered service in 1955. Some were delivered as dual-role RB-52Bs. The B-52C and B-52D were improved versions with increased weight and fuel, while the B-52E and F added further modifications and improvements. The B-52G was the major production model, and was further improved, and introduced wet wings, remotely-controlled tail guns and a shorter, stubbier tailfin. The final B-52H introduced new turbofan engines. The B-52G was the first model armed with a stand-off weapon (the AGM-28 Hound Dog

Right: *The Boeing B-52H Stratofortress was the most capable B-52 variant, with TF33 turbofan engines and advanced systems and avionics.*
Below: *This B-52H served with the 410th Bomb Wing during the 1970s. The Stratofortress has already served for an impressive 47 years.*

cruise missile), while the H was intended to carry the cancelled Skybolt. A total of 744 B-52s were built with the last of 102 B-52H's being delivered in October 1962.

During the 1950s and 1960s, Strategic Air Command's force of B-52s were fully committed to SIOP (the Strategic Integrated Operational Plan), as atomic bombers. They stood ready for a nuclear Armageddon (at a few moments notice, and sometimes even on 'airborne alert'). Some B-52s were used for conventional bombing missions during the Vietnam War, but even these retained their nuclear capability, and remained assigned to SAC's nuclear 'alert' commitment. During the 1970s and 1980s, the B-52Gs and B-52Hs gained new weapons. These

included SRAM, and also the AGM-86 ALCM.

Progress towards Strategic Arms Reduction during the mid- and late-1980s freed some of the USAF's 160 B-52Gs for conventional missions. These aircraft projected power over inter-continental distances, potentially allowing the USAF to mount operations in the Middle East (for example) without requiring bases in the region. The conventional B-52s were also seen as a means of hitting Soviet 'Follow On Forces' in Europe which might be beyond the range of a theater commander's tactical air power.

B-52G crews began intensive low-level training, practising 'Nap of Earth', terrain-following, flying by day, and, using NVGs, also at night.

Under Operation Rapid Shot, SAC began short-notice deployments of B-52 units to austere operating locations for conventional exercises with local commanders. They also began identifying suitable forward operating bases for the type, setting a minimum runway length of 9,000ft (2,743m). SAC mounted its first major conventional exercise (Mighty Warrior) in August 1988.

Above: *Redundant B-52s were stored at Davis Monthan in Arizona, and then were scrapped in large numbers as part of arms limitation treaties in the 1990s.*

Right: *A Boeing B-52D Stratofortress refuels in flight from a KC-135 tanker. The USAF's boom refuelling method allows very high fuel flow rates.*

Right: *This B-52D wears the black undersides which became characteristic of the type during the long involvement in Vietnam.*

Below: *This Boeing B-52G is armed with AGM-69 Short Range Attack Missiles. The first B-52 unit to become operational with the missile was the 42nd Bomb Wing.*

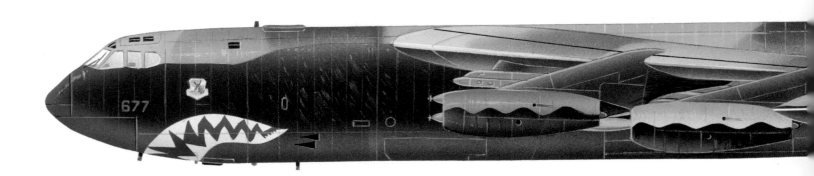

Left: *B-52Hs were extensively used in Desert Storm (as shown here) and during other recent operations.*

Above: *1,000-lb (453-kg) bombs tumble from the bomb bay of a B-52F during the Vietnam War.*

Below: *This shark-mouthed B-52D served with the 43rd Strategic Wing. The B-52D was the mainstay of SAC's contribution to the war in Vietnam.*

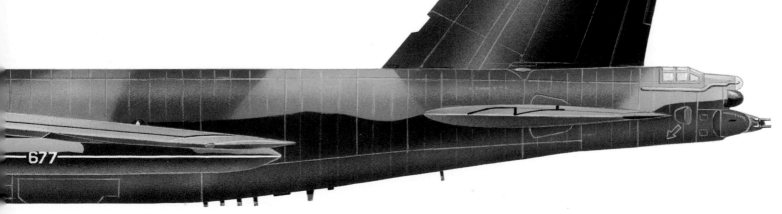

Above: *This Boeing B-52G Superfortress is seen launching a Hound Dog cruise missile, one of the first such weapons deployed by Strategic Air Command.*

Right: *The B-52G switched to conventional duties from the 1980s, following strategic arms reduction talks. The variant has seen active service in the Gulf and Afghanistan.*

For many years thereafter, the USAF operated a force of largely conventionally armed B-52Gs, and nuclear-roled B-52Hs. With the end of the Cold War, and demands for a peace dividend, the older G-models (which had less powerful, less modern turbojet engines) were retired by the end of 1994. The turbofan-powered B-52Hs took over their conventional roles. Only the B-52H remains in the inventory today, with 85 assigned to Air Combat Command and nine to the Air Force Reserves. Only 66 aircraft are officially assigned as ALCM-capable heavy bombers, the remainder being classed as in-use attrition reserves in order to conform to SALT II treaty limitations. The actual frontline force size consists of 50 'Primary Aircraft Authorized'. These aircraft have received a succession of upgrades and modifications. They have transformed their capabilities and turned them into formidable and versatile strike/attack platforms with improved all-weather attack capabilities and more accurate navigation systems. The aircraft also carry the latest precision-guided and stand-off munitions. The B-52 has an unrefuelled combat range in excess of 8,800 miles (14,161km) and this can be extended through the use of aerial refuelling. During Operation Desert Storm in 1991, B-52s attacked a variety of targets, delivering 30 percent of all the weapons dropped by coalition air forces. During the Gulf War B-52s flew the longest bomber mission in history when B-52Gs took off from Barksdale Air Force Base, Louisiana, to launch conventional air-launched cruise missiles at Iraqi targets. They returned to base after a 35-hour, nonstop combat mission. More recently, B-52s saw extensive use in Operation Enduring Freedom over Afghanistan.

Further modifications and upgrades are certain. These may still include re-engining with four underwing RB.211 turbofans. This option, examined in the late 1990s, was rejected on cost grounds. This was before it became apparent that the price of fuel would continue to rise, and when it seemed that only a small number of B-52s would be retained until 2030. The savings now promised by re-engining (with 90 or so aircraft serving an additional 10 years) could be huge.

MYASISCHEV M-4 'BISON'

THE MYASISCHEV M-4 was destined to be over-shadowed by the longer-lived, more widely built turbo-prop Tu-95, although the aircraft, (known as the 'Bison' by NATO) was probably a greater technical and technological achievement. Unfortunately, however, it was probably impossible (using the technology then available) to produce a genuinely intercontinental jet bomber. The M-4s inability to fly round-trips to US targets limited its usefulness in the eyes of the military elite. Only a few of them were built.

In March 1951 work began on what became the M-4. The type was to carry a pair of FAB-9000 9,000-kg (19,841-lb) bombs, or a variety of conventional or nuclear weapons, using radar bombing equipment. The aircraft emerged as a graceful leviathan, with anhedral wings incorporating wingtip outriggers, and a bicycle type main landing gear. The type was also expected to cruise at 700km/h (435mph) over a range of 6,500km (4,039 miles). Myasischev was ordered to get his broadly equivalent jet bomber into the air by early 1953. The first prototype made its maiden flight on January 20, 1953.

The M-4 equipped the 22nd Guards Heavy Bomber Division, comprising the 101st and 203rd Heavy Bomber Divisions, each of which had two M-4 squadrons, and one squadron of Tu-16s. The first Soviet thermonuclear bomb was tested on August 12, 1953, and was quickly sent to the M-4 force. This was later assigned to attack targets around the Great Lakes, by night. Myasischev eventually built 35 M-4s (including prototypes) but these had insufficient thrust and inadequate payload/range capability, and the type was phased out of production. These were followed by 90 3Ms. The first seven production 3Ms were powered by AM-3 engines, but introduced a zero-dihedral tailplane, a lengthened and re-profiled nose, and were accordingly assigned the new reporting name 'Bison-B'. The next 30 were designated as 3MNs and were fitted with more powerful VD-7 engines. Others had the same aerodynamic and structural features, but were powered by RD-3M-500A engines. These were designated 3MS. The 3MNs and 3MSs were built in 18 small batches. The new engines had a lower specific fuel consumption. The aircraft could carry underwing fuel tanks, so the range went up quite considerably.

There were nine 3Ms built as carriers for the K-14 cruise missile, under the designation 3MD, with a new Rubin 1 radar in a more sharply pointed solid nose. These pointed-nosed, VD-7 engined aircraft entered service as bombers, and not as missile carriers. They were assigned the NATO reporting name 'Bison C'. Some aircraft were converted as 3M-5 or 3ME missile carriers, with Rubin 1ME radar and an ECM tailcone in place of the rear turret. These versions, however, never entered service. The surviving M-4s were eventually converted to tanker configuration (principally to serve the 3M bombers).

Right: *A 3MD 'Bison-C' heads a line up of Soviet bombers.*

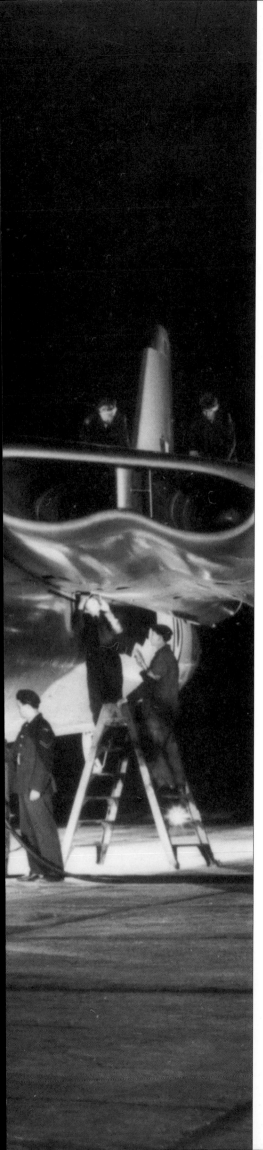

VICKERS VALIANT

THE VICKERS VALIANT was the first of the British V-bombers to enter squadron service. World War II bombers had become dated due to wartime developments. Consequently, in 1947 the Air Ministry issued a requirement for larger, longer-range four-jet bomber to enter service in the strategic role.

The designs selected to meet the requirement eventually became the Avro Vulcan and Handley Page Victor. The Short Sperrin was ordered as a deliberately more conservative 'insurance policy' against the possible failure of the more advanced designs.

Vickers had unsuccessfully submitted its Type 660 to meet the advanced bomber requirement. This rather less radical aircraft, however, was passed over in favor of the Delta-winged Avro 770 and the crescent winged Handley Page bomber. But it soon became clear that the Vickers aircraft would meet most of the requirements in the official Air Ministry specification (except range) and would be available considerably before the Avro and Handley Page designs. The aircraft was therefore ordered straight off the drawing board as an 'interim' bomber, later named as the Vickers Valiant.

The Valiant, although it lacked the space-age appearance of the Avro Vulcan and Handley Page Victor, was

a beautiful-looking and graceful aeroplane. The aircraft was surprisingly modern, similar in configuration to the Tupolev Tu-16 and had superb performance characteristics. It had a large bomb bay which was later used to accommodate a Blue Steel stand-off weapon.

A prototype Vickers Valiant made its maiden flight on May 18, 1951, and the aircraft entered service in February 1955. There were 104 production Valiants built, and these equipped a peak total of ten RAF squadrons.

The type performed the backbone of Britain's A-bomb and H-bomb trials in Australia and the South Pacific in 1956 and 1957. There were also four Valiant squadrons involved in Operation Musketeer—the Anglo-French Suez operation. Their task was to bomb Egyptian airfields and other military targets.

When the new Vulcan and Victor entered service, Valiants became available for conversion to the reconnaissance and tanker roles, equipping three specialized units. From 1961, some three squadrons of Valiants were switched to tactical nuclear strike duties in support of NATO's SACEUR (Supreme Allied Commander Europe), using US nuclear weapons under a 'dual key' arrangement.

The last 'Main Strategic Force' Valiants (using British nuclear weapons) were retired in September 1962. The tactical Valiants switched to the low level role in 1963, but serious fatigue cracks were found in many Valiants' main spars in December 1964. These fatigue crack problems are considered to have been accelerated by the stresses imposed by low level

Left: *This Wittering Wing Valiant is seen in the high speed silver finish used before the V-Force adopted overall anti-flash white.* **Following page:** *A No.214 Squadron Valiant is towed past a battery of Bloodhound SAMs at its Marham base in eastern England.*

operations. The aircraft affected were judged to be uneconomic to repair, and the type was rapidly withdrawn from service.

At one time, it seemed likely that some Valiants would be repaired, refurbished and sold (perhaps to Australia or South Africa). In the event, however, these aircraft were retired and scrapped.

Ironically, a dedicated low-level pathfinder version of the Valiant (strengthened for low level operations), the B.Mk 2, was flown in prototype form from April 11, 1952. The aircraft, however, was not selected for production. The withdrawal of the bomber Valiants had little effect on Royal Air Force readiness, since they could quickly be replaced by Mk 1 Vulcans, Victors, and also Canberras. The aircraft's withdrawal, however, did leave a gap in Britain's tanker capability which took several months to remedy.

Above: *The first Vickers Valiant prototype flew in highly polished natural metal finish, and lacked bombing radar. The prototype first flew in May 1951 and entered service in February 1955.*
Right: *The stresses of low level flight caused fatigue problems which led to the Valiant's premature retirement.*

TUPOLEV TU-95

TUPOLEV'S MIGHTY 'BEAR' became emblematic of the Soviet Union's Cold War bomber force, at least in the West. This was partly because of the aircraft's sheer size and innovative design. It was also because the Tu-95, as the Soviet Union's longest range bomber and reconnaissance platform, was the type most often encountered by Western fighter pilots, and thus the most frequently photographed.

The Tupolev Design Bureau soon realized that the Soviet Union's requirement for a jet-powered intercontinental bomber was not achievable using the technologies then available to them. They also realized that any jet bomber would be deficient in payload and/or range. Thus while the Myasischev Design Bureau manfully struggled to produce a jet-engined intercontinental bomber, Tupolev turned his attentions to a propeller-driven aircraft, the Type 95. Early studies compared aircraft with four or eight turboprop engines, both designs using a scaled-up Tu-88 configuration. This combined a conventional fuselage, with swept wings and tail surfaces very much like those of the smaller Type 88 (Tu-16) with four massive turboprop engines, driving 18ft (5.4m) diameter contra-rotating propellers. While the swept wing may have marginally reduced drag, the main advantage of the wing on the Tu-95 was to give space behind the wing spars for a capacious bomb bay. These features combined to give the new bomber jet-like performance at a fraction of the fuel burn. Even the first prototype (flown on November 10, 1952) achieved a maximum speed of 890km/h (553mph) and a maximum

range of 14,200km (8,823 miles). It also had the ability to carry a bombload of 12,000kg (26,455lb), including the huge FAB-9000 or a first generation atom bomb.

The planned service designation of Tu-20 was not used, and the Type 95 entered service in early 1956 as the Tu-95. The 31 basic Tu-95s were limited to training duties, and the 19 Tu-95Ms with more powerful engines and full operational equipment became the first aircraft to enter front-line service. The early aircraft were later brought up to the same standards. These frontline variants were augmented by a small number of Tu-95A, Tu-95MA and Tu-95V aircraft for atomic weapons testing. Two Tu-116 transports were also built.

There were two Tu-95Ms rebuilt to serve as prototype missile carriers, with a massive flat radome replacing the normal glazed nosecone. These aircraft were redesignated as Tu-95Ks. They were followed by 40 production Tu-95Ks (sometimes known as Tu-95K-20s), which entered service in August 1959. A further 25 were built as Tu-95KDs, with new avionics and inflight refuelling probes (later retrofitted to the Ks). These were known as 'Bear-Bs' to NATO.

Some 40 aircraft were built for Naval Aviation as targeting and mid-course guidance aircraft for ship- and submarine-launched missiles, under the designation Tu-95RTs. These were built between 1963 and 1965, and

Right: *The Tu-95RTs 'Bear-D' was a maritime reconnaissance and mid-course missile targeting platform, with 'Short Horn' and 'Big Bulge' radar.*

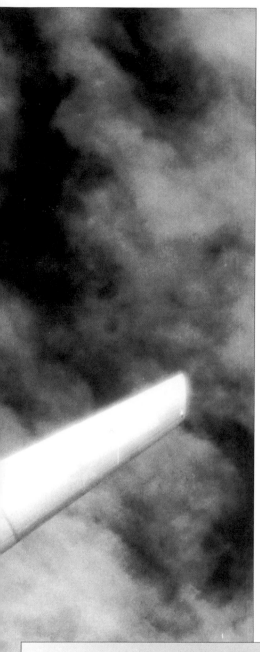

Left: *This 'Bear-D' shows off the type's innovative combination of swept wing and turboprop engines to advantage.*
Below: *The Tu-95RTs accounted for a relatively small proportion of Tu-95 production, but was frequently encountered by Allied navies and air forces.*
Following page: *The basic Tupolev Tu-95M freefall bomber was known to NATO as 'Bear-A'. This aircraft was retired to the Soviet Air Forces' Museum at Monino, near Moscow.*

were assigned the reporting name 'Bear-D' by NATO.

Tupolev Tu-95 production was stopped at Kuibyshev in 1965, when the plant switched to production of the Tu-142 ASW and maritime patrol derivative of the Tu-95 for Naval Aviation. Production of the Tu-142 (known to NATO as the 'Bear-F' or 'Bear-J') totalled about 225 aircraft in five main sub-types, all but the first 35 aircraft being built at Taganrog in southern Russia.

Most of the bomber Tu-95Ms were upgraded during the 1960s with new radar and avionics, an inflight refuelling probe and more powerful engines. Four aircraft were similarly converted as strategic reconnaissance platforms under the designation Tu-95MR ('Bear-E'), three of them with inflight refuelling probes. The Tu-95Ks and Tu-95KDs were similarly upgraded between 1965 and 1970. These became Tu-95KMs, or (in the case of those aircraft which still lacked inflight refuelling capability) Tu-95KU trainers. The KMs gained new radomes along the sides of the rear fuselage, and this led to the allocation of a new NATO ASCC reporting name of 'Bear-C'. All 65 of these first generation missile carriers were subsequently rebuilt again during the 1970s and early 1980s to carry the new supersonic Kh-22 cruise missile. The aircraft also gained new radar, weapons pylons, and even an ECM tailcone in place of the original tail turret. They were re-designated as Tu-95K-22s ('Bear-G').

During the 1980s, 33 surviving Tu-95Ms were converted to Tu-95U trainer standards, with sealed bomb bays and a red stripe around the rear fuselage. The surviving Tu-95K-22 missile carriers lost their nuclear role and were relegated to maritime patrol and conventional overland attack missions. When a new cruise missile (the Kh-55) was developed, a new version of the 'Bear' was developed to carry it. The Tu-95MS, based on the naval

Tu-142 airframe (albeit with a shortened fuselage), entered production in 1982. Some 33 were built as Tu-95MS-6s, with provision for six missiles, all carried internally, while 56 more were Tu-95MS-16s, with provision for an additional ten missiles underwing. All are now believed to carry only internal missiles.

When the START-1 treaty was signed in 1991, 147 'Bear' bombers and missile carriers were still serving with the former Soviet Air Force. These consisted of 84 Tu-95MS 'Bear-Hs', plus 63 Tu-95K-22 'Bear-G', Tu-95K/KD/KM 'Bear-B/C' and Tu-95M 'Bear-A/E' aircraft. This excluded the 37 Tu-95RTs and the AV-MF's Tu-142s. A further 11 TU-95Us were still used for conversion training and were referred to as 'Bear-Ts' following the START I treaty.

A regiment of Tu-95s remained at Uzin in the Ukraine when the USSR broke up, however, with 23 Tu-95MS, one Tu-95K and one Tu-95M aircraft. There were three Tu-95MS bombers transferred to Russia in payment for gas debts. The rest were decommissioned under the provisions of the START-1 treaty. A further 40 Tu-95MSs were based at Dolon, near Semipalatinsk, in Kazakhstan. These aircraft were all transferred to Russia.

The last 10 frontline Tu-95K-22s are believed to have been decommissioned during 1997. Some, however, may remain among the eight Tu-95s based at the LII flight-test institute at Zhukovskii in the Moscow region.

Today, Russian Tu-95 and Tu-95MS bombers are deployed at two air bases. The 121st Heavy Bomber Air Regiment (part of the 22nd Air Division) at Engels air base has 19 Tu-95MS-16s and two Tu-95MS-6s. The 73rd Heavy Bomber Air Division at Svobodny, in the Amur region near the Chinese border, has 16 Tu-95MS-16s and 26 Tu-95MS-6s.

The Tu-95MS is expected to remain operational until 2010–2015. No replacement, however, has been nominated, and the type may serve even longer. Russia is now believed to be working on a new air-to-surface missile to replace the existing Kh-55, and this could be used as the centrepiece of a new 'Bear' upgrade.

Above: *A Soviet Tu-95MS 'Bear-H'. This is the only bomber version still in service with the Russian Air Force.*
Right: *The Tu-95K-20 'Bear-B' was a dedicated missile carrier, armed with the massive AS-3 'Kangaroo' cruise missile.*

McDONNELL DOUGLAS A-4 SKYHAWK

THE DOUGLAS A4D was developed as a replacement for the US Navy's AD1 Skyraider and was optimized for the carrierborne nuclear strike/attack role. The Skyhawk was intended to be a simple, low cost aircraft. Special consideration was given to flight characteristics and size for aircraft carrier operations. The type was nicknamed 'Heinemann's Hot Rod' by the US press, in honor of designer Ed Heinemann.

Construction of the A4D prototype began in September 1953. The prototype first flew on June 22, 1954, and the aircraft entered service with the US Navy in September 1956.

The aircraft, although significantly smaller than most of the fleet air defense fighters it served alongside, was compact and agile. The type enjoyed excellent performance characteristics, and soon picked up the affectionate 'Scooter' soubriquet.

The Skyhawk, re-designated as the A-4 from 1962, was sufficiently compact to be able to do without folding wings, yet could carry a warload of up to 6,000lb (2,721kg) (more on later versions). The aircraft had a maximum range of 1,000 miles (1,609km). A succession of variants introduced improved armament, radar, powered controls and inflight refuelling equipment. The US Navy operated the A-4B, the A-4C, A-4E and A-4F, together with a number of two-seat trainer variants.

The McDonnell Douglas A-4 Skyhawk, although designed to meet a Cold War specification, won its spurs in Vietnam. In this conflict the type won a reputation for rugged dependability and performed with great distinction. In US Navy service, the A-4 was supplanted by Vought's A-7 Corsair in the light attack role. The type, however, remained in service with land-based training and Adversary units. It also served with the USMC, for whom the much-improved, up-engined and re-equipped A-4M Skyhawk II was developed. The A-4M began to enter service in 1970, and served until 1999.

Outside the US armed forces, Skyhawks were delivered to a number of export customers. Some A-4s saw service aboard aircraft carriers (like some of those supplied to Argentina, and Australia) and others were intended for operations from land bases. Large numbers were supplied to Israel, which used the type during the Yom Kippur and Six Day wars. A-4 Skyhawks were also sent to New Zealand, Indonesia, Malaysia, Singapore, and Kuwait.

The 2,690th and final Skyhawk was delivered in February 1979. Some export aircraft, however, were produced by conversion and modernization of earlier versions, retired by the US Navy. Singapore's aircraft, for example, were converted from redundant US Navy A-4Bs. These aircraft have been progressively modified and further modernized in service. They now have a state-of-the-art navigation

Left: *The A-4 Skyhawk, although it was originally optimized to carry a single nuclear weapon, was soon adapted to use a range of ordnance.*

Left: *Later Skyhawks featured a dorsal hump containing advanced avionics, and a more 'square-cut' tailfin.*

Below: *The two-seat McDonnell Douglas A-4 Skyhawk served in the advanced training role, as well as for conversion and weapons training. The type entered service with the US Navy in 1956.*

and attack system, and General Electric F404 turbofan engines.

The Kuwaiti Skyhawks saw active service during Desert Storm in 1991, having fled their bases as Iraq invaded, and thereafter operated from Saudi Arabia. These aircraft were subsequently refurbished, modernized and sold to Brazil (for carrier operation) in 1998. Some 32 A-4Ms were even more comprehensively modernized as A-4AR Fightinghawks for Argentina, entering service in 1997. Export models are still highly regarded and undergoing electronic, engine and weaponry upgrades to maintain their flying prowess into the 21st century.

AVRO VULCAN

THE AVRO VULCAN, with its huge Delta wing, was one of history's most immediately recognisable aircraft, and enjoyed a long and distinguished career in a vitally important role. The aircraft was designed to meet a 1947 Specification for a new strategic bomber. The requirement that resulted in the Avro Type 698 demanded more of an improvement over previous generation bombers than had the requirements which led to the Halifax and Lancaster.

In order to meet the speed, range and bombload figures laid down, the companies who responded to the Air Ministry's specification had to adopt innovative aerodynamic configurations. Avro selected a tailless Delta configuration, and built five sub-scale aerodynamic testbeds as Avro 707s. These were used to explore handling in different parts of the envelope.

As the aircraft were so innovative, there were real fears that one or other of the selected high risk V-bombers might not succeed. Therefore, in addition to the Avro 698 and Handley Page's crescent-winged Victor, the Air Ministry also ordered the Valiant as a stop-gap and 'insurance policy'.

With two competing 'advanced bombers' ordered, as well as an intermediate 'stop-gap', some were surprised that the Vulcan and Victor were not ordered 'off the drawing board'. This would have brought them into service years sooner. Instead, prototypes were ordered and evaluated before production orders were placed.

The first Avro 698 made its maiden flight on August 30, 1952. A few days later the aircraft stunned audiences at the Farnborough Air Show in Britain with an aerobatic display.

With two prototype and two pre-production Vulcans flying, the aircraft was fitted with a new, kinked wing leading edge, to reduce buffet at high g. The aircraft also had sufficient flexibility to accept a succession of more powerful Olympus engines. Soon after it entered service, the Vulcan B.Mk 1 was capable of cruising at 607mph (976km/h) at 50,000ft (15,240m). This gave the aircraft virtual immunity from interception.

The Vulcan B.Mk 1 entered service with No.230 OCU in February 1957, and the first frontline squadron (No.83) formed in July. Only 45 B.Mk 1s were built before production switched to the B.Mk 2 with more powerful 200-series Olympus engines and provision for the new Blue Steel stand-off thermonuclear missile. The B.Mk 2 also had a new redesigned extended span wing, with reduced thickness/cord ratio on the outer panels and with full span elevons instead of the B.Mk 1's separate elevators and ailerons. The new wing was flown on the second B.Mk 1 prototype, before a production B.Mk 2 flew on August 30, 1958. While the adoption of Blue Steel was one reaction to increasingly tough Soviet defenses, another was the provision of advanced ECM equipment in an enlarged and extended tailcone. This ECM tail was subsequently retrofitted to surviving B.Mk 1s, which thereby became B.Mk 1As, serving until withdrawn from frontline

Right: *The Vulcan/Blue Steel combination shouldered Great Britain's strategic deterrent until replaced by Polaris submarines in 1968.*

Left: *The Vulcan's massive Delta wing gave it unmatched high altitude performance, though from 1964, the aircraft was a low level bomber!*

Below: *This Vulcan B.Mk 2 wears the last colour scheme applied to the type, with matt wrap-around camouflage. It also has a fin-top RWR and nose mounted TFR.*

Following page: *Vulcan bombers and Victor tankers share ramp space at Akrotiri in Cyprus.*

duties in 1967.

The new variant entered service with No.83 Squadron in July 1960, and the new Blue Steel missile followed in 1962. It was subsequently claimed that the introduction of Blue Steel made it possible for Bomber Command alone (with no help from SAC) to destroy "70 per cent of worthwhile targets in the USSR in a single raid".

Even before Blue Steel entered service, plans for its successor were well advanced. The planned Blue Streak, however, was cancelled in April 1960 and was replaced by the US Douglas Skybolt. This was flown by Vulcans in mock-up, inert and instrumented test round form before the US Government cancelled the program.

Meanwhile, the growing effectiveness of enemy SAMs led to a switch to low level operations. These saw the Vulcans receiving a coat of disruptive grey/green camouflage on their upper surfaces, although the undersides remained in glossy anti-flash white.

When Blue Steel reached the end of its operational life in 1969, it marked the end of the V-Force as Britain's strategic nuclear deterrent. This commitment was assumed (from midnight on June 30, 1969) by submarines armed with Polaris missiles. This actually represented a reduction in capability, since 48 available V-Bombers (each carrying a Blue Steel) were replaced by two on-station submarines, each carrying 16 missiles. The Vulcans then switched to tactical nuclear strike and conventional bombing duties, with two squadrons forming a Strike Wing at RAF Akrotiri in Cyprus. The Vulcan remained in service in the bomber role until December 31, 1982. Its final year conferred an

XL445

Left: *RAF Vulcan B.Mk 2s received camouflaged topsides during the early 1960s, with the switch to low level tactics.*

Following page: *The RAF's last Vulcans were retired during 1984, having enjoyed a final moment of glory during the 1982 Falklands War.*

opportunity for making history when two aircraft from No.44 Squadron participated in Operation Corporate (Britain's re-capture of the Falklands) flying long-range bombing and defense suppression sorties from Ascension Island. These missions included laying a stick of 21 1,000-lb (453-kg) bombs across Port Stanley airfield, and hitting enemy radar sites using Shrike missiles. The raids were a powerful demonstration of Britain's ability to hit long-range targets with impunity. The fact that they were car-ried out by a nuclear capable bomber must also have given the Argentinian Junta 'pause for thought'. The Vulcan briefly remained in service in small numbers in the strategic maritime radar reconnaissance and tanker roles. It finally retired in March 1984.

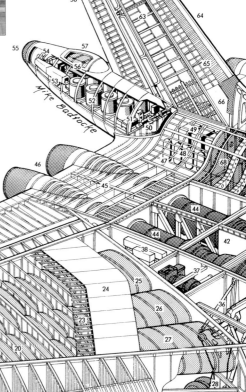

HAWKER SIDDELEY (AVRO) VULCAN B MK 2

1. Wing tip ILS antenna
2. Starboard navigation light
3. A.R.I 18075 'Blue Diver' antenna, port and starboard
4. Outboard aileron
5. Inboard aileron
6. Rear spar
7. Outer wing panel rib structure
8. Front spar
9. Cambered leading edge ribs
10. Cranked leading edge
11. Leading edge corrugated inner skin panel
12. Retractable landing/taxying light
13. Fuel tank fire suppression bottles
14. Outer wing panel attachment rib joint
15. Honeycomb skin panelling
16. Outboard elevator
17. Inboard elevator
18. Elevator hydraulic actuators
19. No. 7 starboard fuel tank, total internal capacity 9,260 imp gal (42,096-lit)
20. No. 5 starboard tank
21. Diagonal rib
22. Leading edge de-icing air duct
23. Wing stringers
24. Parellel chord wing skin panels
25. No. 6 starboard fuel tank
26. No. 4 starboard tank
27. No. 3 starboard tank
28. Main undercarriage leg strut and shock absorber
29. Eight-wheel main undercarriage bogie
30. Mainwheel bay door
31. Fire suppression bottles
32. Inboard leading edge ribs
33. De-icing air supply
34. Fuel collectors and pumps
35. Main undercarriage wheel bay
36. Drag link and retraction actuator
37. Airborne Auxiliary Power Plant (AAPP)
38. Electrical equipment bay
39. Starboard engine bays
40. Rolls-Royce (Bristol) Olympus 301 engines
41. Engine bleed air ducting
42. Engine bay dividing rib
43. Fire suppression bottles
44. Jet pipes
45. Fixed trailing edge structure
46. Exhaust nozzle shrouds
47. Rear equipment bay
48. Oxygen bottles
49. Batteries
50. Rudder power control unit
51. Rear avionics equipment bay
52. ECM equipment packs
53. Avionics cooling air duct
54. 'Red Steer' tail warning radar equipment
55. Aft radome
56. Twin brake parachute housing
57. Parachute door
58. Rudder rib structure
59. Rudder mass balances and seals
60. Fin de-icing air vent
61. Fin tip antenna fairing
62. Passive ECM antennae, fore and aft
63. Two-spar fin torsion box structure
64. Fin leading edge rib structure
65. Corrugated inner skin/de-icing ducting
66. HF antenna
67. Fin de-icing air supply
68. Bomb bay rear bulkhead
69. Bomb bay roof arch frames
70. De-icing bleed air pre-cooler air intake
71. VHF antenna
72. Port Olympus 401 engines
73. Engine bay shroud ribs
74. Port jet pipe fairing
75. Electrical equipment bay
76. Chaff/flare launchers
77. 'Green Satin' doppler navigational equipment bay
78. Elevator mass balances and seals
79. Elevator hydraulic actuators
80. Port inboard elevator
81. Port outboard elevator
82. Port inboard aileron
83. Aileron mass balance and seal
84. Control rods
85. Aileron power control units
86. Ventral actuator fairings
87. Port outboard aileron
88. Wing tip localiser antenna
89. Port navigation light
90. Cranked and cambered leading edge panel
91. Fuel tank fire suppression bottles
92. Outer wing panel joint rib
93. No. 7 port fuel tank
94. No. 5 port tank
95. Leading edge de-icing air duct
96. No. 6 port fuel tank
97. No. 4 port tank
98. No. 3 port tank
99. Port main undercarriage bay
100. Skin support stringers
101. Port airbrake panels
102. Airbrake drive mechanism
103. Intake ducts
104. Wing spar attachment joints
105. Centre-section front spar transverse main frame
106. DF loop antenna
107. Anti-collision light
108. Bomb bay longerons
109. Bomb bay front bulkhead
110. Starboard airbrake housings
111. Boundarylayer bleed-air duct
112. Starboard intake duct structure
113. No. 2 fuselage fuel tanks, divided port and starboard
114. UHF antenna
115. Port engine intake
116. No. 1 fuselage fuel tanks, divided port and starboard
117. Fuselage frame and stringer structure
118. Intake lip structure
119. De-icing air duct corrugated inner skin
120. Intake divider
121. Starboard air intaker
122. Boundary layer splitter plate
123. Forward fuselage section joint frame
124. Rear pressure bulkhead
125. Nosewheel doors
126. Nose undercarriage shock absorber leg strut
127. Hydraulic steering jack
128. Twin nosewheels
129. Avionics equipment bay
130. Rearward facing crew members' stations, Tactical Navigator, Radar Navigator and Air Electronics Officer
131. Cabin side windows
132. Chart table
133. Assisted exit swivelling crew seats
134. Jettisonable cockpit canopy, dinghy stowage beneath
135. First Pilot's Martin-Baker Mk 4 ejection seat
136. Windscreen panels
137. Instrument panel shroud
138. Windscreen wipers
139. Co-Pilot's ejection seat
140. Flight deck floor level
141. Entry hatch
142. Extending boarding ladder
143. Pilot head
144. Ventral bomb aiming fairing, unused on B Mk 2 aircraft
145. Aircraft destructor
146. Air refuelling supply pipe
147. Forward pressure dome
148. Radar mounting structure
149. H2S radar equipment pack
150. Rotating radar scanner
151. Radome
152. Terrain following radar antenna
153. Flight refuelling probe
154. Bomb bay doors
155. Bomb door hydraulic actuators and hinge links
156. 1000-lb (454 Kg) HE bombs
157. 7-round bomb carrier, maximum load-3 (21,000lb)

SUD OUEST VAUTOUR

THE SUD OUEST Vautour (Vulture) was designed to meet a 1951 Armée de l'Air requirement for a multi-role tactical fighter and also a fighter-bomber. From the start the aircraft was planned in three quite separate versions.

The Vautour was strongly reminiscent of the Soviet Yak-28 'Brewer', which it predated. The aircraft had a 'bicycle-type' landing gear (with outriggers in the underslung wing-mounted engine nacelles) and a mid-set tailplane.

There were three Vautour prototypes built (one of each sub-type) together with six pre-production aircraft and 140 production machines. The Vautour IIA was a dedicated single-seat ground attack aircraft, and did not enter regular Armée de l'Air service. The prototype Vautour IIA made its maiden flight on December 16, 1953. The French Air Force ordered 300 examples of the variant but only 30 were built. Israel bought 25 of these aircraft to replace the de Havilland Mosquito.

The Vautour IIB was a tandem two-seater, and had a glazed nose for visual bomb-aiming. It had an internal weapons bay accommodating a single tactical nuclear bomb, or up to 4,500lb (12,041kg) of conventional weapons. This variant, however, lacked the four 20-mm cannon of the IIA and IIN variants.

The type made its first flight in prototype form on December 5, 1954. It

Left: This aircraft was the first prototype for the bomber version of the Sud Ouest Vautour, the Vautour IIB. The type first entered service in 1957.

entered service in 1957, and the 40 procured for the Armée de l'Air continued in use until 1966.

The final Vautour model, and the most widely built, was the IIN. This was a dedicated radar-equipped night-fighter which combined the tandem cockpits of the IIB with a new radar nose. The Vautour IIN prototype was actually the first to fly, on October 16, 1952. The Vautour IIN had a maximum speed of 1,100km/h (686mph) and a range of 4,000km (2,485 miles). The aircraft was armed with four 30mm DEFA cannon. It also had 232 rockets in two packs in fuselage and underwing attachments for four Matra R 511 air-to-air missiles.

Israel received seven of the 70 aircraft built in 1958–59, with radar removed. These aircraft were used alongside Israel's IIAs in the ground attack role. Further aircraft were delivered to Israel following the withdrawal of the Vautour IIN in French service from 1973, following brief use as ECM aircraft.

The first Sud Ouest Vautour arrived in Israel on August 1, 1957. The type was issued to two squadrons. These were the 'Bat' squadron which initially operated the IINs and 'Knights of the Heart' squadron which operated the IIAs and IIBs.

The Sud Ouest Vautour was rendered obsolete by the new types supplied by the United Sates to Israel in the late 1960s. The type was replaced by the A-4 Skyhawk and the F-4 Phantom. These undertook all the roles performed by the Vautour, including photo-reconnaissance and electronic warfare. The Vautour was finally retired in early 1972.

HANDLEY PAGE VICTOR

THE HANDLEY PAGE Victor was one of two aircraft selected by the British Air Ministry for its requirement for a new high speed, high altitude bomber. They picked the boldest and most innovative submissions, in the vague hope that one would eventually demonstrate its superiority, perhaps before both types entered full production. There was also a fear that these very radical new types represented great risk.

The Air Ministry calculated that by selecting two aircraft for further development, that risk might be spread. In the event, as well as the Avro 698 (which became the Vulcan) and the Handley Page 80 (which became the Victor) they also ordered the Vickers Valiant. This aircraft was selected as an interim aircraft, and as a further 'insurance policy'.

The Victor (named by Sir Winston Churchill) was operated in smaller numbers than the Vulcan. By the mid-1960s, it was clearly 'less preferred' by officialdom, and the Vulcan came to dominate the V-Force. The reasons for this apparent lack of official favor remain unclear, and are probably complex. On the face of it, the Victor should have been the firm favorite, since it was aerodynamically efficient and enjoyed the best performance, payload and internal volume of any of the V-bombers.

The Handley Page Victor's low drag, crescent wing delayed shock formation, and gave the aircraft a well-mannered stall without the pitch-up that afflicted many swept-wing aircraft. It also allowed a light structure, with a thick, capacious root.

The Victor weighed the same as the B-47, and had the same span. It was, however, much less 'draggy' and had double the wing area with attendant advantages in maneuverability, altitude performance and take-off and landing characteristics. Its ceiling was 10,000ft (3,0478m) higher than that of the B-47 Stratojet.

The crescent wing also pushed the spar box far forward in the fuselage, giving more room for the bomb bay behind. This was once described by a senior officer as being like a 'poorly furnished railway carriage'. In it the Victor could carry two extra sticks of seven 1,000-lb (453-kg) bombs, giving a total of 35 bombs, compared to the Vulcan's 21 bombs, in three sticks. The original specification had been for only 18 such weapons. The Victor thus had a larger internal bomb bay than the much larger A-model B-52. Remarkably, Handley Page even designed extra external underwing bomb carriers. This could have boosted the aircraft's conventional loadout to a staggering 76,000-lb (34,473-kg), though these were not procured. The engine bays were located entirely behind the wing spars, allowing later, larger engines to be fitted without major structural changes.

The Handley Page Victor prototype first flew on December 24, 1952. Flight tests went well (although there

Right: *The Victor's crescent wing was the key to the type's superb performance and aerodynamic efficiency.*

Following page: *The Victor could carry 50 per cent more bombs than the Vulcan. This No. 15 Squadron aircraft is dropping the maximum load of 35 1,000-lb (453-kg) bombs, in five clips of seven.*

was a fatal accident) and the aircraft was found to be exceptionally easy to land. On June 1, 1957 a Handley Page Victor even achieved Mach 1 in a very shallow dive. Handley Page built 50 Victor B.Mk 1s, and 24 of them were upgraded with new ECM equipment as B.Mk 1As.

Funding for the Victor program was slow and sporadic, and production was pitifully sluggish and unhurried. Thus the USAF had received its 1,000th B-47 Stratojet before the Vulcan or Victor had even been cleared for service.

The Victor B.Mk 1 did finally enter service with No.232 OCU in November 1957 (two years later). The type joined its first operational squadron (No.10) in January 1958.

Despite the success of the Victor B.Mk 1, when orders were placed for the B.Mk 2, the aircraft was plainly 'second' to the Vulcan. While the RAF ordered 89 Vulcan B.Mk 2s the order

for 51 Victor B.Mk 2s was subsequently reduced to only 34. The Victor B.Mk 2 used the 20,600-lb (9,344-kg) Rolls Royce Conway instead of the 11,050-lb (5,012-kg) Sapphire. The two engines were dimensionally similar, and virtually the same weight. They had the same specific fuel consumption, but the Conway had 60 per cent greater thrust. The new engine required new intakes, while the new variant also had a large intake on the leading edge of the tailfin, and extended wingtips.

The first Victor B.Mk 2 made its maiden flight on February 20, 1959. The type entered service with No.232 OCU in 1961, and with No.139 Squadron in May 1962. Later, the B.Mk 2s had large fairings (known as 'Küchemann carrots' or 'Whitcomb bodies') added to their wing trailing edges from 1963–64. These aircraft contained window dispensers, but also reduced drag.

The Handley Page Victor B.Mk 2R (Retrofit) added Blue Steel capability to 21 Victor B.Mk 2s, which also received more powerful engines. Blue Steel Release trials had to be conducted at 51,000ft (15,544m). This was because the Javelin chase aircraft could climb no higher, so the performance penalty with the missile must have been negligible. The Blue Steel missile climbed to 70,000ft (2,136m) after release, and attained a speed of Mach 2.5. Test rounds regularly demonstrated an accuracy of within 300ft (91m)—quite enough with a thermonuclear warhead in the megaton range!

The Victors transitioned to the low level role in 1964. Four Victor B.Mk 1s had been assigned to a Radar Reconnaissance Flight in 1958. A dedicated photo-reconnaissance version (the SR.Mk 2) was produced by converting B.Mk 2s to replace reconnaissance-roled Valiants when they were

prematurely retired from service.

Victor B.Mk 1s were converted as tankers from 1962, as they were retired from frontline service. The program was accelerated when the Vickers Valiant was withdrawn. There were 30 aircraft converted by 1967.

Victor production was constrained by the aircraft's supposed inability to carry Skybolt, and by government hostility. In fact, the Victor could carry two Skybolts underwing, and Handley Page produced studies of an advanced Victor carrying four Skybolts.

Sir Frederick Handley Page resolutely refused to consider joining a larger combine or to allow his company to be swallowed by Hawker Siddeley, in pursuit of the government's drive towards rationalization. Handley Page was given an order for 27 extra Victor B.Mk 2s (in addition to the 29 already on order) as a sweetener, but only five were built. The order was otherwise cancelled in the face of Sir Frederick's

continuing intransigence.

With each Avro Vulcan able to carry a pair of Skybolts, the government sought to reduce the size of the V-force. The Victor B.Mk 2R was therefore retired at the end of 1968, all suffering fatigue cracks due to their low level use.

The reconnaissance aircraft continued until 1974, by which time the redundant bombers had been refurbished and converted to tanker configuration. As a tanker, the Handley Page Victor out-lasted the Avro Vulcan, participating with great distinction in the Falklands and Gulf conflicts. The Handley Page Victor was finally retired in October 1993.

Left: *This Victor B.Mk 1 trialled the underwing tanks and inflight refuelling probe of the Victor tankers.*
Above: *A formation of Handley Page Victor K.Mk 2 tankers, photographed shortly before the type's final retirement in October 1993. The type first entered service in November 1957.*

REPUBLIC F-105

THE F-105 WAS the final product of Republic's 'Thunder Factory' and the successor to the F-84 Thunderjet and the F-84 Thunderstreak. The aircraft was in much the same mould—a dedicated fighter-bomber optimized for the delivery of a single nuclear weapon against a tactical target. It also had respectable conventional attack capabilities.

The type was developed as a private venture and was intended to be capable of exceeding Mach 2, carrying its single nuclear bomb internally, or heavier loads of iron bombs externally. It was therefore of advanced design, with a highly-swept wing, forward swept variable geometry intakes, full-span leading edge flaps, ailerons for low-speed roll control and spoilers for high speed. The aircraft also had an automatic flight control system and an afterburning Pratt and Whitney J75 turbojet engine.

The first of two prototypes made its maiden flight on October 22, 1955, and the production F-105B entered service in 1958. Only 78 production F-105Bs were built. The D-model was much improved, with a more powerful engine, strengthened airframe and undercarriage. It also had a new integrated flight and fire control system, including a new search and ranging radar in the extended nose.

Republic built 610 F-105Ds, the first making its maiden flight on June 9, 1959. From the −25RE production block, the F-105Ds were delivered with extra hardpoints for 12 more

Left: The F-105 may have had an 'F-for-Fighter' designation, but was all bomber, proving its potential in the Vietnam War.

conventional weapons. Early aircraft were subsequently brought up to the same standards.

During its early career, the F-105 suffered a succession of problems, and the type was grounded several times. Some of the problems were solved by the introduction of a two-seat trainer version, the F-105F.

The F-105 flew 75 per cent of the airstrikes against North Vietnam between 1964 and 1969. It carried more ordnance in the Vietnam War than any other aircraft type, from the Navy or the Air Force. They suffered correspondingly heavy losses but demonstrated great resilience. Many pilots owed their lives to the aircraft's robust structure and reliable systems. F-105s also shot down 24 enemy MiGs during the war.

The F-105 lacked sufficient precision capability for some conventional missions. The aircraft were often despatched to 'bomb on command' with a B-66 'lead ship'. To remedy some of these deficiencies, 30 F-105Ds received Thunderstick II modifications, with a new inertial navigation system, LORAN, a solid-state version of the R-14A radar, and Doppler.

The best known conversions were the 612 two-seat F-105Fs which were converted to F-105G standards as dedicated defense suppression aircraft. They were rushed into service to counter the North Vietnamese SAM threat, and were equipped to detect, identify, locate and attack enemy air defense and SAM radars. This type was the last in frontline service. After retiring in 1978 they served with the Georgia Air National Guard until May 1983.

LOCKHEED F-104C/G STARFIGHTER

T HE LOCKHEED F-104 Starfighter was designed as a dedicated air-to-air fighter interceptor, incorporating lessons learned during the Korean War. Designer Clarence 'Kelly' Johnson placed great emphasis on performance, but incorporated a 20-mm M61A1 Vulcan rotary cannon and a search/ranging radar in the nose, with a pair of AIM-9 Sidewinder AAMs on the wingtips. He also intended to minimize its cost, size and maintenance requirement. Both North American and Republic had submitted designs. Both companies, however, were already involved in major fighter development and production programs. Lockheed's proposal was therefore cautiously selected.

The first XF-104 prototype made its maiden flight on March 4, 1954, and was a very space-age aircraft, with its stubby, 'steak-knife sharp' wings and needle nose. It was soon being referred to as the 'Missile with a Man in it'. The first production F-104As were delivered to the USAF in late 1958.

The F-104A was succeeded on the production line by the F-104C, which added limited fighter-bomber capability. This variant was delivered to TAC from October 1958, subsequently seeing active service in the Vietnam War.

While the F-104C had limited fighter-bomber capability, the F-104G was specifically developed for the United States' NATO allies for use as a multi-role, all-weather strike fighter. It was driven by a West German Luftwaffe requirement, although Canada, Japan, the Netherlands, Belgium and Italy soon signed up for the aircraft, too.

In West German service, the F-104G did suffer from a high accident rate, and this led to much ill-informed criticism of the aircraft. In fact, the Germans suffered an even higher accident rate with the F-84, while other NATO Starfighter operators found the aircraft to be no problem. But lazy journalists were soon dubbing the F-104 as a 'Widow Maker' or 'Flying Coffin', and this reputation took decades to live down. The main problem was that Germany sent its young and very inexperienced pilots off to the United States to learn to fly the aircraft. These pilots went to convert to the F-104, in perfect weather in the Arizona desert. When they returned to a European winter, casualties were probably inevitable.

The first F-104G (one of 182 built by Lockheed) made its maiden flight on June 7, 1960. The first West German-, Belgian-, Dutch- and Italian-built F-104Gs soon followed suit.

Lockheed set up a massive production program. There were five separate groupings of factories from five countries building 1,322 F-104Gs and CF-104Gs, 126 TF-104G two-seat trainers, and 194 RF-104G reconnaissance aircraft. Some were delivered to other allied nations, including Denmark, Greece, Norway, Spain, Turkey, and later to Taiwan.

The aircraft was used in the fighter, reconnaissance, nuclear strike and

Left: : *The USAF's Lockheed F-104C Starfighter had limited air-to-ground and nuclear strike capabilities. The type was used by TAC from 1958.*

Above: *The USAF used the Lockheed F-104 Starfighter primarily in the air defense role, although this F-104C is armed with underwing bombs.*

Right: *NATO's Lockheed F-104Gs were dedicated multi-role fighter bombers, with a vital low level strike/attack role. These aircraft are Belgian.*

attack roles. They proved highly effective, giving way to the F-16 during the 1970s and 1980s in most of its customer countries.

The aircraft lingered on for rather longer in Greece, Turkey and Taiwan. The similar F-104J was used mainly in the air defense role in Japan, while the F-104S (with an increased thrust engine and BVR missile capability) was a dedicated interceptor built in Italy only for the AMI. It was further upgraded to F-104ASA standards during the 1980s. The F-104 remains in service in Italy, but only in the air-to-air role.

CONVAIR B-58 HUSTLER

THE DEVELOPMENT OF what became the supersonic Convair B-58 Hustler began in 1949, and the aircraft's basic Delta-winged configuration was finalized in January 1951. The USAF's operational requirement was issued that December, and the design was selected for production in October (beating a competing B-59 design offered by Boeing). At that stage, it was expected that there would also be a dedicated reconnaissance version of the aircraft.

The B-58 Hustler was designed for Mach 2 performance, it had an area-ruled fuselage and made considerable use of bonded honeycomb sandwich panels for temperature resistance. The four J79-GE-1 engines were hung below the thin wing, while weapons were carried in a massive ventral pod, which also housed 4,172 US gal (15,792 litres) of fuel. Despite its high performance, the B-58 Hustler was fitted with a defensive 20-mm cannon in the tailcone. The aircraft carried a crew of three in tandem seated in individual cockpits. One special feature of the B-58 was the individual escape capsules fitted for crew members to use in emergencies while flying at supersonic speeds.

The XB-58 prototype made its maiden flight on November 11, 1956 (less its pod, which was flown under the aircraft from February 16, 1957). The 13 YB-58s were followed by 17 YB-58As (the last of which was completed to full production standards). During the extensive flight test program, which involved 30 aircraft, a total of seven aircraft were lost. Production orders were placed for 86 further Convair B-58As. There were 11 YB-58As later brought up to the same standards. Production of the B-58As ceased in the Fall of 1962.

Modifications were made to eight of the trials aircraft to convert them into dual-control trainers. These had dual controls and extra transparencies in the second (rear) cockpit. The first of these flew on May 10, 1960.

The aircraft began to be delivered to the Strategic Air Command's 43rd Bomb Wing at Carswell Air Force Base, Texas, in December 1959. The first squadron then became operational in March 1960. Hustlers were subsequently delivered to the 305th Wing in May 1961. But while many were impressed by the B-58's performance, and by the succession of record-breaking flights (including New York-Paris and Tokyo-London) the aircraft had an atrocious accident rate (with 18 lost in service!). It was viewed by many as being a profligate waste of money, since each one cost more than three B-52Gs.

The final nail in the Convair B-58's coffin came with the switch from high-level to low altitude penetration, since the B-58's low level performance was hampered by its short range and relatively flimsy wing structure. The first Convair B-58 Hustler was retired in November 1969, and all had been retired by January 1970.

Left: : *The Convair B-58 Hustler carried its weapons in an enormous, jettisonable ventral pod, which also contained some 4,000 gallons of fuel.*

Previous page: *This Convair B-58A Hustler served with the 43rd Bomb Wing at Little Rock, Arkansas, but was photographed during a 1969 visit to Mildenhall in eastern England.*

Previous page, inset: *The first B-58 Hustler prototype wore Convair's house colours, including a scarlet tailfin.*

Right: *Most Convair B-58s wore a 'Milky Way' band around their noses, with the Strategic Air Command badge superimposed on the port side.*

Below: *Most B-58s ended their days at Davis Monthan, scrapped after only a brief period in storage.*

McDonnell Douglas F-4 Phantom

T HE F-4 Phantom has become a byword for multi-role versatility, and has seen extensive service in the air-to-ground role. The F-4 has flown close air support missions in Vietnam, SAM-killing missions in Desert Storm, and even helped to maintain the Cold War nuclear deterrent. It was originally, however, designed as a carrierborne fighter interceptor.

The aircraft (originally designated F4H-1) with its anhedral tail and up-turned wingtips, was never a beautiful aircraft. Its drooping radar nose and twin downward pointing jetpipes, however, made it look a purposeful and aggressive aircraft.

The prototype made its maiden flight on May 27, 1958, and the type was quickly breaking records. The McDonnell Douglas F-4 Phantom entered frontline US Navy service in February 1961. The aircraft was also quickly adopted by the USAF, with whom the type entered service in late 1963. At one time, it seemed likely that the USAF's Phantom aircraft would be known as F-110s. But with the adoption of a unified tri-service designation system in 1962, they became simply F-4Cs.

The USAF, US Navy and USMC all used the F-4 Phantom to great effect in the Vietnam War, in both the air-to-air and air-to-ground roles. The F-4 Phantoms carried up to 16,000lb (7,257kg) of external stores. The aircraft could deliver a variety of bombs, rockets, ASMs and other weapons. The USAF Phantoms frequently carried external gun pods for strafing ground targets.

Combat experience in the Vietnam War resulted in the development of the F-4E, which finally gained an integral, internal 20-mm cannon, with a new radar in a more slender nose. The F-4E proved the most popular Phantom variant, although the US Navy and USMC continued to take delivery of improved versions based on the original nose shape.

The first export customer for the Phantom was Britain, which ordered Spey-engined aircraft to equip the aircraft carrier HMS *Ark Royal*. These Phantoms would operate in the fighter role, alongside Blackburn Buccaneers. As well as these Royal Navy F-4Ks, Britain received similar land-based F-4Ms for the Royal Air Force. These aircraft served with No.38 Group in the fighter-bomber role, and with RAF Germany in the tactical strike role. Replacing Canberras from 1971, the RAF Germany Phantoms were themselves replaced by Jaguars from 1975. The aircraft were then 'cascaded' to the air defense role, in which they served until 1992.

McDonnell Douglas Phantom 'bombers' has seen extensive combat service in the Middle East. They have served in Israel's many wars with its neighbors and during the long war between Iran and Iraq.

The United States Air Force used the specialized F-4G in the defense suppression, 'Wild Weasel', role and these

Right: *The McDonnell Douglas F-4E was the most versatile multi-role variant of the Phantom, and saw extensive service in the Vietnam War.*

Above: *'Wild Weasel' F-4Gs performed with distinction during Operation Desert Storm, providing defense suppression for coalition air forces.*

Left: *This McDonnell Douglas F-4E's assymmetric loadout includes a Paveway II LGB—a common F-4 weapon during the Vietnam War.*

aircraft enjoyed great success until their retirement following Operation Desert Storm. Their retirement was driven by the need to make force cuts. Few disagreed with those who suggested that the F-4G was a better 'Wild Weasel' than the aircraft which replaced it.

The McDonnell Douglas F-4 Phantom remains in frontline service in the tactical fighter and fighter-reconnaissance roles in Greece, Turkey, Iran, Israel, Japan and South Korea, and in the air defense role in Germany. Spain retains a handful of reconnaissance-roled Phantoms. The McDonnell Douglas F-4 enjoys competitive performance characteristics and packs an impressive punch. Many surviving Phantoms have been modernized and upgraded for service well into the 21st Century.

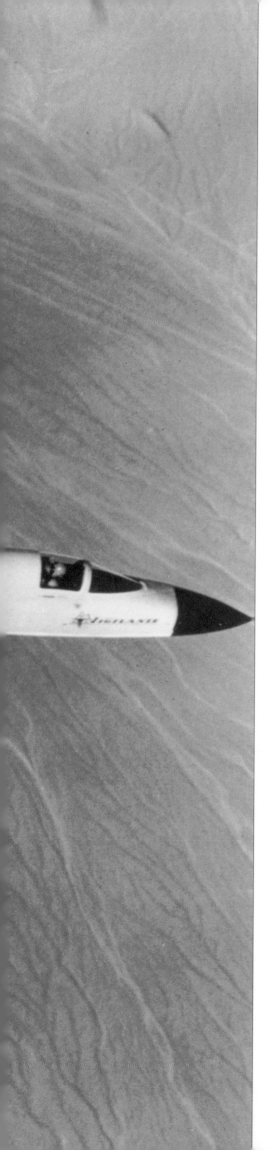

NORTH AMERICAN A-5 VIGILANTE

THE RAPID EVOLUTION of aircraft design in the 1950s led to new aircraft types with sleek lines and impressive performance. One such aircraft was the North American A-5 Vigilante. The aircraft was designed to replace the North American AJ Savage and the Douglas A-3 Skywarrior. The US Navy had issued a requirement for a supersonic replacement in the heavy attack role, and the Vigilante was developed to meet this.

The first of two YA3J-1 prototypes made its maiden flight on August 31, 1958. It was an astonishingly futuristic aircraft, from its needle-tipped radar nose and raked, fully-variable intakes, to its spoilers and slab tailerons. The aircraft incorporated one-piece wing-skins machined from aluminum lithium alloy, and major portions of the structure were made from titanium alloys.

The Vigilante had an advanced inertial navigation system, and was the first US combat aircraft to use an airborne digital computer for navigation and weapons aiming. The monopulse attack radar incorporated terrain avoidance features. The Vigilante's pilot viewed the world through one of the first Head Up Displays, and a stretched acrylic windshield proven to be able to withstand a birdstrike even at Mach 2.

The aircraft also had a unique linear bomb bay, which took the form of a straight, tubular 'tunnel' between the engine bays. This bay usually accommodated a nuclear weapon forward, with fuel tanks behind. These linked items were catapault-ejected rearwards along fixed rails in the 'tunnel' after the tailcone was jettisoned.

The North American A-5's enjoyed a long reach due to the massive internal volume it had for fuel. For most missions it therefore did not require its neat retractable inflight refuelling probe. The type was ordered into production in 1959, and made its first carrier landing (becoming the largest aircraft type ever to achieve this) in July 1960.

North American built 57 production A3J-1s, these being re-designated as A-5As in 1962. The first of these entered operational service with VAH-7 in January 1962, and VAH-1 also equipped with the type.

In an effort to extend the Vigilante's range, North American designed an upgraded version, the A3J-2 (later A-5B). This had a humped fuselage spine, increased area blown flaps, more powerful engines and new underwing hardpoints. In the event, the US Navy relinquished the strategic bomber role (with some reluctance) and all of the 18 A3J-2s were eventually converted to RA-5C reconnaissance configuration.

The A-5 was retired from the bomber role after a final deployment in October 1964. There were 43 surviving A-5As subsequently converted to RA-5C standards, and used for reconnaissance. This variant served until 1979, when the type was finally replaced by F-14s.

Left: *The Vigilante enjoyed only the briefest career as a bomber, finding its forte as a reconnaissance aircraft.*

BLACKBURN BUCCANEER

THE ADMIRALTY IN Britain selected Blackburn's sleek and powerful NA39 to fulfil its medium attack requirement. By contrast the US Navy received the sluggish Intruder to fulfil the same role. Both types were designed to counter the Soviet's new *Sverdlov*-class cruisers. The Buccaneer relied on being able to slip undetected under enemy radar at extremely low altitude and very high speed, delivering a single nuclear weapon over a radius of more than 400 nautical miles (740km). The Admiralty accepted that in order to overcome the problems of fatigue at very low level the Buccaneer would have to be extremely heavily built, and that as such, would not be capable of supersonic speed. Blackburn incorporated flap blowing and boundary layer control to increase lift and reduce wing area. It also had area-ruled the fuselage to reduce drag, giving a distinctive coke-bottle shape.

The NA39 was surrounded by secrecy, to the extent that the aircraft was decorated with roundels of non-standard size. It was not photographed with objects which could be used to scale the aircraft, or in any pose which showed the wing's planform. Despite this, the first 3-view published in the aviation press was correct within a few inches!

The NA39 made its maiden flight on April 30, 1958, and quickly proved to be extremely promising. The type entered service, as the Buccaneer, in July 1962. Even before this event, the Royal Navy had placed orders for the improved Buccaneer S.Mk 2. This had more powerful Spey engines, and the new variant entered service in 1966. The rundown of the Royal Navy carrier fleet led to transfers of RN aircraft to the RAF. The last RN Buccaneer squadron, used on HMS *Ark Royal*, kept its aircraft until November 1978.

Amateurish salesmen were probably responsible for the failure to sell the Blackburn Buccaneer to the US Navy and the German Bundesmarine. There were 16 supplied to South Africa before an arms embargo prevented delivery of a second 20-aircraft batch. Even the supply of a replacement aircraft for one Buccaneer from the first batch which was lost en-route to South Africa.

The Buccaneers sent to South Africa saw extensive operational service during the long war in Angola. It was probably the designated platform for South Africa's nuclear weapons program. The type was finally retired in

Right: *The Buccaneer was an unsurpassed low level, strike attack aircraft, and served until 1994. This RAF Germany aircraft is seen over the Rhine.*

Following page, left: *Crews from No.801 Squadron confer after flying their Buccaneer S.Mk 1s from the deck of HMS Ark Royal to RNAS Yeovilton. The Royal Navy used Buccaneers until November 1978.*

Following page, top right: *The Buccaneer could carry a heavy load of bombs, internally and externally.*

Following page, bottom right: *Weapons options spread out in front of a Royal Navy Buccaneer. The type could carry nuclear or conventional weapons. These included bombs, rockets, and Bullpup, Sea Eagle or Martel missiles.*

April 1991, by which time attrition and fatigue had reduced the fleet to four aircraft.

Blackburn designed a version of the NA39 to meet the RAF's requirement for a Canberra replacement (a requirement met by the TSR2). It then drew up another version (thin-winged, cleaned-up, supersonic, and powered by reheated engines, and with advanced sensors and avionics) when the TSR2 was cancelled. Eventually, some standard Buccaneer S.Mk 2s (with provision for a bulged belly tank) were purchased for the RAF in 1968. There was also the transfer of Royal Navy aircraft rendered surplus by the premature withdrawal of HMS *Victorious* and HMS *Eagle*.

RAF Buccaneers carried the new WE177 nuclear bomb, instead of Red Beard (used by naval Buccaneers). They did not, however, have the new reconnaissance pack or 430-gallon (1,954-litre) underwing tanks designed for the aircraft.

The RAF used the Buccaneer in the maritime strike/attack role (using a variety of weapons, including Martel and later Sea Eagle ASMs, WE 177 and Paveway II LGBs). It was also used in the overland strike role, with two squadrons based in RAF Germany. Latterly, the Buccaneers also became 'spikers' (laser designation platforms) for other types, and were used as such during Operation Desert Storm. A series of fatal accidents in 1979 and 1980 led to the discovery of major fatigue problems, and the fleet was grounded. A costly repair scheme was designed and incorporated on the least affected aircraft.

The Buccaneer served on until March 1994, when the type was finally replaced in the maritime role by shorter-ranged, less suitable but more modern Tornados rendered surplus by post-Cold War defense cuts. A handful of Buccaneers served on with the MoD (PE) until February 1995, and two remain airworthy as civilian warbirds in South Africa.

Right: *The use of 'flap blowing' gave the Buccaneer useful low speed handling capabilities, enabling it to operate from the Royal Navy's tiny carriers.*
Below: *This Buccaneer served with No.24 Squadron, South African Air Force. Buccaneers sent to South Africa saw extensive service in Angola. The type was finally retired in 1991.*
Following page: *Buccaneers launch from the deck of the carrier HMS* Victorious *in the Gulf of Aden.*

TUPOLEV TU-22

THE TUPOLEV Tu-22 'Blinder' was actually built in larger numbers than the bomber versions of the 'Bear', yet is a much less familiar aircraft in the West. The Soviet Union's first successful supersonic medium bomber, the Tu-22 first flew on June 21, 1958, and entered service two years later.

The aircraft, although assigned against strategic targets, were never intended to be intercontinental bombers. Instead they were assigned against theater targets in Europe and the Far East—including US Navy carrier groups. They effectively replaced the subsonic Tu-16 'Badger' in exactly the same way that the US B-58 was intended to replace the B-47 Stratojet.

Tupolev's initial supersonic bomber studies focused on a scaled-up and cleaned up four-engined derivative of the Tu-16, but by 1954, attention had switched to a more radical configuration. This had boldly-swept wings and engines mounted above the rear fuselage, 'sandwiching' the tailfin. The aircraft was sized to carry 24 500-kg (1,102-lb) bombs or a single FAB-9000 9,000-kg (19,841-lb) weapon. This capacity also allowed it to carry most of the Soviet Union's contemporary nuclear weapons. The type suffered severe teething problems and an alarming accident rate. Only 15 Tu-22B bombers were built, together with 127 Tu-22R dual role bomber/reconnaissance aircraft.

When the new bomber made its first public appearance, NATO assigned

Left: The Tupolev Tu-22RD 'Blinder-B' was a dual role bomber and reconnaissance aircraft, with nose mounted inflight refuelling probe.

the reporting name 'Bullshot', but this was felt inappropriate by the United States, and was changed to 'Beauty'. This reporting name, however, was deemed too complimentary, and was finally changed to 'Blinder'. Soviet crews called it the 'Awl'.

The Tupolev Tu-22Bs and Tu-22Rs were augmented by some 46 Tu-22U trainers. These had a raised instructor's cockpit taking the place of the navigator's station behind the pilot's cockpit. From about 1964, production switched to the Tu-22K missile carrier, whose primary armament consisted of the Kh-22 cruise missile. There were 76 missile carriers built, most with refuelling probes under the designation Tu-22KD. The Tu-22K and -KD were never very effective, carrying only a single missile, and the Tu-16 (which carried two) continued to form the backbone of the theater strike force. A complementary 'Blinder' variant, the Tu-22P, was also developed, to provide targeting for the missile carriers, and stand-off and escort jamming capability. Some 47 of these aircraft were built, equipping one squadron in each Tu-22K Regiment. These jammers remained in use after the withdrawal of the Tu-22K, providing the same 'service' to Tu-22M 'Backfire' units. Some Tu-22Rs were upgraded with inflight refuelling probes as Tu-22RDs, and with Shompol SAR as Tu-22RDMs. The latter also received a tail-mounted ECM package in place of the original tail-mounted remotely controlled gun turret. The Tu-22P and Tu-22R both participated in the Soviet occupation of Afghanistan, and were finally withdrawn in the mid-1990s.

Above: *The prototype Tupolev Tu-22K, carrying a Kh-22 cruise missile under its belly, during an airshow flypast. Tupolev production switched to this version from about 1964.*

Left: *The Tu-22's unusual engine location, highly swept wing and needle nose are all evident in this rare photograph.*

The Tupolev Tu-22 was unpleasantly heavy to fly, and suffered a range of faults and deficiencies which led to a high accident rate. This, coupled with the aircraft's downward-firing ejection seats, made the Blinder unpopular with many aircrew.

The Tu-22 Blinder was retired during the mid-1990s. A handful of Tu-22Rs, however, may remain active in Ukraine.

Small numbers of redundant Soviet Tupolev Tu-22Rs were rebuilt for export. There were 12 sent to Iraq, and between seven and 18 delivered to Libya. Both countries used their Tu-22s in action, Iraq during the long-running war against Iran, and Libya in operations against Chad. A handful of these aircraft may remain in service, although neither nation is believed to have a genuine operational capability using the aircraft.

GRUMMAN A-6 INTRUDER

THE A-6 WAS designed to meet a USN/USMC requirement for an all-weather attack aircraft to 'fit between' the A-1/A-4 light attack aircraft and the A-3/A-5 heavy attack aircraft. It was ordered in 1957, following evaluation of 12 competing designs, including VTOL and even turboprop designs.

The prototype Grumman Design 128, then designated as the A2F-1, made its maiden flight on April 19, 1960. The first examples entered service in February 1962. The type was soon in combat service in Vietnam.

The basic A-6A was soon augmented by the dedicated defense suppression A-6B (with anti-radar missiles) and the A-6C with improved all-weather and night attack capability. From 1969, these early versions gave way to the A-6E, with a new multimode all-weather radar, and solid state avionics.

Many A-6Es were newly built, but others were produced through conversion of earlier variants. From 1970, US Navy squadrons began to receive A-6As converted to KA-6D buddy tanker configuration.

The Grumman A-6E was the longest-serving version of the Intruder, and was upgraded and modernized in service. The A-6E's sophisticated radar and target recognition/attack multisensor (TRAM) system, with its chin-mounted forward-looking infra-red (FLIR) system, gave the aircraft an unparalleled all-weather, low-level attack capability. The A-6E also had an impressive payload and long range. The aircraft's slow speed and lack of agility, however, made it extremely vulnerable. The ageing Intruder was maintenance-intensive and difficult to support, becoming the Navy's most expensive frontline aircraft to operate.

At one time the US Navy planned to replace its Grumman A-6Es with a new A-6F version, with new F404-GE-400D engines, a new Synthetic Aperture Radar, and digital avionics. This was cancelled in 1988, shortly after the prototype's maiden flight. Plans to re-wing the remaining A-6Es were cancelled, and the type was simply retired, although not before it had added to its laurels with a superb performance in combat during Operation Desert Storm. The last Intruder unit, VA-75 'Sunday Punchers', was disbanded in early 1997. This left the US Navy's Carrier Air Wings without a sophisticated, long-range, all-weather strike attack aircraft. Instead, the Navy deployed an air-to-ground conversion of the F-14, unofficially known as the Bombcat.

The basic Grumman A-6 Intruder formed the basis of the EA-6. This dedicated ECM version for the USMC had a profusion of receiver antennas scattered over its airframe, some of them in a massive fin-top football fairing. This was in turn developed into the EA-6B Prowler, which had four

Right: *Laden with Rockeye Cluster Bombs, this A-6E of VA-196 aboard the USS* Coral Sea *lacks the TRAM turret which distinguished later Intruders.*

Following page: *This A-6 of Air Wing Three carries rockets, retarded bombs and an AGM-88 HARM missile.*

Left: *Two Grumman A-6 Intruders of VA-52 'Knight Riders', assigned to the USS Kitty Hawk and laden with 500-lb (226-kg) bombs.*

Below: *VA-42 was the East Coast training unit for A-6 aircrew, and was the first Intruder unit to form. The first Intruders entered service in 1962.*

seats, and which became the US Navy's standard EW and defense suppression platform.

The EA-6B entered service in 1972, and has undergone a succession of improvements and upgrades since then. These have dramatically expanding the aircraft's capabilities and combat effectiveness. Since the 1980s, the EA-6B has attacked and engaged enemy radars as well as detecting and jamming them, using AGM-88 HARM missiles. And while the A-6 Intruder is now no more than a memory, every US Navy aircraft carrier that puts to sea does so with a squadron of Prowlers, while USMC Prowler units deploy in support of every expeditionary force.

DASSAULT MIRAGE IV

WHEN FRANCE DECIDED to create an independent nuclear deterrent, or 'Force de Frappe', it was always clear that the force would include land-based and submarine-launched missiles, and manned bombers. The Mirage IVA was essentially a scaled up, twin-engined derivative of the successful Mirage III fighter configuration. The prototype first flew on June 17, 1959. This was followed by three pre-production aircraft and 62 production machines between December 1963 and November 1966.

The general configuration of the aircraft strongly resembled that of a Mirage III. Less obvious differences included the tandem cockpit for the pilot and navigator, and main gear bogeys with four tires each. Despite the fact that the aircraft was crammed with fuel tanks, and was generally fitted with twin 2,500-litre (660 US gallon) drop tanks, it could only just reach Soviet airspace. The aircraft therefore relied on inflight refuelling in order to fly 'round trip' missions against Soviet targets. The Mirage IV consequently featured a sturdy nose-mounted inflight refuelling probe. A fleet of 12 Boeing KC-135F tankers were used to refuel the aircraft.

The Mirage IV force always maintained aircraft on QRA alert, ready to go at a moment's notice, and regularly

Left: The Mirage IV served as a freefall bomber, then as a cruise missile carrier, and is now operating in the reconnaissance role.
Following page: This Mirage IV, with an AN-22 nuclear weapon under its belly, wears the original natural metal colour scheme. In the late 1980s, 19 aircraft were converted as ASMP cruise missile carriers.

practised deployed operations from other Armée de l'Air bases. In emergencies the Dassault Mirage IV was planned to operate from farmland strips, specially hardened using chemicals, and with RATOG (rocket assisted take-off gear).

The Mirage IV was designed to carry the AN-22 nuclear weapon fitted in the recess in the fuselage. The AN-22 was modified from 1967 to be parachute-retarded, after it was realized that the aircraft could not penetrate Soviet airspace at high altitude. In the late 1980s, 19 aircraft were converted as ASMP cruise missile carriers, under the designation Mirage IVP ('P' for 'Penetration'). The new weapon had a stand-off range in excess of 150 miles (241km) at high level, and a yield of 30- or 150-kT. The conversion also saw the addition of new navigation equipment and defensive avionics.

The aircraft switched to full-time reconnaissance (previously a secondary role) in 1996. Since then the aircraft have been used in action over Kosovo in 1999, carrying ECM and BOZ pods underwing. The reconnaissance version of the Mirage IVP carries its reconnaissance sensors in an external centerline CT53 pod, which can carry a variety of payloads for low-level or medium level missions. These include optical cameras and an IRLS. There are five Mirage IVPs still operational with Escadron de Reconnaissance Strategique 1/91 at Mont de Marsan in southwest France. The type is expected to be retired during 2005, or soon afterwards. The Mirage IVP played a quiet but vital role during Operation 'Enduring Freedom' (November 2001–2002).

BAC TSR2

THE TSR2 WAS developed to meet a 1957 RAF requirement for a low-level Mach 1.7 tactical strike and reconnaissance aircraft to replace Canberras and tactical V-bombers. The specification was refined and tightened in May 1959, adding Mach 2 (or even Mach 2.25) capability, and the ability to take-off from 'firm grass' during deployed operations (not just concrete!). Low level flight was defined as being 200ft (609m) or less. The Air Staff demanded a 1,000 mile (1,609km) radius of action and a ferry rang of 2,500nm (4,630km).

The program was used as a means of forcing aircraft companies to merge and integrate. English Electric and Vickers were eventually selected to produce a collaborative design. The design combined features of the respective companies' P-17A and Type 571, with assemblies being built at three sites in England.

The resulting aircraft had an extremely slender cross-section, and incorporated advanced materials and manufacturing techniques. The aircraft had a high-set Delta wing, with distinctive down-turned wingtips and full-span blown flaps for better STOL performance. The design incorporated a range of new systems which have since become standard, including a HUD, a moving map, terrain following, ground mapping and side-looking radar. It had an internal bomb bay for up to 6,000-lb (2,721-kg) of bombs. This could consist of six 1,000lb (453kg) HE bombs or two tactical nuclear weapons, each weighing 2,100lb (952kg). The TSR2 also had four underwing hardpoints for additional fuel or weapons. The bomb bay could also accommodate an optional reconnaissance pack, containing cameras and linescan equipment.

The first prototype made its delayed first flight at Boscombe Down, southern England, on September 27, 1964. The second was scheduled to fly on April 6, 1965. This was grounded after the program's cancellation was announced that day. TSR2 had survived an initial defense review in November 1964, but was then cancelled. The type had been expected to enter OCU service at Coningsby, eastern England, in 1968.

The cancellation of TSR2 was a bitter blow to British industry, and to the RAF. In the years since then, it has become clear that the aircraft should not have been cancelled, and was vastly superior to the F-111 which was intended to replace it. As such the aircraft represented a real challenge to US industry. Pressure from the United States to cancel the aircraft was intense, with a strong linkage being made between the program and a much-needed International Monetary Fund loan. Britain's incoming Labour government was hostile to the aircraft and the program because of its origins under the previous administration. Mountbatten, the Chief of the Defense Staff, saw the program's high cost as being a threat to funding for his

Right: *XR219 was the only TSR2 prototype to fly, making its maiden flight on September 27, 1964. The second prototype, however, was grounded after the program was cancelled in April 1965.*

Following page: *The TSR2 was packed with advanced systems and avionics, including terrain following radar.*

Left: *Minor undercarriage problems prevented the TSR2 from retracting its undercarriage for the first few flights.*
Below: *This TSR2 did not fly before the program was cancelled. The TSR2 should have replaced Canberras and the tactical V-bombers.*

beloved Royal Navy and its priority programs, perhaps including Polaris. He made great efforts to undermine the aircraft's sale to Australia, making it clear that he expected it to be cancelled. Even some senior RAF officers approved of cancellation, dazzled by the promise of the supposedly lower cost F-111. This, however, would be years late, far more expensive than TSR2, and much less capable.

The aircraft's price looked high only because those of its rivals were often under-stated, and since it was the first British military aircraft program 'accounted' as a complete weapons system. The cost also seemed high because a whole new generation of avionics and systems were 'charged' to TSR2 even though they would later be used by every other new combat aircraft. Completing production of the first batch of TSR2s would have cost little more than the government's demands that every aircraft, component and tool should be destroyed. This might have ensured the first export order (from Australia) after which the TSR2s future would have been assured. There were nine aircraft complete or nearing completion at the time, and many more assemblies were waiting to be mated. The TSR2 was in some respects superior to the later Tornado, with a longer low level radius of action. There is little doubt that it would still be in service today.

GENERAL DYNAMICS F-111

THE F-111 ORIGINATED in studies for a replacement for TAC's F-100 Super Sabres and F-105 Thunderchiefs in the tactical strike role. TAC wanted an aircraft which could operate from shorter runways. They also required a longer ferry range as overseas deployments by F-100s were often limited by refuelling problems. The aircraft would also be optimized for very low-level penetration, including a final 200nm (370km) 'dash' at Mach 1.2. It would be a multi-role aircraft, capable of Mach 2.5 at high level in the interceptor role. This made it inevitable that the successful design would have a variable geometry, swing wing.

'Glueing on' the fighter role and the demand for Mach 2.5 capability immediately made the F-111 designers' jobs more difficult. Their task, however, would soon be immeasurably complicated by the incoming Secretary of Defense, Robert McNamara. He directed that the USAF (whose primary requirement was still for a low-level strike aircraft) and the US Navy (who needed a long-range carrierborne interceptor) should acquire a common aircraft. This became known by the acronym TFX.

Both services initially welcomed the joint common fighter, until it became clear that no single airframe could meet all the different requirements. By then, however, the bit was between McNamara's teeth, and he drove the program forward. Boeing and General Dynamics competed for the lucrative TFX contract, which was awarded to the latter company (the military favored the Boeing submission) in November 1962. The General Dynamics design was more of a compromise, and the US Navy and USAF versions were variants of a common airframe. The Boeing aircraft, however, was tailored more closely to the USAF requirement, while the Boeing Navy version had relatively little commonality with the USAF variant. McNamara was later accused of having bought the "second best airplane at the higher price".

Technical difficulties, barely controlled weight growth and massive cost escalation characterized the remainder of the TFX's development. During wind-tunnel testing severe drag problems were encountered. Weight reduction programs on the naval version reduced commonality to a mere 28 per cent or so, before the F-111B was cancelled altogether, and replaced by the F-14 Tomcat.

The first F-111A made its maiden flight on December 21, 1964, and soon ran into further problems, not least of which was the TF30 engine. This would later severely compromise the F-14 program as well!

Once the aircraft entered service with the USAF's evaluation unit, the General Dynamics F-111 began to win friends. The aircrews were 'blown away' by the aircraft's performance and its automatic terrain following capability. Engineers were impressed by its reliability and maintainability.

Left: *Two General Dynamics F-111As of the 428th TFS, 474th TFW, the USAF's first F-111 Wing, previously known as the 4480th TFW.*

Opposite, top: *This 429th TFS F-111A was none of those which took part in the type's second combat deployment to Takhli in Thailand.*

Opposite, bottom: *Two Wings of FB-111s were used by Strategic Air Command as strategic bombers, using AGM-69 SRAM missiles.*

Below: *A General Dynamics F-111D of the 27th TFW approaches the tanker. The F-111D introduced a new digital computer and advanced avionics.*

Even before CAT 1 testing was complete, in March 1968, six aircraft were deployed to Vietnam for the Combat Lancer evaluation. These soon demonstrated their combat effectiveness. But things soon went wrong after three aircraft failed to return from routine

Below: *This aircraft was the first production General Dynamics F-111A, flying for the first time on December 21, 1964. The F-111 bombers went on to serve with the USAF until 1996. This grey and white color scheme never reached the frontline.*

missions. They had all crashed due to structural fatigue failures. This eventually led to a fleet-wide grounding and a cripplingly expensive series of modifications and 'fixes'.

The engine intakes were redesigned, and avionics were improved, resulting in a succession of sub-variants. The 'definitive' F-111D finally entered service in October 1971. The further improved F-111F (with more powerful engines, improved avionics and Pave Tack pods for laser designating) followed in early 1972. Strategic Air Command even acquired two Wings of FB-111s. These were dedicated strategic nuclear strike aircraft, each carrying a pair of SRAMs. These aircraft were eventually converted to F-111G standards and were returned to the tactical role.

The Australians must have rued their selection of the General Dynamics F-111 over the BAC TSR2 during the long years of delay and disappointment. The 24 aircraft, which should have cost A$112 million, were supposed to have been delivered from 1967. Instead, the aircraft were delivered from 1973, and cost almost twice as much! The RAF did not have the opportunity to regret its involvement in the F-111 program, since none were ever delivered. Britain had cancelled its 50-aircraft order mainly because the United States could not give a fixed price!

During the final years of its USAF

career, the Aardvark finally lived down its unfortunate early history. It was, however, never capable of the kind of austere-strip STOL operations once envisaged for it. The F-111 was tied to long concrete runways as its predecessors had been. Time and again, the F-111 proved invaluable in precision attacks against vital targets. After attacking targets in Libya in 1986, the F-111F played a vital role in the Gulf War. Some claimed that the elderly Aardvark was actually the USAF's most effective and accurate PGM and LGB delivery platform.

Unfortunately, though, Operation Desert Storm proved to be something of a final swansong for the General Dynamics F-111.

With pressure for post-Cold War defense economies becoming increasingly difficult to resist, the USAF finally withdrew its last F-111 bombers in July 1996. The EF-111A EW and defense suppression aircraft followed during 1998. This allowed the USAF to stop supporting an entire aircraft type, with corresponding savings in logistics support costs.

The F-111 remains in service with the RAAF, who use the aircraft in the attack and reconnaissance roles. The RAAF's aircraft have been comprehensively upgraded and modernized with digital avionics, and are able to use the latest precision-guided munitions. Australia's original batch of 24 F-111Cs (four of them locally converted to RF-111C standards). These aircraft were then augmented by four F-111A attrition replacements delivered in 1982, and by 15 ex-USAF F-111Gs delivered in 1993. These will allow the Australian F-111 fleet to be maintained in service until 2020.

NORTH AMERICAN XB-70 VALKYRIE

THE XB-70 WAS conceived as a replacement for the B-52 in the strategic bombing role, but was always a much more ambitious aircraft, with a requirement for Mach 3 performance and also a 70,000ft (21,336m) ceiling. The USAF hoped to procure some 250 B-70s. The ambitious nature of the aircraft made it extremely expensive, however, and development of the aircraft as a bomber was cancelled in late 1959, after a full-scale mock-up had been approved, only to have funding restored in 1960.

As the aircraft had to be capable of cruising at supersonic speed, it broke much new ground aerodynamically. It had an innovative delta-Canard configuration, folding wingtips (which folded down for supersonic cruise), a retractable 'nose ramp' or visor, and massive twin fins. The XB-70 was effectively designed to ride on its own supersonic shock wave, using what was referred to as compression lift, in which pressure was increased below the wing, independently of what was going on above it. The XB-70 also introduced new structural materials and construction techniques, using an unparallelled proportion of expensively made stainless steel honeycomb (welded using ingots of sterling silver!), and 8 per cent titanium (by weight). Almost every system had to be designed afresh, in order to minimize weight and ensure performance at XB-70 speeds and altitudes. The aircraft was intended to have an integrated and active defensive system, including decoys and missiles.

After the election of President John F. Kennedy in January 1961, Robert McNamara took over as Defense Secretary. McNamara was an opponent of manned bombers. The aircraft started to be presented in a new light, as a more flexible aircraft with a new multi-sensor payload which would allow it to find and hit targets missed in previous strikes. McNamara, however, resisted all attempts to keep the program alive.

Only two of the three XB-70 prototypes were flown. The third (intended to carry a full four-man crew with bombardier navigator and defensive systems operator) was cancelled and scrapped before completion, when it became clear that it could not be completed within the imposed cost cap.

In the end, those who believed that missiles made the manned bomber obsolete had their way. The Valkyrie never entered production. Funding was instead diverted to McNamara's own pet project, the TFX (later to become the F-111) and to the RS-71 (later re-designated as the SR-71).

The first prototype made its maiden flight on 21 September 1964, but did not manage to exceed Mach 1 until its third flight. It reached Mach 2.14 on the eighth flight, and Mach 3 on flight 17. The second XB-70 (which sustained Mach 3 for over 30 minutes on its 39th flight) was lost in a collision in June 1966. The first XB-70 prototype served on in the research role until February 4, 1969.

Right: *Powerful vortices stream from the wingroots of the second prototype XB-70.*

GRUMMAN F-14 'BOMBCAT'

THE F-14 WAS designed as a dedicated fleet air defense interceptor, following the cancellation of the naval version of the F-111. As such, it was always even more closely tailored to the air-to-air mission, and less well-suited to air-to-ground operations than was the F-111B. It was always apparent that the F-14 had a number of attributes which offered great potential in the air-to-ground role, including its two-man cockpit, impressive payload, and relatively long range. But this potential remained latent, and the aircraft's secondary, reversionary air-to-ground capability was for many years not exploited by the US Navy.

When the original VFX specification was first released in June 1968 it included an important secondary close air support role, with a payload of up to 14,500lb (6,577kg). Early Grumman publicity material for the winning design (303E) included illustrations of the aircraft carrying heavy loads of air-to-ground ordnance.

The type made its maiden flight on December 21, 1970. During the F-14 flight test program at least one preproduction Tomcat was photographed carrying fourteen 500-lb (226-kg) Mk82 bombs. But for as long as A-6 Intruders were deployed aboard US Navy carriers, there was simply no incentive to add the air-to-ground role to the Tomcat's repertoire. When the

Left: The Tomcat is often referred to as the Turkey, due to the ungainly 'flapping' of its extensive high lift devices on approach. The type entered service in 1974.

F-14 entered service in 1974 it was as an air defense fighter, pure and simple.

Once the Intruder needed replacing, Grumman turned its attention to unlocking the latent air-to-ground potential of the Tomcat. The company proposed a succession of ambitious air-to-ground versions, derivatives and conversions of the Tomcat. These failed to find favour with the US Congress, since generally they lacked the capabilities offered by the F/A-18, yet would have cost a great deal. The US Navy finalized its plans to develop the F/A-18E/F Super Hornet instead. But while the Super Hornet filled the Navy's long term requirement for an A-6 requirement, the withdrawal of the Intruder left a capability gap. In order to partially plug this, the US Navy finally activated the F-14's long dormant air-to-ground capability, cheaply converting Fleet Tomcats to 'bombcat' standards.

Air-to-ground testing culminated in the dropping of two inert 2,000-lb (907-kg) Mk 84 iron bombs by a test Grumman F-14A in November 1987. Frontline trials and training began during 1990. Weapons clearance trials proceeded slowly, but Fleet Tomcat squadrons started dropping bombs in 1991–1992.

The "bombcat" finally saw combat service on September 5, 1995, when two F-14As from VF-41 participating in Operation Deliberate Force over Bosnia-Herzegovina dropped LGBs on an ammunition dump in Eastern Bosnia. The "bombcat" also soon gained LANTIRN targeting pods, to allow self designation of LGBs. The aircraft soon used bombs, LGBs, rockets and CBUs.

A number of important weapons routinely carried by both the Grumman A-6E and the McDonnell Douglas F/A-18, however, could not be used by the upgraded Grumman F-14 Tomcat. These included the AGM-65 Maverick anti-armor missile, the AGM-88 High-speed Anti-Radiation Missile (HARM), the AGM-84 Harpoon antiship missile, the Walleye guided bomb, and the Stand-off Land Attack Missile (SLAM).

The LANTIRN-equipped Bombcat made its combat debut during Operation Desert Fox at the end of 1998. F-14Bs from the USS *Enterprise* were involved in the first wave of attacks on December 16, 1998. These dropped GBU-12s and GBU-24s on Iraqi air defense installations. The LANTIRN Tomcat was soon in action again, with VF-41 flying combat missions over Kosovo in support of Operation Deliberate Force.

Integration of the GPS-guided JDAM on the F-14 has been planned for many years. This was finally achieved in time for use by Bombcats participating in Operation Enduring Freedom over Afghanistan (2001-02).

Some believe that Iran's F-14s (delivered before the revolution which toppled the Shah) also have a secondary attack role. These aircraft would use freefall bombs, CBUs, and AGM-65 Maverick missiles, and perhaps have a laser-guided ASM based on a locally-manufactured Phoenix airframe. Iranian Tomcats may have been used in the maritime attack role, carrying Chinese C-802 missiles, and the indigenous Sattar-2 extended range LGB.

Right: *Armorers prepare a variety of weapons aboard a US carrier for operations over Afghanistan.*

Opposite, bottom: *Paveway laser guided bombs are loaded aboard a LANTIRN-equipped F-14 Tomcat during Operation Enduring Freedom.*

Below: *This Grumman F-14 wears the markings of VF-103 'Jolly Rogers', a pioneering LANTIRN squadron. The aircraft is taking off from the flight deck of USS* George Washington.

SEPECAT JAGUAR

THE JAGUAR, WAS originally designed to fulfil a French requirement for an advanced trainer and light fighter-bomber and a British requirement for an advanced trainer. It emerged, however, as a heavier, more sophisticated, longer-range strike attack aircraft, and other types (the Alpha Jet and Hawk) were eventually selected to meet the original requirements. Even so, the Jaguar is a remarkably compact aircraft, with a wingspan smaller than a clipped-wing Spitfire! Despite this, the aircraft can carry a maximum bombload of 10,500-lb (4,762kg).

The aircraft is not a true all-weather aircraft in the same way as the Tornado. It is, however, optimized for attacking targets with great precision, at low level, and in foul weather, using sophisticated navigation and weapons aiming systems.

Even after the Jaguar made the transition from the trainer to the fighter-bomber role, British and French requirements remained quite different. The RAF wanted what was, in effect, a single-seat, shorter-ranged TSR2, a highly sophisticated all weather strike/attack aircraft. The Armée de l'Air wanted a simpler, cheaper aircraft, more like an updated Super Mystere or Hunter. Despite this, the two nations managed to agree a common airframe, with avionics providing the main difference. The engine was a similarly collaborative venture, between Rolls Royce and Turbomeca.

The French single- and two-seat versions were respectively designated Jaguar A and E (for Attack and Ecole).

The British versions were designated Jaguar S and B, with Royal Air Force service designations GR.Mk 1 and T.Mk 2. A Jaguar M version was designed (and flew in prototype form) for use aboard French aircraft carriers, but this lost out to Dassault's rival Super Etendard.

The first Jaguar prototype (a French two-seater) made its maiden flight on September 8, 1968, and the first single-seater followed on March 29, 1969. The first British single-seater flew on October 12, 1969. The first British two-seater made its first flight on August 30, 1971.

The Jaguar officially entered Armée de l'Air service in June 1973, and RAF service one year later. The first frontline RAF Jaguars equipped a three-squadron Wing at RAF Coltishall in eastern England, while the first frontline French aircraft equipped a wing at St. Dizier, southeastern France.

Royal Air Force Jaguars were upgraded to GR.Mk 1A and T.Mk 2A standards during the late 1970s, with more powerful engines and a new navigation /attack system.

The SEPECAT Jaguar enjoyed only a brief career in the strike role. The five squadrons of Jaguars with RAF Germany were replaced by Tornados by 1988. The Armée de l'Air Jaguars lost their strike commitment in 1991. This was, however, far from the end of the Jaguar's career, since its rugged dependability and deployability made

Right: *A No.20 Squadron Jaguar, carrying a Phimat chaff dispenser, a AN/ALQ-101 ECM pod, and 1,000-lb laser guided bombs.*

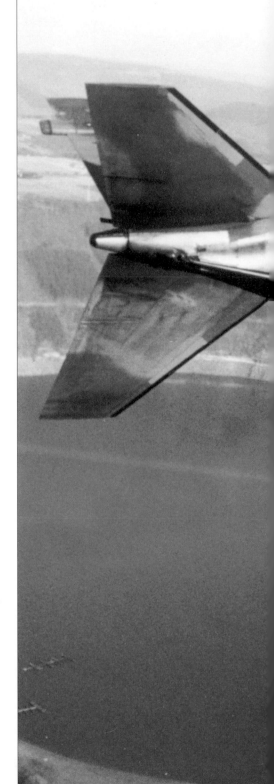

it unusually well suited to post-Cold War peace-keeping and peace-enforcement missions. The type therefore remained in RAF service with the original three-squadron wing at RAF Coltishall in eastern England, while the French Jaguar force shrank more slowly, remaining at two wing strength for some time.

The type performed with distinction in Operation Desert Storm for which RAF Jaguars were extensively modified, receiving overwing AIM-9L Sidewinder AAMs, and a host of avionics improvements. Armée de l'Air Jaguars also saw action in Desert Storm, and in a number of operations in former French colonies. When the RAF found itself short of laser designator platforms for Balkan operations, the Jaguar was selected (almost by default) to remedy the deficiency. This arose as integration of TIALD on Tornado was already underway, and the Harrier was just being modified to undertake the night attack role. There were 11 single seat aircraft upgraded to GR.Mk 1B standards. These had a new HUD, HOTAS controls, GPS, a TERPROM terrain reference navigation system, a new display, and with provision for a TIALD laser designator. Two twin-stickers were also upgraded to T.Mk 2B standards.

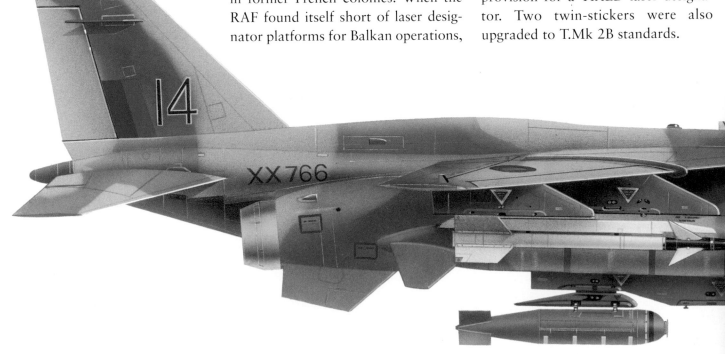

Unusually, the upgrade was not performed by the aircraft's original manufacturer, but by an innovatively managed team drawn from industry, Britain's Defence Evaluation and Research Agency, and the RAF itself. This resulted in an upgrade which was cheap, popular with the frontline, operationally effective and swift.

Extension of the modification program across the Jaguar Fleet resulted in the interim Jaguar 96 (GR.Mk 3) and Jaguar 97 (GR.Mk 3A), the latter now being in service in substantial numbers. These modifications were accompanied by the introduction of a helmet mounted sight, an NVG compatible cockpit, a sophisticated new PC-based mission planner, wiring for ASRAAM missiles and a host of further improvements.

The RAF's Jaguar is now receiving a new engine, the Adour 106, which will result in massive savings in support costs. Early promises of considerable thrust increases, however, now seem unlikely to materialize. Moreover, control of the upgrade process has

Opposite: *Carrying a centreline reconnaissance pod, a Jaguar approaches the tanker during Operation Desert Shield.*
Above: *This RAF Jaguar T.Mk 2 carried out successful rough-field take off and landing trials at Boscombe Down in southern England.*
Below: *This Jaguar, carrying BL 755 cluster bombs underwing, wears the markings of No.226 OCU, the Jaguar training unit.*

Above: *The view from the backseat of a Jaguar T.Mk 2.*
Left: *Jaguars of No.6 Squadron in formation, each carrying a different weapon fit. The nearest carries a Paveway II Laser Guided Bomb.*

now been effectively handed back to BAe. The heady days of value-for-money and speed seem to have been left behind.

The RAF's Jaguars are expected to serve until 2008-09. Their lives could easily be extended further, and the type will remain a useful, highly deployable and versatile fighter-bomber and tactical reconnaissance platform. The Eurofighter will be unlikely to match the Jaguar's capabilities in some areas for some timee.

French Jaguars have never been comprehensively upgraded. The French aircraft are compatible with a range of advanced weapons however, including LGBs and AS30 missiles. The remaining single squadron of Armée de l'Air Jaguars is expected to disband during 2004. Elsewhere, the SEPECAT Jaguar remains in service in Ecuador, Oman and five Indian Air Force squadrons with more expected to form.

SUKHOI SU-24 'FENCER'

THE SU-24 REMAINS a powerful long-range, low-level strike attack aircraft with real all-weather precision attack capability. With its variable geometry 'swing wing' and side-by-side cockpit, the Su-24 is inevitably compared with the US General Dynamics F-111. The aircraft was never intended or used as a strategic bomber, however, a fact obscured by such comparisons. The Su-24 is more broadly equivalent to the Anglo-German-Italian Tornado.

The Fencer was designed to replace the Yak-28 in the all-weather low-level tactical strike and attack roles. It was intended to carry free-fall TN-1000 and TN-1200 nuclear bombs, and a variety of conventional free-fall bombs, rockets and guided ASMs to attack fixed and mobile targets with pinpoint accuracy. While optimized as a supersonic bomber the aircraft was also intended to have a secondary photographic reconnaissance role, and to replace the 'Brewer' in the EW role.

The design of what became the Sukhoi Su-24 began in the early 1960s. Sukhoi, however, abandoned its initial design (an enlarged, twin-engined aircraft based loosely on the Su-7 configuration, but with a tandem cockpit) in favour of the compound Delta T6. This featured fuselage-mounted lift jets for enhanced STOL performance. The lift jets were heavy and bulky, however, and the T6 was redesigned six months later.

The resulting T-6-2IG prototype had no lift jets (leaving increased space for fuel and weapons) but did feature a

VG 'swing' wing. This was added to improve take-off and landing performance. The aircraft made its maiden flight during May 1970 and was ordered into production as the Su-24 in late 1970.

The production Su-24 entered front-line service in 1973. The Su-24 was deployed with the Group of Soviet Forces in Germany in 1979, and in Poland. From 1984 the Su-24 saw active service in Afghanistan.

The original Su-24 underwent slight changes in configuration during production, and this led NATO's ASCC to assign three reporting names ('Fencer-A' through to '-C'). The aircraft was fast and stable at low level, and could carry an impressive warload (though only at the expense of range) but its avionics were backward and unreliable. The aircraft was thus never as capable as Western attack aircraft.

The improved Su-24M 'Fencer-D' was a much better aircraft, and entered service in 1986. The Su-24M introduced upgraded avionics, with separate 'Orion-A' forward-looking attack and 'Relief' Terrain Following Radars. It also had a Kaira 24 laser and TV sighting system which gave PGM compatibility. The 'Fencer-D' had a retractable refuelling probe above the nose, and could carry a buddy refuelling store on the center-line. At least 670 Su-24s have definitely been built. The overall total is probably between 900–1,200. 'Fencer-Bs', '-Cs', '-Ds' and '-Es' remain in widespread front-line use in Russia, and various former Soviet states. Downgraded, non-nuclear capable export Su-24MKs have been delivered to Algeria, Iran, Iraq, Libya and Syria.

Left: *The Sukhoi Su-24 'Fencer-C' remains in widespread use.*

FAIRCHILD A-10

THE A-10 WAS conceived as a low-level tankbuster, close air support and counter-insurgency aircraft, using its formidable internally mounted 30-mm cannon or guided missiles as its primary armament. In recent years, however, it has come to prominence in a medium level bombing role, and has been used against a wider range of targets. In many respects, the Fairchild A-10 has made the transition from being a latter-day P-47 to being a latter-day A-26. In the post-Cold War world, the A-10 is prized for its rugged dependability, relatively good loiter time, and easy deployability. There is less appreciation for its low level, slow speed agility, or for its armor-plated and multiply redundant invulnerability to ground fire.

As a relatively low-cost and simple aircraft, the USAF's proposed AX was developed competitively, to the extent of having an evaluation (or 'fly-off') between two competing designs. These were the Northrop YA-9 and Fairchild's YA-10.

The first of two YA-10 prototypes flew first, on May 10, 1972 and was generally favoured by the evaluation pilots. The YA-9, however, was judged to have better handling, and better air-to-ground target tracking capabilities. The YA-10 was much closer to being a production aircraft. Its easily accessible hardpoints, existing TF34 turbofan engines (used by the USN's S-3 Viking), promised reliability and maintainability swung the decision in Fairchild's favor.

The prototype Fairchild YA-10s were followed by six pre-production YA-10As. These aircraft were used for extensive trials and tactical/doctrinal development. In 1974 an initial order for 22 A-10s was placed. The type entered service in January 1979, and initially equipped units in USAFE and the ANG. By April 1979 some 200 A-10s had been delivered.

Officially dubbed 'Thunderbolt II', the A-10 is more generally known as the 'Warthog'. This is an affectionate tribute to the aircraft's lack of grace and relative ugliness.

As the Fairchild A-10 was designed to operate at low level, within range of enemy fire, it is heavily armored, and most important systems are also duplicated. The pilot famously sits in an armored titanium 'bathtub'. The aircraft has the capacity to fly on even if the engine pod or tailfin is shot off.

The type's original role also dictated that the aircraft should be able to operate from austere and fairly primitive forward airstrips. This has made it much easier to forward deploy the aircraft during post-Cold War operations. The aircraft is a flexible, economic bomb truck. It is capable of carrying a wide range of ordnance, including up to 28 500-lb (226-kg) Mk 82 bombs. The A-10 is fitted with a GAU-8 Avenger cannon. This can fire up to 60 rounds a second. Surviving examples of the A-10 are being upgraded to allow them to serve on well into the 21st Century.

Right: *The Fairchild A-10 was designed for survivability, with careful duplication of systems and components for maximum redundancy.*

Following page: *The A-10A N/AW was a one-off two-seater, designed as a night/all-weather attack version of the aircraft. The type is a flexible, economic bomb truck.*

TUPOLEV TU-22M

THE TU-22M, DESPITE its designation, is an all-new aircraft, and not merely a new variant of the original 'Blinder'. Dissatisfaction with the Tu-22 (and poor relations with Soviet premier Nikita Kruschev) was such that Tupolev was not even invited to tender for a follow-on for the aircraft. The Bureau, however, did develop the Type 135 as a private venture, refining this into the smaller, lighter Type 125. But even this failed to find favor, and Sukhoi's innovative T-4 was selected for further development.

The Tupolev OKB regained its ascendancy with the accession of President Leonid Brezhnev. The further modified, lower-cost Type 145 (disingenuously presented as being a simple, low-cost upgrade of the Tu-22) finally received development funding. The aircraft was based around the existing Kh-22 missile (rather than the new Kh-45 planned for the rival T-4) but was in most respects a 'clean sheet of paper' design.

The fly-by-wire, titanium T-4 was expensive and over-ambitious and in November 1967 the Type 145 was selected in its place. The prototype made its maiden flight on August 30, 1969. The new aircraft looked vaguely like a 'Blinder' with a variable geometry 'swing wing', and with conventional intakes 'feeding' side by side

Left: The Tupolev Tu-22M-3 'Backfire-C' was identifiable by its new raked air intakes which 'fed' new NK-25 turbofan engines.
Following page: *This aircraft, under escort by a Norwegian F-16, is a Tupolev Tu-22M-2 'Backfire-B', 211 of which were built. This variant could carry up to three Kh-22 missiles or various free-fall weapons.*

engines buried in the rear fuselage. The Tu-22M, however, was allocated the new ASCC reporting name 'Backfire'. Western intelligence erroneously believed that the new type was officially known as the Tu-26, a designation which is still applied in some quarters. The aircraft retained a remotely controlled tail gun, but this was used solely for firing IR decoy flares and chaff cartridges, and so did not need to be accurately 'aimed'. Nine pre-production Tu-22M-0 aircraft retained trailing edge fairings for the undercarriage, but the production Tu-22M-1 had conventional inward-retracting main gear units, with bays in the wing roots. Only nine aircraft were built before Tupolev switched to production of the Tu-22M-2 ('Backfire-B'), building 211 'Dvoikas' (Deuces) at Kazan for the Air Forces and Naval Aviation.

As the Tu-22M-2 entered service it became enmeshed in controversy. The United States insisted that the aircraft should be counted as an intercontinental 'strategic' bomber, whereas the Soviet side insisted that it was not. Eventually compromise was reached, under which 'Backfires' lost their nose-mounted inflight refuelling probes as the Soviet Union had insufficient tankers for these to be significant. Production was capped at 30 aircraft per year.

The Tu-22M-2 was capable of carrying one, two, or even three Kh-22 missiles, and could also carry a variety of free-fall weapons. The type's introduction finally allowed the retirement of the Tu-16 missile carriers, although 'Badger' EW aircraft continued to support Tu-22M operations.

The Tupolev Tu-22M-2 suffered some reliability problems, and during the 1980s the opportunity was taken to develop an improved version. This, the Tu-22M-3 ('Backfire-C') introduced new NK-25 engines. These were fed by new box-like raked intakes which together gave increased thrust and a massive 33 per cent hike in mission radius.

The new Tu-22M variant remained compatible with the existing (but by now obsolescent) Kh-22 missile, but also introduced a number of new weapons. These included the Kh-15 'Kickback', and the variant entered service in 1983. Kazan built 268 Tu-22M-3s up to 1993, when funding constraints brought the program to a premature halt.

The Tu-22M itself was an expensive aircraft, and the decision was taken not to produce a dedicated trainer version, but instead to rely on a converted version of the Tu-134 airliner. It is only relatively recently that the type has been adapted for the reconnaissance role, with 12 Tu-22M-3s being built with Shompol SAR as Tu-22M3(R)s. A further 12 more Tu-22M-2s are being converted to a similar mission fit. There were three Tu-22M-3s also converted to Tu-22MP configuration as prototypes for a dedicated escort jammer variant, although this has not been procured.

No Tupolev Tu-22Ms have been exported, though there have been repeated reports that sales (to China, India, Iran and/or Libya) are 'close'. An Indian contract now seems likely to be finalized during 2002. About 150 Tupolev Tu-22Ms remain in service in Russia, with more in service in the Ukraine.

Right: *This Tu-22M-2, with its wings swept forward, carries a single Kh-22 cruise missile under its belly.*

Inset, right: *The Russian Air Forces' Tupolev Tu-22M-2s had their inflight refuelling probes removed as part of arms limitation talks. Russia and Ukraine still use the type.*

PANAVIA TORNADO IDS AND ECR

THE TORNADO CARRIES a smaller weaponload than the F-15E or the F-111, and has a shorter range. The aircraft lacks the newer F-15E's formidable air-to-air capabilities and its avionics are more primitive. But despite this, the Tornado enjoys some advantages, especially in terms of its low-level performance. During Operation Desert Storm the aircraft performed low-level airfield attacks which could not be emulated by any other coalition aircraft.

The aircraft resulted from multinational studies for an F-104 Starfighter replacement in the strike/attack role, which eventually focused around a joint Anglo-German-Italian requirement. The resulting MRCA design drew heavily on BAC's UKVG and MBB's NKF. This was largely driven by British range requirements, albeit with stringent German demands for STOL performance and an Italian insistence on Mach 2 performance driving some aspects of the design. The MRCA emerged as a small neat bomber with twin engines side by side in the rear fuselage, a high-set variable geometry wing with outboard pivots, massive two-dimensional intake ramps and an array of high lift devices and powerful thrust reversers. The aircraft carried all of its weapons externally (apart from a pair of 27-mm cannon), most of them on the broad flat underside of the fuselage.

The MRCA was originally conceived as a family of aircraft, with a single-seater Panavia 100 for Italy and the Luftwaffe and a two-seater Panavia 200 for the RAF and Marineflieger. It was was briefly known as the Panavia Panther, although this name was quickly discarded. The single-seat version was also quickly dropped.

The aircraft was a genuinely collaborative program, with different sub assemblies being produced in all three countries before being assembled on national production lines. The program suffered more political difficulties than technical, and in West Germany opposition to the aircraft reached worrying levels. Some referred to it scathingly as the 'English Aeroplane' while others poked fun at claims of multi-role versatility by calling it 'Die Eierlegende Wollmilchsau' (The egg-laying, wool-bearing, milk-giving pig). Fortunately, the aircraft soon proved itself, and opposition slowly evaporated.

The first of 15 prototype and preproduction aircraft made its maiden flight on April 8, 1974, and production aircraft entered service with a Trinational Tornado Training Establishment in 1980. The type entered frontline service during 1982. Apart from the ADV (Air Defence Variant) fighters for the RAF, the Tornado IDS (Interdictor Strike) versions delivered to the three customer nations enjoyed a remarkable degree of commonality. There were different weapons options. The RAF aircraft

Right: *The Trinational Panavia Consortium produced just short of 1,000 Tornados, making it one of the most successful postwar bomber programs.*

Left: *Although Germany and Italy use a dedicated Tornado ECR for SEAD duties, the RAF uses ALARM missiles on the basic IDS.*

Below: *An RAF Tornado GR.Mk 1 in temporary desert camouflage for Operation Desert Storm. Britain subsequently used the type in Balkan operations.*

used WE 177 nuclear bombs, the JP233 runway denial weapon and British bombs and CBUs. Italian and West German aircraft used mainly US weapons, B61 nuclear bombs and Kormoran anti-ship missiles.

The RAF's Tornados also included a number of GR.Mk 1As with an internal reconnaissance suite replacing the usual cannon, and some GR.Mk 1Bs with provision for Sea Eagle anti-ship missiles. Some GR.Mk 1As and GR.Mk 1Bs were built as such, while others were converted from former standard 'bombers'. With no change in designation, some RAF Tornados were also adapted to carry the ALARM anti-radar missile, and these were used in the 'Pathfinder' and SEAD roles by Nos. 9 and 31 Squadrons in RAF Germany.

West Germany, and later Italy, produced another version, the ECR (Electronic Combat and Reconnaissance), for defense suppression.

TORNADO GR. MK 4

1 Air data probe
2 Radome
3 Lightning conductor strips
4 Terrain following radar antenna
5 Ground mapping radar antenna
6 Radar equipment module, hinged position
7 Radome hinged position
8 IFF antenna
9 Radar antenna tracking mechanism
10 Radar equipment bay
11 UHF/ TACAN antenna
12 Laser Ranger and Marked Target Seeker (LRMIS), starboard side
13 FLIR housing
14 Ventral doppler antenna
15 Incidence probe
16 Canopy emergency release
17 Avionics equipment bay
18 Front pressure bulkhead
19 Windscreen rain dispersal air ducts
20 Armoured windscreen panel, gold film coated
21 Retractable, telescopic flight refuelling probe
22 Probe retraction link
23 Windscreen open position, instrument access
24 Pilot's wide-angle HUD
25 Instrument panel
26 Radar 'head-down' display
27 Instrument panel shroud
28 Control column
29 Rudder pedals
30 Battery
31 Cannon barrel housing, cannon deleted from port side
32 Nosewheel doors
33 Taxiyng light
34 Nose undercarriage leg strut
35 Torque scissor links
36 Forward retracting twin nosewheels
37 Nosewheel steering unit
38 Nosewheel leg door
39 Electrical equipment bay
40 Ejection seat rocket pack
41 Engines throttle levers
42 Wing sweep control lever
43 Radar hand controller
44 Side console panel
45 Pilot's Martin-Baker Mk 10 'zero-zero' ejection seat
46 Safety harness
47 Ejection seat headrest/ drogue container
48 Upward hinging cockpit canopy
49 Canopy centre arch
50 Navigator's radar display
51 Navigator's instrument console and weapons control panels
52 Foot rests
53 Canopy external latch
54 Pitot head
55 Additional avionics equipment in port cannon bay
56 Mauser 27-mm cannon
57 Cold air unit ram air intake
58 Transverse ammunition magazine, 180-rounds
59 Liquid oxygen converter
60 Cabin cold air unit
61 Stores management system computer
62 Port engine air intake
63 Intake lip
64 Cockpit framing
65 Navigator's Martin-Baker Mk 10 ejection seat
66 Starboard engine air intake
67 Intake spill duct
68 Canopy jack
69 Canopy hinge point
70 Rear pressure bulkhead
71 Intake ramp actuator linkage
72 Navigation light
73 Two-dimensional variable are intake ramp doors
74 Suction relief doors
75 Wing glove kruger flap
76 Intake by-pass air spill ducts
77 Intake ramp hydraulic actuator
78 Forward fuselage fuel tank, total internal capacity 1285-Imp gal (5842-lit, 1542-US gal)

79 Wing sweep control screw jack
80 Flap and slat control drive shafts
81 Wing sweep, flap and slat central control unit and motor
82 Wing root glove integral fuel tank
83 Air system ducting
84 Anti-collision light
85 UHF antennae
86 Wing pivot box carry-through, electron beam welded titanium structure
87 Starboard wing pivot bearing
88 Flap and slat telescopic drive shafts
89 Starboard wing sweep control jack
90 Leading edge sealing fairing
91 Wing root glove faorong
92 494-Imp gal (2250-lit, 694-US gal) 'Hindenberger' external fuel tank
93 AIM-9L Sidewinder air-to-air self-defence missile
94 Canopy open position
95 Canopy jettison unit
96 Pilot's rear view mirrors
97 Starboard three-segment leading edge slat, open
98 Slat screw jacks
99 Slat drive torque shaft
100 Swivelling wing pylon angle control rod
101 Inboard pylon pivot bearing
102 Starboard wing integral fuel tank
103 Wing fuel system access panels
104 Outboard pylon pivot bearing
105 BOZ chaff/ flare launcher pod
106 Outboard swivelling wing pylon
107 Starboard navigation and strobe lights
108 Wing tip fairing
109 Double-slotted Fowler-type flaps, extended
110 Flap guide rails
111 Starboard spoilers, open
112 Flap screw jacks
113 External tank tail fins
114 Wing swept position trailing edge housing
115 Dorsal spine fairing
116 Aft fuselage fuel tank
117 Fin root antenna fairing
118 HF antenna
119 Heat exchanger ram air intake
120 Starboard wing fully swept position
121 Airbrake, open
122 Starboard all-moving tailplane (taileron)
123 Airbrake hydraulic jack
124 Primary heat exchanger
125 Heat exchanger exhaust duct
126 Engine bleed air ducting
127 Fin attachment point
128 Port airbrake rib structure
129 Fin heat shiels
130 Vortex generators
131 Fin integral furl tank
132 Fuel system vent piping
133 Fin rib and machined skin panel structure
134 ILS antenna
135 Towed Radar Decoy (TRD)
136 Forward passive ECM housing
137 Fuel jettison and vent valve
138 Fin tip antenna fairing
139 VHF antenna
140 Tail navigation light
141 Aft passive ECM housing

142 Obstruction light
143 Fuel jettison
144 Rudder
145 Rudder honeycomb core structure
146 Rudder hydraulic actuator
147 Dorsal spine tail fairing
148 Thrust reverser bucket doors, open
149 Variable area afterburner nozzle
150 Nozzle control jacks (4)
151 Thrust reverser door actuator
152 Honeycomb core trailing edge structure
153 Port all-moving tailplane (taileron)
154 Tailplane rib structure
155 Leading edge nose ribs
156 Tailplane pivot bearing
157 Tailplane bearing sealing plates
158 Afterburner duct
159 Airbrake hydraulic jack
160 Turbo-Union R.B. 199-34R Mk 101 afterburning turbofan engine
161 Tailplane hydraulic actuator
162 Hydraulic system filters
163 Hydraulic reservoir
164 Airbrake hinge point
165 Intake frame/ rear fuselage production joint
166 Engine bay ventral access panels
167 Engine oil tank
168 Rear fuselage fuel tank
169 Wing root pneumatic seal
170 Airframe mounted accessory equipment gearbox, port and starboard, shaft driven from engines
171 Integrated drive generator (2)
172 Hydraulic pump (2)
173 Gearbox interconnecting shaft
174 Starboard side KHD Auxiliary Power Unit (APU)
175 Telescopic fuel pipes
176 Port wing pivot bearing
177 Flexible wing sealing plates
178 Wing skin panelling
179 Rear spar
180 Port spoiler housings
181 Spoiler hydraulic actuators
182 Flap screw jacks

183 Flap rib structure
184 Port Fowler-type double-slotted flap, extended
185 Port wing fullt swept position
186 Wing tip structure
187 Fuel vent
188 Port navigation and strobe lights
189 Leading-edge slat rib structure
190 GEC-Marconi Avionics 'Sky Shadow' ECM pod
191 Outboard swivelling pylon
192 Pylon pivot bearing
193 Front spar
194 Port wing integral fuel tank
195 Machined wing skin/ stringer panel
196 Machined wing rib structure
197 Swivelling pylon control rod
198 Port leading edge slat segments, open
199 Slat guide rails
200 Port 'Hindenberger' external fuel tank

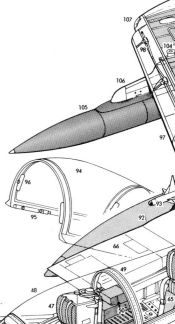

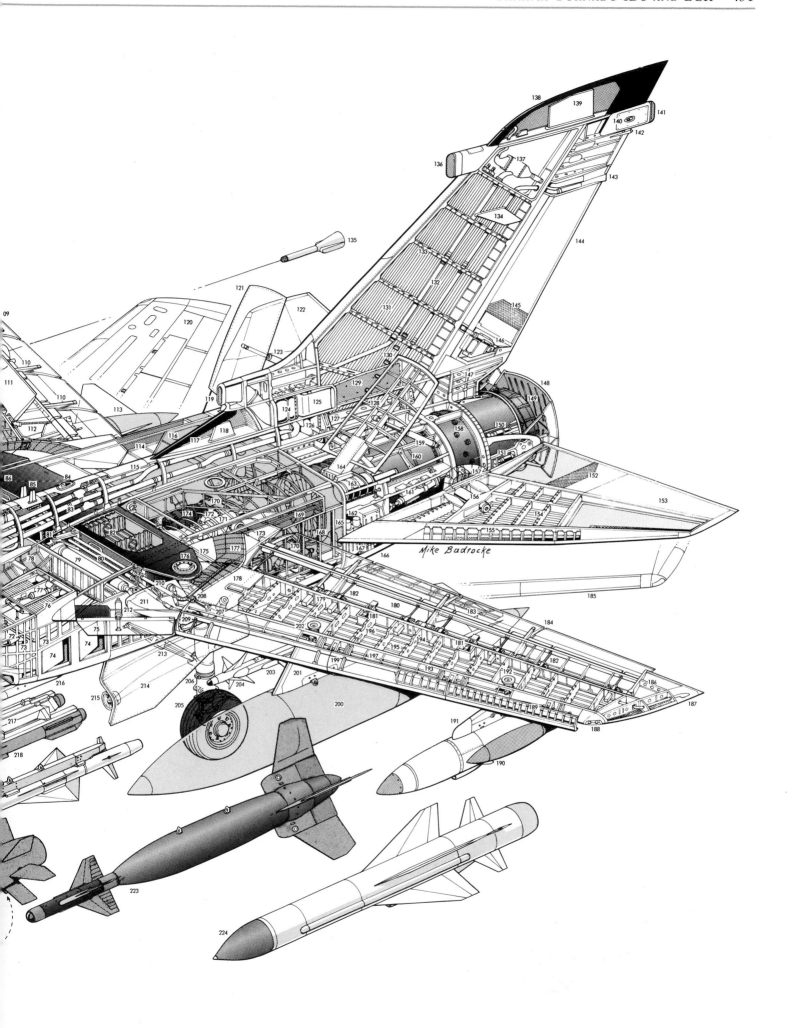

Mike Badrocke

Previous page: *A Tornado dispenses runway cratering and anti-personnel minelets from its underfuselage JP233, now banned under anti-landmine treaties.*
Left: *A Tornado GR.Mk 1 from the Royal Air Force's No.27 Squadron, now a Chinook helicopter unit.*
Inset: *The Tornado's load carrying capability is belied by its small size. RAF Tornados are being upgraded to GR.Mk 4 standard*s. *They carry a range of new precision guided weapons, including Paveway III laser guided bombs.*

The new version was fitted with FLIR and IRLS. It also had an advanced emitter locator system and AGM-88 Harm anti-radiation missiles.

The only export customer for the Tornado so far has been Saudi Arabia, which took delivery of 96 IDS aircraft, some of them in reconnaissance configuration. Tornados never saw active service during the Cold War. British, Italian and Saudi Tornados, however, were used during Operation Desert Storm. They proved devastatingly effective in both low-level and medium-level roles. Some RAF Tornados were hastily modified as laser designators, using the GEC TIALD pod, and this modification was subsequently applied to further aircraft postwar. Great Britain, Germany and Italy subsequently used their aircraft in Balkan operations, including the Kosovo conflict.

RAF Tornados are being upgraded to GR.Mk 4 standards with FLIR, GPS and improved avionics and systems, including an NVG compatible HOTAS cockpit. The new version also has expanded compatibility with a range of new precision guided weapons. These include Paveway III laser guided bombs, Brimstone anti-tank guided missiles and Storm Shadow ASMs.

German and Italian Tornados are also being upgraded with similar modernized systems, sensors and weapons. The Tornado is expected to remain in service until 2020 or later.

McDonnell Douglas F/A-18A-C Hornet

THE F/A-18 HORNET was a naval-ized derivative of Northrop's unsuccessful contender for the USAF's LWF requirement—for which the General Dynamics F-16 was selected. The Hornet closely followed the configuration of the Northrop YF-17 (with Northrop a principal sub-contractor on the Hornet team), but was rather larger and heavier, stressed for carrier operation and with an enlarged nose to accommodate a 28-in (71-cm) radar dish. The F/A-18 was also a very advanced aircraft, with CRT cockpit displays and a ground-breaking digital fly by wire flight control system.

The US Navy selected the multi-role Hornet as a replacement for the A-7 light attack aircraft, while the US Marine Corps selected the aircraft to replace A-4M Skyhawks and F-4 Phantoms. For both services, the Hornet would also have a vital air-to-air capability, allowing the aircraft to augment the more expensive F-14.

The basic F/A-18 Hornet airframe and engine combination made the aircraft arguably the best air-to-air fighter of its generation. It was fast, incredibly agile, fast accelerating with better low speed and high Alpha handling than even the F-16. Once a Hornet has dropped its bombs, it is thus an extremely potent dogfighter.

The Hornet, while able to carry a hefty air-to-ground role, could also carry a load of AIM-7 Sparrow and AIM-9 Sidewinder air-to-air missiles.

Left: *The 'Stingers' of VFA-113 were the first frontline United States Navy F/A-18 Hornet squadron.*

The aircraft's built-in M61A1 20-mm cannon was a versatile and flexible tool for strafing ground targets or for air-to-air combat. Its APG-65 radar has multiple air-to-air and air-to-ground modes, with innovative software which allows simple switching between modes. The Hornet was also easy enough to fly for it to be genuinely possible for aircrew to be proficient in both roles simultaneously.

The F/A-18 was thus a very much more multi-role aeroplane than any of the types it replaced, and unlike any previous aircraft, was a multi-role aircraft on every mission it flew. It could 'swing' from the air-to-air role to air-to-air combat at the press of a switch. This was an unexpected bonus for the Navy, who had anticipated procuring slightly different Hornet sub-variants to equip separate VA- attack and VF-fighter squadrons, but who were instead able to equip VFA- fighter attack squadrons with a single variant.

The Hornet prototype made its maiden flight on November 18, 1978 and the type entered service with the first USN training unit in May 1980. The first frontline Hornets were those of the US Marine Corps' VMFA-314, which was declared operational with the type in January 1983.

The Hornet was sometimes criticized for a lack of range, although it could outrange an F-4 in the same configuration when clean. Moreover, the Hornet was a much more accurate gunnery and bombing platform. Its was widely felt to be able to achieve more on its more limited fuel load, and its range shortfall (compared with

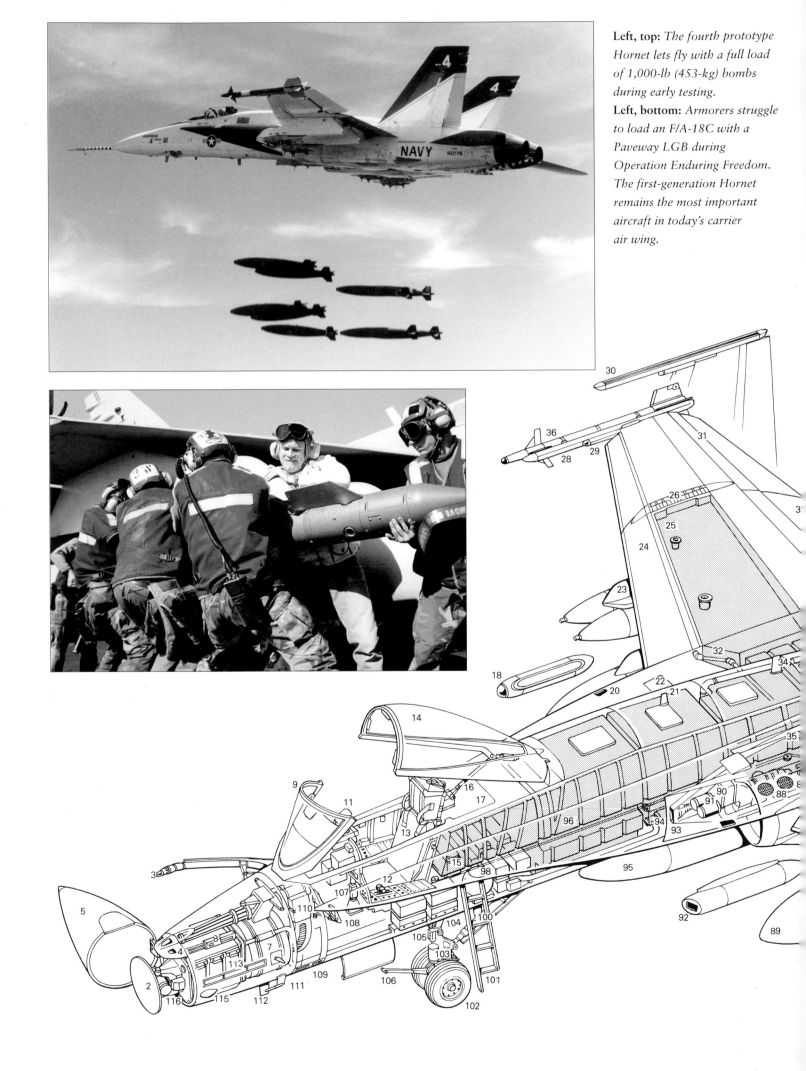

Left, top: *The fourth prototype Hornet lets fly with a full load of 1,000-lb (453-kg) bombs during early testing.*

Left, bottom: *Armorers struggle to load an F/A-18C with a Paveway LGB during Operation Enduring Freedom. The first-generation Hornet remains the most important aircraft in today's carrier air wing.*

McDONNELL DOUGLAS F/A-18 HORNET

1 Radome
2 Planar array radar scanner
3 Flight refuelling probe, retractable
4 Gun gas purging air intakes
5 Radar module withdrawal rails
6 M61A1 Vulcan 20mm rotary cannon
7 Ammunition magazine
8 Angle of attack transmitter
9 Hinged windscreen (access to instruments)
10 Instrument panel and cathode ray tube displays
11 Head-up display
12 Engine throttle levers
13 Martin-Baker Mk10L 'zero-zero' ejection seat
14 Canopy
15 Cockpit pressurization valve
16 Canopy actuator
17 Structural space provision for second seat (TF-18 trainer variant)
18 ASQ-137 Laser Spot Tracker
19 Wing root leading edge extension (LEX)
20 Position Light

21 Tacan antenna
22 Intake ramp bleed air spill duct
23 Starboard wing stores pylons
24 Leading edge flap
25 Starboard wing integral fuel tank
26 Wing fold hinge joint
27 AIM-9P Sidewinder air-to-air missile
28 Missile launch rail
29 Starboard navigation light
30 Wing tip folded position
31 Flap vane
32 Leading edge flap drive shaft interconnection
33 Starboard drooping aileron
34 UHF/IFF antenna
35 Boundary layer bleed air spill duct
36 Leading edge flap drive motor and gearbox
37 Engine bleed air ducting
38 Aft fuselage fuel tanks
39 Hydraulic reservoirs
40 Fuel system vent pipe
41 Fuel venting air grilles
42 Strobe light

43 Tail navigation light
44 Aft radar warning antenna
45 Fuel jettison
46 Starboard rudder
47 Radar warning power amplifier
48 Rudder hydraulic actuator
49 Starboard all-moving tailplane
50 Airbrake
51 ECM antenna
52 Radar warning antenna
53 Formation lighting strip
54 Variable area afterburner nozzles
55 Afterburner duct
56 Engine fire suppression bottles
57 Arrester hook jack and damper
58 Port all-moving tailplane
59 Afterburner nozzle actuator
60 Tailplane pivot bearing
61 Arrester hook
62 Tailplane hydraulic actuator
63 General Electric F404 afterburning turbofan engine
64 Engine digital control unit
65 Formation lighting strip
66 Engine fuel system equipment
67 Port drooping aileron
68 Single slotted Fowler-type flap
69 Aileron hydraulic actuator
70 Wing fold rotary actuator and gearbox
71 Port navigation light
72 AIM-9P sidewinder air-to-air missile
73 Leading edge flap rotary actuator
74 Port leading edge flap
75 Airframe mounted engine accessory gearbox, shaft driven
76 Leading edge slat drive shaft
77 Auxiliary power turbine

78 Flap hydraulic jack
79 Twin stores carrier
80 Outboard stores pylon
81 Aft retracting mainwheel
82 Mk 83 general purpose bombs
83 AIM-7 sparrow air-to-air missile
84 Mainwheel shock absorber strut
85 Inboard stores pylon
86 Main undercarriage pivot bearing
87 Hydraulic retraction jack
88 Radar equipment cooling air spill valves
89 External fuel tank
90 Air conditioning system heat exchanger
91 Radar equipment liquid cooling units
92 AAS-38 forward looking infra-red (FLIR) pod
93 Boundary layer splitter plate
94 Air conditioning system water separator
95 Centerline fuel tank
96 Forward fuselage fuel tanks
97 Avionics equipment bay
98 Liquid oxygen converter
99 Nose undercarriage hydraulic retraction jack
100 UHF antenna
101 Retractable boarding ladder
102 Forward retracting nosewheels
103 Nosewheel steering unit
104 Landing/ taxiing lamp
105 Carrier approach lights
106 Catapult strop link
107 Control column
108 Rudder pedals
109 Gun gas vents
110 Ammunition feed mechanism
111 Pitot head
112 UHF/IFF antenna
113 Radar equipment module
114 Formation lighting strip
115 Forward radar warning antenna
116 Radar scanner tracking mechanism

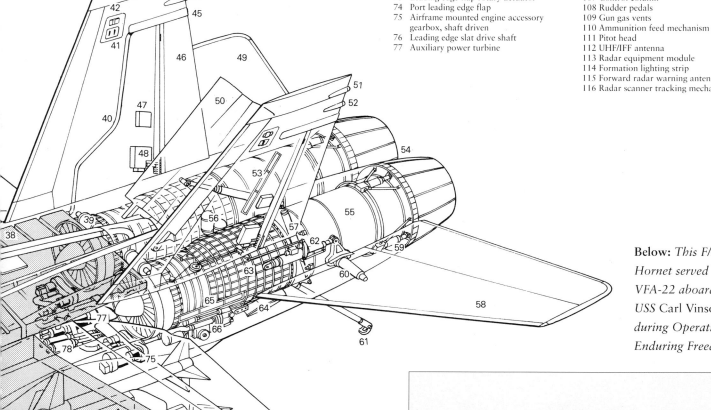

Below: *This F/A-18C Hornet served with VFA-22 aboard the USS Carl Vinson during Operation Enduring Freedom.*

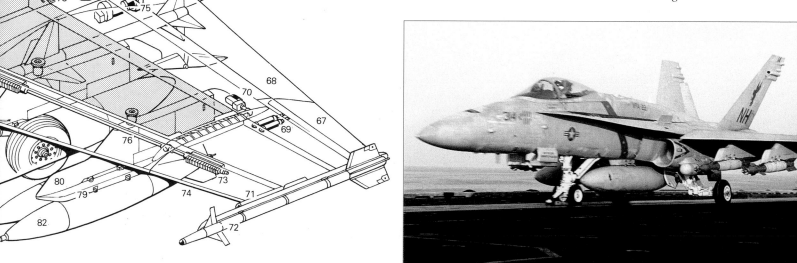

the specification) was less than 20 miles (32km).

The Marines were particularly enthusiastic about the Hornet, and quickly increased their orders for the new aircraft, replacing their A-6 Intruders with the two-seat Night Attack capable F/A-18D. The basic single-seat F/A-18A was augmented by the F/A-18C from 1986, with improved avionics and displays, and most C models also had enhanced night attack capabilities. The oft-derided A-model was a very much better aircraft than many of its critics would allow, especially in the basic air-to-air and day attack roles. It could, however, also carry a laser spot tracker and a navigation FLIR.

Hornets formed the backbone of every carrier air wing. Some experimental air wing compositions included four F/A-18 squadrons, with no F-14s embarked, presaging the new air wing composition which is about to become standard in the next decade. The aircraft has seen extensive combat service, first in operations over Libya in

Right: *Canadian Hornets are officially CF-188s. The Hornet name does not translate into French.*
Below: *A VFA-94 Hornet carrying a pair of GBU-12 LGBs during Operation Enduring Freedom in Afghanistan.*
Inset: *Close-up of the large and drag-inducing twin store rack and pylons as armorers practice bombing up a Hornet.*

1986, and subsequently during Operation Desert Storm and over the Balkans. Progressively upgraded and improved in service, the Hornet has received AIM-120 AMRAAM air-to-air missiles and will gain JHMCS helmet sights, while in the air-to-ground role, the aircraft has gained compatibility with a wide range of advanced weapons. These include JSOW, JDAM, SLAM-ER and the WCMD. Later Hornets have gained upgraded APG-73 radar, and improved FLIR and laser designator equipment.

The Hornet was widely exported. Export Hornets, especially those in Canada, have been used in action in the air-to-ground role.

LOCKHEED F-117A

THE LOCKHEED F-117A, officially known as the Nighthawk, is perhaps best known as the Stealth Fighter. It is, however, a fighter only in the same sense as the F-111 and has only the most limited air-to-air self defense potential, and this has never been exploited. Theoretically, the F-117 could carry a Sidewinder for self defense, but no such fit has ever even been trialled, and the F-117 remains a dedicated single-role aircraft. The Stealth Fighter is a bomber—pure and simple. The aircraft's sole raison d'etre is to deliver up to two 2,000-lb (907-kg) PGMs against high value targets. It achieves this by penetrating enemy air defenses without fighter escort or SEAD cover, relying on a degree of 'invisibility' to radar, or Stealth, in order to achieve this.

The aircraft is primarily tasked with destroying elements of an enemy's air defense network, and with clearing 'corridors' through which conventional attack aircraft and bombers can pass en route to their targets. This is because of its ability to evade and avoid detection by enemy air defenses. Stealth is sometimes fundamentally misunderstood. Stealth aircraft are not invisible to enemy radar, they just appear much smaller to it, and thereby effectively reduce the range of that radar. The aircraft may slip through unnoticed, or detection by radar may thereby be delayed to the extent that the enemy defenses do not have time to react to their presence. Stealth is also difficult to achieve. This is because a ten-fold decrease in radar range requires a ten-thousand fold reduction in target radar cross section (RCS)!

The Stealthy aircraft cannot have a low RCS when viewed from every aspect. The 'trick' is to present only the least visible sides of the aircraft to enemy radars. If a F-117 (for example) turns belly-on to an enemy radar, exposing its large, flat underside, it will become more likely to be seen. The really impressive thing about the F-117 is its mission planning system, which calculates routes between enemy radars which minimize the aircraft's exposure to them. Everything can go wrong, if a look-down Airborne Early Warning radar shows up in the wrong place, or if a mobile air defense radar unexpectedly plugs a gap between fixed radar sites. The F-117A may then be detected in time to be hit by guns, SAMs or fighters.

The Stealth fighter was designed as the culmination of years of effort to reduce the RCS of military aircraft. Previous aircraft, including the SR-71 Blackbird and the Ryan AQM-91 Firefly drone, had featured reduced RCS. This was combined with extreme high speed or high altitude performance in order to survive. DARPA's 1975 project Harvey (named after the invisible rabbit in the eponymously named Jimmy Stewart movie) aimed to create an aircraft that might penetrate enemy air defenses by dint of its invisibility to radar alone.

In September 1975, Lockheed and Northrop were given contracts to design Stealth demonstrators, known as XSTs (Experimental Survivable

Right: *This F-117A of the 4450th Tactical Group is seen at the top secret base at Tonopah, south-central Nevada, the first home of the USAF's Nighthawks.*

Left: *The Lockheed F-117 Stealth Fighter's highly swept wing reduces radar cross section rather than drag.*
Below: *A Lockheed F-117 Stealth lands with the aid of its braking parachute. The aircraft's faceted fuselage scatters radar energy, thereby reducing the aircraft's apparent radar cross section.*

Testbeds). Both companies built and tested mock-ups and models, but it was Lockheed that won the contract to build two flying XSTs under the designation 'Have Blue'.

These aircraft remain more highly classified than the production Lockheed F-117s which followed.

This is because they are closer to the uncompromized 'optimum' shape for minimum RCS. This is a highly-swept 'bevelled' diamond, with the external shape of the aircraft consisting of flat plates or facets, carefully tailored so as to reflect incoming radar energy away from its source.

Left: *The Lockheed F-117A has forward-and downward-looking infra red sensors in the nose. These are used for finding and designating targets which are then hit with up to two 2,000-lb (907-kg) PGMs.*
Below: *The F-117A uses the USAF's standard 'boom' refuelling method.*

The first 'Have Blue' demonstrator made its maiden flight on December 1, 1977, and the two aircraft quickly proved undetectable by most US radars (excepting that of the E-3 Sentry AWACS, and that only at short ranges). Even before they flew, Lockheed had received a contract to develop the concept to produce an operational attack aircraft, then known simply by the program name 'Senior Trend'.

The Senior Trend aircraft had larger, outward canted twin tailfins, reduced wing sweep and a shorter nose. The aircraft used systems and components from a variety of in-service types, in order to reduce cost and timescale and to maintain security. Ordering extra F/A-18 HUDs, ejection seats and F404 engines, and F-15 and A-10 landing gear components attracted less attention than ordering new items.

There were five development aircraft ordered, and later 59 F-117As were built, allowing the USAF to equip two frontline squadrons and a training unit. The first prototype made its maiden flight on June 18, 1981. The type then became operational with the shadowy 4450th Tactical Group at Tonopah, a secret airfield deep inside Nevada's Nellis range complex, in October 1983. The aircraft operated in total secrecy until November 1988, when the type's existence was formally acknowledged.

This disclosure was made in part to allow the unit to begin training by daylight, and also for political reasons (it was weeks before a Presidential election). It allowed the F-117A to move to Holloman AFB, New Mexico, where the operating unit became the 37th TFW (later re-designated as the 49th FW). The aircraft has participated in various combat operations, including the US intervention in Panama, Desert Storm, Kosovo and Afghanistan.

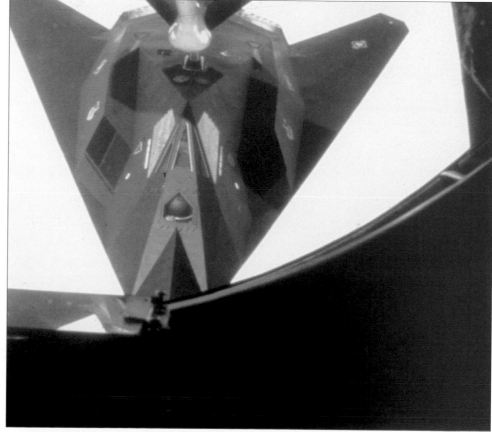

ROCKWELL B-1B

WORK ON A new strategic manned bomber (the AMSA or Advanced Manned Strategic Aircraft) began in the early 1960s, even as ICBMs began to take over the primary strategic deterrent role. It became clear that the use of both manned bombers and ICBMs would complicate matters for an enemy, and would provide better capability against small and mobile targets. This combination made it difficult for an enemy to simultaneously knock out both elements of the US airborne deterrent. This is because bombers can be scrambled (or even be on airborne alert) when enemy missiles are first detected, and can be underway before their bases are wiped out.

North American Rockwell submitted the best and cheapest proposal to meet the Pentagon's 1969 Request for Proposals, and received the contract to build five B-1 prototypes for flight testing. There were two more for static testing, while General Electric received the vital contract for engines

for the new aircraft.

The B-1 was designed to be able to operate from a 6,000-ft (1,828-m) runway, with no special ground facilities. This allowed it to use literally hundreds of small airfields scattered throughout the United States. This in turn dictated the use of a variable geometry 'swing wing'.

The aircraft was designed to be able to cruise at Mach 2.05-2.1 at high level. It was also intended to survive nuclear warfare, with all of its avionics and systems hardened to survive electro-magnetic pulse, over-pressure, radiant heat, radiation and neutron flow. The type was supposed to penetrate using its very low RCS and powerful defensive avionics, and was even intended to be capable of detecting and destroying enemy AWACS platforms. Furthermore, it was designed to penetrate at low level in the most heavily defended airspace.

The requirements were downgraded in early 1971, allowing a reduction in low level penetration speed from Mach 1.2 to Mach 0.85, and reducing the number of test aircraft from five to three. The development schedule was also allowed to stretch and slip. These measures all saved money, and provided time while the USAF studied various alternatives. These included a stretched FB-111G and a re-engined B-52 derivative.

Left: *The 'spider's web' of white lines on the nose of this B-1B are designed to help the tanker's boom operator to find the aircraft's refuelling receptacle.*
Below: *An early artist's impression showing a B-1B carrying cruise missiles externally. The first production B-1B made its maiden flight on October 18, 1984.*

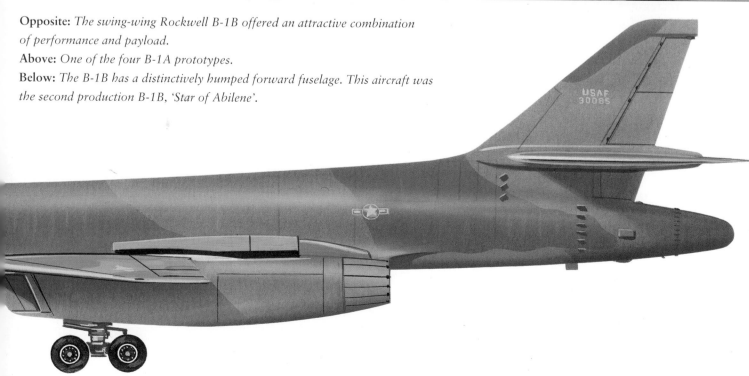

Opposite: *The swing-wing Rockwell B-1B offered an attractive combination of performance and payload.*
Above: *One of the four B-1A prototypes.*
Below: *The B-1B has a distinctively humped forward fuselage. This aircraft was the second production B-1B, 'Star of Abilene'.*

The Rockwell B-1A made its maiden flight on April 1, 1976. This was followed by two more prototypes and a fourth aircraft which was effectively a pre-production machine. This had conventional ejection seats replacing the original 'escape capsule', and with a full EW fit. President Jimmy Carter, however, cancelled the entire program on June 30, 1977.

Rockwell did not give up, however, and explored a number of lower-cost derivatives of the aircraft, even including one design with a fixed wing. While the USAF turned its attention to the advanced, stealthy ATB (Advanced Technology Bomber, later the B-2) it became clear that there would be a need for an interim bomber. This aircraft would plug the gap between the B-52 and the ATB. Rockwell proposed an austere B-1 LRCA (Long Range Combat Aircraft) derivative of the B-1A as an interim bomber. This aircraft had increased gross weight, but with a slower maximum speed (down to Mach 1.2) and simplified intakes.

As the Rockwell B-1B, the new aircraft was ordered into production by incoming President Ronald Reagan in October 1981. He announced that 100 B-1Bs would be procured as part of the Strategic Modernization Program, to be followed by 132 Northrop B-2As. There were two B-1As modified to serve as prototypes for the new B-1Bs. The first of these flew in its new configuration on March 23, 1983.

The first production B-1B made its maiden flight on October 18, 1984, although it utilized B-1A components, and was filled with instrumentation. The aircraft was destined never to

Right: *The two antennas behind the cockpit served the Rockwell B-1B's sophisticated ECM system which supported penetration of hostile airspace.*

Following page: *The Rockwell B-1B originally had refuelling alignment markings applied to the nose in black, but these proved too hard to see.*

Left: *An early Rockwell B-1B taxying with its wings swept fully forward. The type remains the backbone of the USAF's long-range bomber force.*
Below: *The third and fourth B-1A prototypes flew in three-tone camouflage. A long dorsal fairing containing a Crosseye jamming system was later fitted.*

enter frontline service. The type finally entered service with the 96th BW at Dyess Air Force Base in Texas, on December 21, 1983. Early problems included leaking fuel tanks and engine failures, while the complex defensive avionics led some to dub the B-1B as the 'Self-Jamming Bomber'.

The type was not used during Operation Desert Storm in 1991, since it then still had a wholly nuclear role. By 1997, however, the Rockwell B-1B had completely transitioned to the conventional role. Since then, the B-1B has become a key element in the United States Air Force's new expeditionary warfare forces, equipping the composite 366th Wing.

The Rockwell B-1B has performed with distinction in a series of US combat operations. Most recently the type has been deployed over Afghanistan during 2001–2002.

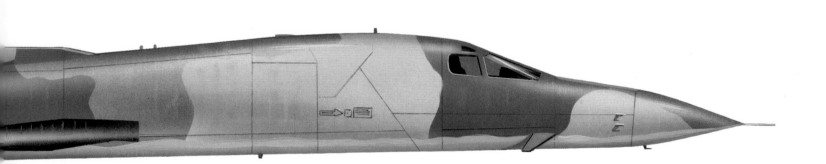

TUPOLEV TU-160

THE TU-160 ENJOYS the dubious distinction of being the largest and heaviest bomber ever built, yet was almost not selected for production at all. The requirement for a supersonic long-range bomber to replace the ageing Myasischev 3M and the Tu-95 attracted bids from Sukhoi (with a scaled up derivative of the T-4) and Myasischev. The latter had been reconstituted in 1967, following its dissolution under Khruschev in 1960.

The first design submitted by the Tupolev OKB bore some resemblance to the Tu-144 supersonic airliner, with a similar ogival planform wing. Tupolev hoped to exploit the expertise it had attained during the Tu-144 SST program, hoping that this would provide cost and time savings. The Air Forces felt that this was too conservative, and during one very emotional meeting, the Commander of Long Range Aviation, Colonel General Reshetnikov, angrily accused the OKB of "trying to sell us virtually a passenger aeroplane!" Moreover, while the Tu-144 was efficient enough in a long-range supersonic cruise, it could not provide adequate range at subsonic speeds, and had inadequate take off and landing performance.

Sukhoi's bid was reluctantly set aside because the OKB was already engaged in too many other vitally important programs. These included the Su-24 tactical bomber, the Su-25 Shturmovik and the T-10 (which became the Su-27 tactical fighter). It was felt that the T-4 would be an unwelcome distraction.

Myasischev's proposed M-18 and M-20 projects both featured a VG wing. The M-18 design had a canard configuration, while the M-20 followed the configuration of the US B-1 bomber. The Myasischev OKB designs were favored by Reshetnikov, because they promised exceptional performance characteristics and impressive operational capabilities.

There were doubts, however, about the re-formed Myasischev OKB after its long enforced 'lay-off', and the loss of many of its senior engineers. Not all of them returned to it when it was re-established. The OKB had limited resources and lacked the large production facilities required, while the age and independent character of the chief designer (70 years) was also felt to present problems.

After the Air Forces' rejection of its ogival wing project, Tupolev turned to the Type 70 bomber project. This incorporated the favoured VG wing (giving benign low-speed handling and high supersonic speed) and was approved for development in 1975. The new type soon gained influential support, while there was never any doubt that the OKB had the required experience in the design and development of large aircraft types in general, and bombers in particular.

A mock-up was produced with engines mounted in vertical 'stacked' pairs. This arrangement, however, soon gave way to a more conventional layout, with paired engines in underwing nacelles below the fixed wing section like those of the B-1.

The engines used were Kuznetsov

Right: *The Tu-160 is the world's largest bomber, and enjoys both high-altitude and low-level capabilities. It has also set a succession of world records.*

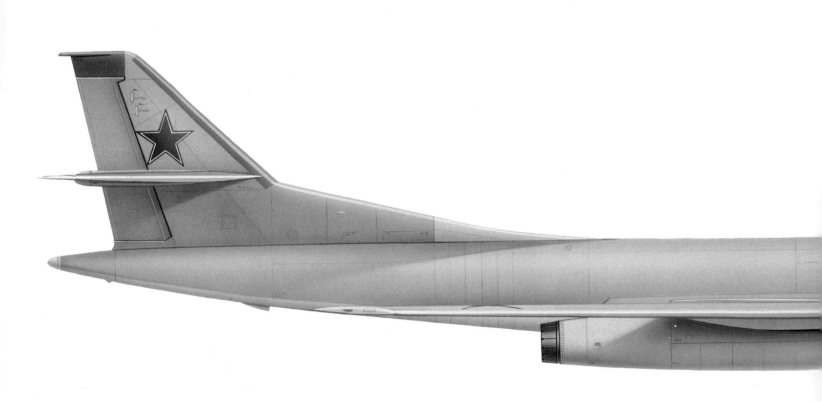

Left: *The Tu-160 was designed to meet a requirement for a supersonic long-range bomber to replace the ageing Myasischev 3M and the Tu-95 whose origins lay in the technology of the 1940s.*

Below: *An early artist's impression of the Tupolev Tu-160. The aircraft was first photographed by US agents in 1981.*

NK-32s, derivatives of the NK-144 used by the Tu-144 and of the NK-22/25 used by the Tu-22M-2 and Tu-22M-3. These offered a low radar and IR signature, not least thanks to a screening unit which shielded the first stage of the engine compressor.

The Tu-160 was heavily influenced by the original Rockwell B-1A, which was designed to penetrate at high level, relying on its high-speed, high-altitude performance and a highly sophisticated ECM suite. The B-1A was cancelled, and replaced by the cheaper, simpler B-1B, which relied on low-level subsonic flight and reduced RCS to penetrate. The Tu-160 can penetrate at low-level at transonic speed, or at high-level at supersonic speeds. The aircraft was built using new construction methods and materials including new high strength aluminum and titanium alloys. The design was also tailored to give reduced radar and IR signature.

The aircraft was primarily designed as a dedicated cruise missile carrier, with two tandem fuselage weapons bays. These each contained a rotary carousel for six RK-55 (AS-15 'Kent') or 12 Kh-15P (AS-16 'Kickback') cruise missiles or a wide range of free-fall guided and unguided bombs.

The Tupolev Tu-160 cockpit is spacious and comfortable. The aircraft incorporates a folding bed, a cooker and toilet for long-range operations. The pilots use fighter-type control columns and conventional analogue instrument displays, with no MFDs, CRTs and no HUD, which were all planned for later versions of the Tu-160. Most avionics systems were adapted from those used by the Tupolev Tu-22M.

The Tu-160 was equipped with terrain following and attack radar, as well as a forward-looking TV camera for visual weapon aiming. The aircraft is also fitted with a retractable refuelling probe giving genuine intercontinental range.

The development program of the Tupolev Tu-160 was extremely protracted. Following a first flight on December 19, 1981, series production eventually began at Kazan, central Russia, in 1986. This continued until termination in January 1992. The first photographs of the Tupolev Tu-160 were taken by US agents on November 25, 1981. This was 26 days before the aircraft made its maiden flight.

Between 32 and 39 Tupolev Tu-160s are believed to have been built. This figure probably includes the two Tu-160 prototypes, although early plans were for the delivery of 100 aircraft—to exactly match the number of Rockwell B-1Bs delivered to the USAF's Strategic Air Command.

There were 19 Tupolev Tu-160s delivered to the first operational unit (the 184th Heavy Bomber Regiment) at Priluki in Ukraine from 1987. Even after the aircraft entered service, problems continued to severely restrict operations. These problems included a shortage of basic flying equipment, difficulties with the aircraft's K-36A ejection seats and poor reliability of engines and systems.

Despite these problems, the Tu-160 demonstrated its capabilities by setting a succession of 44 world records. These included 1,000- (621 miles) and 2,000-km (1,242 miles) closed circuit speed records.

The first regiment was left under Ukrainian command after the break-up of the Soviet Union, but eight of its aircraft were later transferred back to Russian control in payment for natural gas debts. The remainder were scrapped (or, in the case of three aircraft, demilitarized for use as civilian satellite launch platforms).

There were six newer Tupolev Tu-160s delivered directly from the factory to Engels, which had been intended to be the second Tu-160 base. These Tupolev Tu-160s were joined by the eight ex-Ukrainian aircraft in 2001. One incomplete aircraft was later finished and delivered in 2000. Further aircraft may be built using incomplete aircraft stored at the Kazan factory in Russia.

DASSAULT MIRAGE 2000N/D

Dassault FIRST STARTED work on a strike version of the Mirage 2000 (which first flew in 1978, and entered service in the fighter role from 1982) in 1979, building a pair of prototypes of the Mirage 2000P (for Penetration). The new version was based on the airframe of the Mirage 2000B trainer and had local strengthening for prolonged low level flight. The 2000P was quickly re-designated as the Mirage 2000N (for Nucléaire) and featured a new CSF Antilope 5 ground-mapping and terrain following radar, with a dedicated WSO's station in the rear cockpit. The cockpit is compatible with night vision goggles.

The Mirage 2000N prototype made its maiden flight on February 3, 1983, and entered service in July 1988. The first 31 Mirage 2000N-K1s were solely dedicated to the nuclear strike role, carrying the ASMP cruise missile, but thereafter the next 44 aircraft had conventional and nuclear capabilities. These aircraft were delivered as the Mirage 2000N-K2. The early aircraft were later given conventional attack capabilities, becoming K2s themselves.

The aircraft was fitted with a SNEC-MA M53-P2 afterburning turbofan powerplant. It had a maximum range of 700km (434 miles) and a service

Left: *This desert camouflaged Mirage 2000N of the 4th Escadre was photographed during an exercise at Nellis AFB, Nevada. This aircraft carries the massive tanks characteristic of this strike/attack version.*

Following page: *The Mirage 2000N entered service in 1988.*

ceiling of 16,460m (4,000ft).

Some 75 later Mirage 2000Ns were delivered with no nuclear or ASMP capability, but with enhanced avionics, sensors, displays and navigation systems. This conventional strike derivative of the Mirage 2000N was briefly known as the Mirage 2000N Prime, before being re-designated as Mirage 2000Ds. The prototype made its maiden flight on February 19, 1991. Further production resulted in an eventual total of 86 Mirage 2000Ds being supplied to the Armée de l'Air.

The Dassault Mirage 2000D has laser-guided weapons. These can be delivered with the PDL-CT laser designator pod which is fitted with an infra-camera. The aircraft is also able to carry out all-weather blind attacks on coordinates.

The Armée de l'Air have used the Dassault Mirage 2000D intensively in international operations. These include Operation Desert Storm (1991) and Operation Deliberate Force in Bosnia (1995).

An export version of the conventional attack Dassault Mirage 2000D has been marketed as the Mirage 2000S. Some single-seat export Mirage 2000s are used in dual air-to-air and air-to-ground roles. These include those aircraft supplied to Egypt, Peru and India.

The Indian Air Force aircraft even have the same Antilope terrain following radar. These aircraft were used to deliver PGMs in the 1999 conflict with Pakistan over disputed region of Kashmir on the Indo-Pakistan border.

Above: *The Mirage 2000D is a conventional attack version of the 2000N. This aircraft carries AS30L missiles and an ATLIS laser designator. This derivative of the Mirage 2000N was briefly known as the Mirage 2000N Prime.*

Right: *A Mirage 2000D of EC 2/3 Champagne refuels from an RAF VC 10.*

McDONNELL DOUGLAS F-15E

The basic F-15 Eagle was originally intended to perform both air-to-air and air-to-ground missions. The latter role, however, was very much secondary, and was abandoned (primarily as an economy measure) in 1975. The YF-15A prototype had made its maiden flight on July 27, 1972. The fighter F-15 was always a long-range aircraft. The type had sufficient range to permit it to self ferry to Europe without inflight refuelling. This would later facilitate the development of a dedicated air-to-ground version of the F-15.

Development of the F-15E (known to its manufacturers, but not the USAF, as the Strike Eagle) began in the early 1970s, to meet the USAF's ETF (Enhanced Tactical Fighter) requirement for an F-111 replacement. The ETF requirement outlined an aircraft which would be able to fulfil the strike mission without escort, EW or AWACS support. And although it later became clear that such an aircraft was already being developed as the F-117, the F-15E was developed as a fallback, in case the technically risky Stealth Fighter ran into problems. This was not revealed (no-one could even talk about the F-117) and the new aircraft was pushed as being a way of augmenting the inadequate number of F-111Fs then available. The requirement was re-named as the Dual Role Fighter (DRF).

McDonnell Douglas and Hughes together used the second two-seat TF-15A prototype as a demonstrator and prototype for the Strike Eagle. The aircraft had FAST pack conformal fuel tanks and a belly-mounted Pave Tack laser designator. The prototype was fitted with a new APG-63PSP version of the basic Eagle's radar, with Synthetic Aperture and ground mapping capabilities. It also had a new rear cockpit, with new MFDs and hand controllers for the WSO. The aircraft flew in its new form on July 8, 1980, and was then evaluated against the rival F-16XL. This aircraft was an F-16 derivative with a new cranked Delta wing, before being selected for production in 1984.

The production McDonnell Douglas F-15E was extensively redesigned to cope with increased take-off weights. It was also intended to accommodate new EW systems and external hardpoints for the bombload of up to 24,250lb (10,999kg), and for LANTIRN targeting and navigation pods. The aircraft has an extended fatigue life (to 16,000 flying hours) and can sustain 9 g at heavy all-up weights. The new version also featured the new APG-70 radar. The conformal fuel tanks can be removed, but are routinely carried as part of the standard 'fit'.

The aircraft retains the full air-to-air capabilities of the F-15C interceptor, and is arguably the world's most capable multi-role fighter. The first true F-15E flew on December 11, 1986. Since much development had been completed using the TF-15A and a fleet of converted F-15Bs and F-15Ds,

Right: *Without a load of air-to-ground ordnance, the McDonnell Douglas F-15E retains all of the performance and agility of the F-15 Eagle.*

deliveries to the first training unit began on April 12, 1988. The McDonnell Douglas F-15E entered frontline service with the United States Air Force in December 1989.

The McDonnell Douglas F-15E played a vital role during Operation Desert Storm in 1991. The USAF Strike Eagles proved especially effective in the Scud-hunting role, using their APG-70 radar to detect and track these elusive targets in Iraq. Although efforts were made to clear the Strike Eagles to carry nuclear weapons, it is believed that the strike role was abandoned before any F-15E units became operational.

The Strike Eagle has been exported to both Saudi Arabia and Israel, as the F-15S and F-15I respectively. The F-15S was down-graded at Israeli request, although apart from the deletion of nuclear capability, only a few APG-70 radar modes were 'de-tuned'. Some ECM equipment was replaced by older kit. The same equipment was similarly removed from F-15Is, and replaced by indigenous Israeli equipment. Saudi Arabia has received 72 F-15S aircraft, while Israeli deliveries total 25 aircraft.

Variants of the McDonnell Douglas F-15E have also been marketed to Greece, Korea and the UAE. The high price tag of the Strike Eagle, however, severely limits its appeal.

Opposite: *The third production F-15E, with its low-intensity formation lights aglow, and carrying a load of 500-lb (226-kg) bombs.*
Left: *An F-15E test aircraft fires an AGM-65 Maverick ASM during early trials.*
Below: *F-15Es from the 4th TFW at Seymour Johnson AFB, North Carolina, with a KC-10 Extender. The Fourth played a vital role in Operation Desert Storm.*

NORTHROP B-2

THE B-2 WAS designed to meet the same kind of low-observable 'stealthy' requirement as the smaller, angular 'faceted' F-117. The aircraft, however, looks very different with its smooth, rather bulbous and curvacious whale-lake fuselage.

The reason for the apparently very different shapes of the two aircraft may lie in the rapid advance in the processing power of modern computers. When the F-117 was designed, its creators could only calculate radar cross section by using the RCS of individual flat panels. Some suggest, however, that the B-2's designers were able to accurately calculate the RCS of three-dimensional curved shapes. Others suggest that Northrop arrived at their 'stealthy' shape by trial and error. The truth probably lies somewhere in the middle—that Northrop began looking at 'curved' stealth shapes during the 'Have Blue' program which resulted in the F-117. They then refined them during the 'Assault Breaker' program for a stealthy battlefield surveillance aircraft (which resulted in the 'Tacit Blue' demonstrator), before further refining its approach for the Advanced Technology Bomber (ATB).

The Northrop B-2 was never surrounded by the same degree of secrecy as the F-117, because it was never

Left: Northrop's approach to RCS reduction used smooth curves rather than the angular facets used by Lockheed on the F-117.
Following page: *The B-2 prototype refuels from an Air Force KC-10 Extender tanker. The first B-2 prototype made its maiden flight in July 1989. Five more development and 15 production aircraft followed.*

intended for the same kind of 'deniable' semi-covert role. Rather, the B-2 was to be part of the US strategic deterrent, and as such was always intended to be highly visible and deliberately, intimidatingly threatening.

The aircraft was designed to meet arguably the most challenging military requirement in history, since its primary purpose was to penetrate Soviet airspace unseen. It was then intended to destroy mobile ICBMs and other high priority targets. The B-2 was to execute such strikes before the Soviet Union even realized that it was under attack, and perhaps before US ICBMs and other assets could degrade the enemy's air defenses!

This requirement for a 'stealthy' bomber was authorized in 1979. A design study, capped at $2 million was commissioned (any project costing more than this would have had to have been reported to Congress). The B-2 was designed to be much more than a one-mission bomber, and was designed to be able to return to any airfield capable of handling a Boeing 727 to be re-armed and re-fuelled for a second strike.

Northrop's proposed Senior Ice reportedly beat Lockheed's competing Senior Peg design in almost every area. After Reagan replaced Carter as US president in November 1980, the decision was taken to build an interim force of 100 B-1s. This was to be followed by 132 Northrop B-2 Advanced Technology Bombers.

The basic flying wing configuration was selected at an early stage, initially with vestigial inward-canted fins above the centre section. This migrated outwards towards the wingtips

NORTHROP B-2A SPIRIT

1 Retractable starboard navigation light
2 ILS antenna
3 Split drag rudder/airbrake with elevon function
4 Drag rudder internal rotary actuators
5 Elevon hydraulic actuators
6 Outer wing panel integral fuel tank
7 Leading edge suppressed antennae
8 Graphite composite skin panelling
9 Outboard elevon hydraulic actuators
10 Starboard outboard elevon
11 Dual inboard elevons
12 Inboard elevon hydraulic actuators
13 Trailing edge integral wing tank
14 Wing panel inboard integral tank
15 Starboard main undercarriage, stowed position
16 Starboard engine bays
17 Intake suction relief doors/ secondary intakes
18 Airframe mounted auxiliary equipment gearbox
19 Rotary flight refuelling receptacle
20 Cockpit sloping rear pressure

bulkhead
21 Avionics equipment racks, port and starboard
22 Space provision for third crew member
23 Third crew station escape hatch
24 Starboard engine combined air intake
25 Boundary layer diverter
26 Cockpit roof escape/ ejection hatches, port and starboard
27 Two-crew standard flight deck
28 Mission Commander's Aces-II ejection seat
29 Pilot's ejection seat
30 Control column, conventional stick and rudder actuating quadruplex digital fly-by-wire flight control system
31 Instrument panel with full-colour, multi-function CRT displays
32 Instrument panel shroud
33 Single curvature windscreen panels with low-observable gold film coatings
34 Starboard AN/APQ-181 low-probability of intercept (LPI)

electronically scanned, multi-function J-band radar unit
35 Flush airflow data sensors, above and below
36 Cockpit front pressure bulkhead
37 Nosewheel leg door
38 Nosewheel leg strut
39 Hydraulic steering unit
40 Twin nosewheels, aft retracting
41 Dual taxying lights
42 Rear breaker strut
43 Crew door mounted telescopic boarding ladder
44 Port AN/APQ-181 radar unit
45 Astro-navigation sensor
46 Cockpit hatch emergency release
47 Weapons bay retractable spoiler panels
48 Port weapons bay outer door
49 Environmental control system equipment bay
50 Port intake boundary layer diverter
51 Boundary layer secondary air intake to air systems heat exchanger
52 Intake S-duct common to both engines with by-pass to bay cooling and exhaust duct mixers
53 Allied Signal Auxiliary Power Unit (APU)
54 APU intake
55 Port engine-driven auxiliary equipment gearbox
56 Engine intake compressor face
57 General Electric F118-GE-100 non after burning turbofan engines

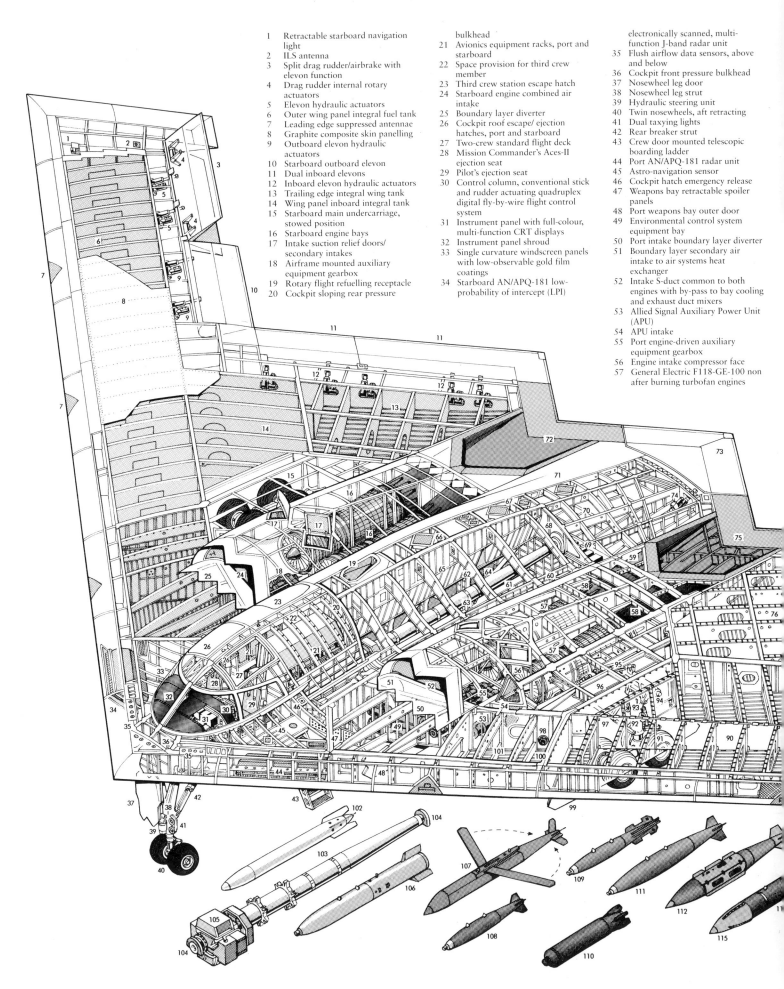

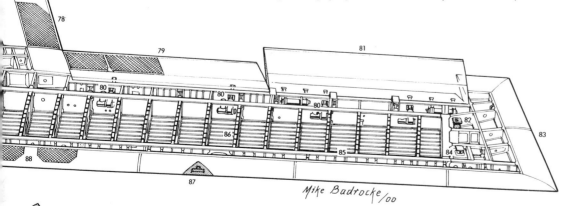

58 Exhaust mixing ducts incorporating flame-jet generators
59 Jet pipes, flattened towards exhaust ducts
60 Engine/ weapons bay firewall and structural bulkhead
61 Port weapons bay
62 Machined transverse bay roof beams
63 Weapons bay rotary launcher
64 Starboard weapons bay
65 Centre-fuselage keel structure
66 Global Positioning System (GPS) antenna
67 Flush communications antennae
68 Weapons bay rear bulkhead
69 Rear equipment bay
70 Aft fuselage structure
71 All-composite skin panelling

72 Exhaust duct carbon composite thermal protection lining
73 Gust Load Alleviation System (GLAS) 'beaver' tail surface
74 'Beaver' tail hydraulic actuators, port and starboard
75 Port engine exhaust duct
76 Rear integral fuel tank bay
77 Inboard elevon actuators, two per surface
78 Port dual inboard elevons
79 Outboard elevon
80 Outboard elevon hydraulic actuators, two per surface
81 Port split drag rudder/ airbrake, open
82 ILS localiser antenna
83 Composite wing tip edge member

84 Port retractable navigation light
85 Front spar, continuous from centerline to wing tip
86 Port outer wing panel integral fuel tank
87 Leading edge flush antennae
88 Leading edge structure, composite skin panelling with honeycomb substrate
89 Wing graphite composite bottom skin/ stringer panel
90 Rear main spar
91 Four-wheel main undercarriage bogie, forward retracting
92 Leg-mounted dual landing lights
93 Articulated mainwheel leg strut
94 Mainwheel leg pivot mounting
95 Hydraulic retraction jack

96 Port mainwheel bay
97 Main undercarriage drag/ breaker strut
98 Pressure refuelling connection via mainwheel bay
99 Single-piece composite mainwheel bay door
100 Wing panel/ centre section main joint rib
101 Inboard fuel tank bay
102 B61 nuclear weapon
103 Weapons bay Advanced Rotary Launcher (ARL)
104 Launcher mounting adaptors
105 Rotating drive unit and sequenced weapons release mechanism
106 B83 nuclear weapon
107 Joint Stand-Off Weapon (JSOW), may be configured with sub-munitions or 500-Ib HE unitary warhead
108 Mk 82 500-Ib HE bomb
109 Mk 62 mine with 'snakeye' retardation tail kit
110 GBU-89 Gator sub-munition dispenser
111 Mk 84 2000-Ib HE bomb
112 GBU-31 2000-Ib Joint Direct Attack Munition (JDAM)
113 GATS/GAM (GPS-Aided Targeting System/ GPS-Aided Munition) GAM-113
114 2000-Ib bomb based GAM-84
115 Grooved aerodynamic nose jacket keeps weapon at constant angle throughout trajectory.

Above: *The B-2 prototype was rolled out amid great ceremony, in contrast to the secretive introduction of the Stealth Fighter.*

Above, left: *The undercarriage doors of the Northrop B-2 have saw-cut edges to minimize radar cross section.*

Above, right: *The intakes of the Northrop B-2 are carefully tailored to hide the compressors from radar, and to minimize radar cross section.*

Following page: *The Northrop B-2 prototype being towed out from its hangar on the occasion of its ceremonial rollout. Since the B-2 became operational it has served in every significant US operation, including the war in Afghanistan.*

before being dropped altogether. The W-shaped trailing edge was adopted in order to give sufficient extra strength and rigidity for low level penetration, should it ever become necessary. The aircraft uses an advanced, 'Low Probability of Intercept' radar to find and attack its targets.

The first B-2 prototype made its maiden flight on July 17, 1989, about two years late. This was followed by five more development aircraft (all later converted to the full Block 30

operational standard) and 15 production aircraft. B-2 production plans had been slashed from 132 to only 75 under the Pentagon's 1990 Major Aircraft Review. This 43 per cent cut in aircraft numbers saved 19 per cent in total program costs. Worse was to follow, with President George Bush seeking funds for only five extra B-2s (bringing the total to 21) in 1992.

A 1994 offer by Northrop to build 20 more B-2s at a guaranteed unit price of $566 million was turned

down by President Bill Clinton's administration, with USAF support. The USAF have been happy with the B-2, but regard the present single wing force as adequate, while they have pressing priorities elsewhere, not least with the F-22 fighter.

The B-2 was declared operational in the conventional role in January 1997. It has since played a significant part in every major US operation, having seen active service in the Kosovo campaign and in operations over Afghanistan.

The aircraft has an unparallelled ability to hit difficult targets with great force and precision from its US base. This freed the United States from reliance on basing in friendly allied countries, or even from gaining over-flight permission from reluctant allies.

The Northrop B-2 is claimed to represent an extremely cost-effective airpower solution. The aircraft can operate with minimal tanker support, and without the need for SEAD or fighter escort, and it can penetrate

enemy defenses and drop cheaper weapons with great accuracy. The aircraft is capable of flying extremely long-duration missions. A toilet and rest bunk are routinely carried.

Despite the existence of the B-2 never being a secret, mystery continues to surround the aircraft. Some even believe that the B-2 incorporates a unique electrical charging ('electro-gravitic') system, whose effect is said to be to reduce aircraft weight by countering gravity!

McDonnell Douglas (Boeing) F/A-18E/F Super Hornet

THE SUPER HORNET is a maritime attack aircraft which entered frontline service in 2001. It is entirely appropriate that this aircraft, and not the B-2, should be the last entry in this book. Lightweight tactical attack aircraft out-number dedicated strategic bombers many times, and have played the most important role in all of the world's recent conflicts. The Super Hornet has the additional advantage of being a near-perfect representative of the kind of multi-role tactical fighter beginning to dominate the air-to-ground role. As the derivative of an aircraft originally designed for the fighter role, the Super Hornet is arguably even more 'typical' of the modern 'bomber'. The fact that it is not a 'brand new' design is also appropriate, since upgrading and improving is becoming increasingly common.

Even before the end of the Cold War, the US Navy selected a derivative of the Hornet to fill the gap left by the cancellation of the A-12, and thus to replace the A-6 Intruder. It was always clear that any F/A-18 derivative would lack the range and payload of the A-6. The Hornet's ability to self escort, and new medium range tactics reduced this disadvantage, while the end of the Cold War led to an increasing emphasis on 'littoral' operations closer in to enemy shores, further reducing this perceived weakness. The new Super Hornet increasingly came to be seen as an F-14 replacement in the Fleet Air Defense role, as well as for the A-6.

McDonnell Douglas had been looking at improved derivatives of the Hornet for some years. What we now know as the F/A-18E/F was a low risk derivative of the basic Hornet, retaining the same basic configuration, with a scaled up wing and LERX and a longer fuselage, new engines (loosely derived from the existing F404) and greater payload and fuel capacity. The aircraft also had a much greater maximum landing weight, allowing it to 'bring back' more weapons, without having to jettison them before landing.

The F/A-18E/F represented a remarkable compromise between the low risk adoption of an existing airframe and systems, and dramatic new capabilities. It had a much reduced radar cross section, revised forward fuselage structure, and reduced maintenance requirements. The aircraft has new displays and a much enhanced avionics system, and is being built in single-seat (F/A-18E) and two-seat (F/A-18F) forms.

The prototype made its maiden flight on November 29, 1995. It was followed by six more EMD aircraft.

The introduction of the F/A-18E/F will lead to a situation in which every USN carrier will embark four Hornet squadrons, two with Super Hornets and two with the 'Heritage Hornet'.

Right: *The prototype F/A-18E taking off from St Louis. The Super Hornet is a bigger and more capable machine than the 'Heritage Hornet'.*

INDEX

PICTURE CREDITS & ACKNOWLEDGEMENTS

Cutaways on pages 358/359, 450/451 and 496/497 by Mike Badrocke. All other pictures are Chrysalis Images except the following which have been credited by page number and position on the page: (T) top, (C) centre, (B) bottom:

Patrick Bunce/Chrysalis Images : 17(T), 50/51, 56/57, 128/129, 131(T), 134(Both), 136/137, 198(Both), 199(T), 218, 220/221, 222/223(All), 224/225(All), 226/227, 228/229, 234/235, 239(B), 243(T), 247(T), 264/265, 266/267, 269, 270/271, 272(T), 273(T), 276/277, 278/279(T), 280(T), 281(T), 282/283(Both)

Philip Jarrett: 26/27, 34/35, 37(B), 38/39(B), 48/49, 60/61, 62(T), 64(B), 66/67, 68/69, 70/71, 72/73, 75(T), 76/77, 78/79, 80/81, 86, 88/89, 102/103, 122/123, 152/153, 170/171, 171(B), 172/173, 178/179, 190/191, 195(B), 256/257, 262/263, 274/275, 286/287, 288/289, 290/291, 296/297, 302/303, 306/307, 308, 309(Both), 332/333, 342/343, 343(B), 347(B), 362/363, 364/365, 366/367, 368/369, 369(T), 370/371, 376/377, 378(T), 386/387, 388/389, 391(Both), 392/393(T), 396/397, 398/399, 408/409, 410/411, 412/413, 414(T), 436/437, 438/439, 440/441, 444/445, 445(B), 478/479

Richard Napper/Chrysalis Images: 24(B), 304/305, 305(B), 464(T), 464/465, 498, 498/499

Navy Visual News: 424/425, 426/427, 427(Both), 458(C), 459(B), 460(B), 461(B)

M.B. & D.O. Passingham: 28/29(B), 30/31, 62/63, 258/259

PRM Aviation: 76(B), 292/293, 294/295(Both), 316/317, 340/341, 346/347, 378/379, 380/381(Both), 414/415, 480(T), 482/483, 484/485

Antony Shaw: 486/487(T), 212/213

Brian Strickland Collection: 232/233, 233(T)

Hanny & Leo Van Ginderen Collection: 400/401

The Editor would like to thank Mike Badrocke, Ashley Brent, Paul Brewer, Stella Caldwell, Charlotte Davies, Terry Forshaw, Colin Gower, Philip Jarrett, Peter R. March, Stephen Mitchell, Pamela Mumbi, Malcolm Passingham, Susannah Straughan and the US Navy Visual News Service for their contributions to the production of this book.